Just The

facts101

Textbook Key Facts

e-Study Guide

by cram101

Textbook NOT Included

Just The facts101 Textbook Key Facts

Textbook Outlines, Highlights, and Practice Quizzes

The American Nation: A History of the United States, Volume 1

by Mark C. Carnes, 14th Edition

All "Just the Facts101" Material Written or Prepared by Cram101 Publishing

---

Title Page

Practice Test Options

"Just the Facts101" is a Cram101 publication and tool designed to give you all the facts from your textbooks. Visit Cram101.com for the full practice test for each of your chapters for virtually any of your textbooks.

Cram101 has built custom study tools specific to your textbook. We provide all of the factual testable information and unlike traditional study guides, we will never send you back to your textbook for more information.

YOU WILL NEVER HAVE TO HIGHLIGHT A BOOK AGAIN!

Cram101 StudyGuides

All of the information in this StudyGuide is written specifically for your textbook. We include the key terms, places, people, and concepts... the information you can expect on your next exam!

Want to take a practice test?

Throughout each chapter of this StudyGuide you will find links to cram101.com where you can select specific chapters to take a complete test on, or you can subscribe and get practice tests for up to 12 of your textbooks, along with other exclusive cram101.com tools like problem solving labs and reference libraries.

Cram101.com

Only cram101.com gives you the outlines, highlights, and PRACTICE TESTS specific to your textbook. Cram101.com is an online application where you'll discover study tools designed to make the most of your limited study time.

By purchasing this book, you get 50% off the normal subscription free!. Just enter the promotional code **'DK73DW19772'** on the Cram101.com registration screen.

www.Cram101.com

ISBN(s): 9781478408659. PUBI-5.201279

Learning System

The American Nation: A History of the United States, Volume 1
Mark C. Carnes, 14th

CONTENTS

CHAPTER OUTLINE: KEY TERMS, PEOPLE, PLACES, CONCEPTS

Chapter 1

Alien Encounters: Europe in the Americas

________ Maya Lin

________ Vietnam Veterans Memorial

________ Beaver

________ Horses

________ Indian American

________ Paleo-Indians

________ Central America

________ Mesoamerica

________ South Carolina

________ Ancient Pueblo People

________ Aztec

________ Christianity

________ Columbian Exchange

________ Pueblo

________ Cahokia

________ Mississippian culture

________ Wampum

________ West Africa

________ Napoleonic Wars

Henry the Navigator

American Revolution

Inca

Lucayan

Ferdinand Magellan

New Spain

Francisco Pizarro

Francisco Vasquez de Coronado

Pueblo people

Yellow fever

Nova Scotia

Plains Indians

Richard Hakluyt

Louisiana

Louisiana Purchase

Roanoke Colony

Spanish Armada

London Company

Pocahontas

Chapter 1. Alien Encounters: Europe in the Americas

- John Smith
- Western
- Powhatan
- England
- William Bradford
- Mayflower
- Mayflower Compact
- New England Colonies
- Pilgrim
- Plymouth Colony
- Puritan
- John Robinson
- Virginia Company
- Cape Cod
- John Mason
- Massachusetts
- Massachusetts Bay Colony
- Plymouth Company
- Squanto

Border

Boston

Roger Williams

Anne Hutchinson

Providence Plantations

William Hutchinson

Pequot War

Factory

Connecticut

Connecticut Colony

New Netherland

North Carolina

Albemarle Settlements

Fur trade

New France

Three-Fifths Compromise

Berkeley

Charles Ridgely II

Henry E. Hudson

Chapter 1. Alien Encounters: Europe in the Americas

_______________ Land grant

_______________ Middle Colonies

_______________ Peter Minuit

_______________ New Amsterdam

_______________ New Sweden

_______________ Patroon

_______________ Quakers

_______________ York

_______________ Delaware Colony

_______________ Iroquois

_______________ William Hepburn Russell

Maya Lin	Maya Ying Lin is an American artist and architect who is known for her work in sculpture and landscape art. She is the designer of the Vietnam Veterans Memorial in Washington, D.C. Personal life Maya Lin, a Chinese American, was born in Athens, Ohio. Her parents immigrated to the United States from People's Republic of China in 1949 and settled in Ohio in 1958, one year before Maya Lin was born.
Vietnam Veterans Memorial	The Vietnam Veterans Memorial is a national memorial in Washington, D.C. It honors U.S. service members of the U.S. armed forces who fought in the Vietnam War, service members who died in service in Vietnam/South East Asia, and those service members who were unaccounted for (Missing In Action) during the War. Its construction and related issues have been the source of controversies, some of which have resulted in additions to the memorial complex. The memorial currently consists of three separate parts: the Three Soldiers statue, the Vietnam Women's Memorial, and the Vietnam Veterans Memorial Wall, which is the best-known part of the memorial.
Beaver	The beaver is a primarily nocturnal, large, semi-aquatic rodent. Castor includes two extant species, North American Beaver (native to North America) and Eurasian Beaver (Eurasia). Beavers are known for building dams, canals, and lodges (homes).
Horses	'Horses' is often cited as one of the greatest albums in music history. In 2003, the album was ranked number 44 on Rolling Stone magazine's list of the 500 greatest albums of all time. NME named the album number 1 in its list '20 Near-as-Damn-It Perfect Initial Efforts'.

Chapter 1. Alien Encounters: Europe in the Americas

Indian American	Indian Americans are Americans who are of Asian descent and have ancestors who are born or are native to India. To make a clear distinction and difference between Indians of Asian origin and Indians 'named as' who are Indigenous peoples of the Americas, the U.S. Census Bureau popularized the term Asian Indian to avoid confusion with 'American Indian'. History The term: Indian In North America the term Indian has an ambiguous meaning.
Paleo-Indians	Paleo-Indians or Paleoamericans is a classification term given to the first peoples who entered, and subsequently inhabited, the American continent during the final glacial episodes of the late Pleistocene period. The prefix 'paleo' comes from the Greek adjective palaios (παλαι?ς) meaning 'old.' The term Paleo-Indians applies specifically to the lithic period in the Western Hemisphere and is distinct from the term Paleolithic. Evidence suggests big-game hunters crossed the Bering Strait from Asia (Eurasia) into North America over a land bridge (Beringia), that existed between 45,000 BCE - 12,000 BCE (47,000 - 14,000 years ago).
Central America	Central America is the central geographic region of the Americas. It is the southernmost, isthmian portion of the North American continent, which connects with South America on the southeast. When considered part of the unified continental model, it is considered a subcontinent.
Mesoamerica	Mesoamerica is a region and culture area in the Americas, extending approximately from central Mexico to Belize, Guatemala, El Salvador, Honduras, Nicaragua, and Costa Rica, within which a number of pre-Columbian societies flourished before the Spanish colonization of the Americas in the 16th and 17th centuries.

South Carolina	South Carolina is a state in the Deep South that borders Georgia to the south and North Carolina to the north. Originally part of the Province of Carolina, the Province of South Carolina was one of the 13 colonies that declared independence from the British Crown during the American Revolution. The colony was originally named by King Charles II of England in honor of his father Charles I, as Carolus is Latin for Charles.
Ancient Pueblo People	Ancient Pueblo People, were an ancient Native American culture centered on the present-day Four Corners area of the United States, comprising southern Utah, northern Arizona, northwest New Mexico, and southern Colorado. They lived in 'houses' called pueblos in which they lifted up ladders during enemy attacks, providing the Pueblo peoples security. The cultural group has often been referred to in archaeology as the Anasazi, although the term is not preferred by contemporaryPueblo peoples.
Aztec	The Aztec people were certain ethnic groups of central Mexico, particularly those groups who spoke the Nahuatl language and who dominated large parts of Mesoamerica in the 14th, 15th and 16th centuries, a period referred to as the late post-classic period in Mesoamerican chronology. Aztec (Aztecatl) is the Nahuatl word for 'people from Aztlan', a mythological place for the Nahuatl-speaking culture of the time, and later adopted as the word to define the Mexica people. Often the term 'Aztec' refers exclusively to the Mexica people of Tenochtitlan (now the location of Mexico City), situated on an island in Lake Texcoco, who referred to themselves as Mexica Tenochca or Colhua-Mexica. Sometimes the term also includes the inhabitants of Tenochtitlan's two principal allied city-states, the Acolhuas of Texcoco and the Tepanecs of Tlacopan, who together with the Mexica formed the Aztec Triple Alliance which has also become known as the 'Aztec Empire'.
Christianity	Christianity is a monotheistic religion based on the life and teachings of Jesus as presented in canonical gospels and other New Testament writings. Adherents of the Christian faith are known as Christians. Christianity teaches that Jesus is the Son of God, God having become human and the saviour of humanity.

Chapter 1. Alien Encounters: Europe in the Americas

Columbian Exchange	The Columbian Exchange was a dramatically widespread exchange of animals, plants, culture, human populations (including slaves), communicable diseases, and ideas between the Eastern and Western hemispheres (Old World and New World). It was one of the most significant events concerning ecology, agriculture, and culture in all of human history. Christopher Columbus' first voyage to the Americas in 1492 launched the era of large-scale contact between the Old and the New Worlds that resulted in this ecological revolution, hence the name 'Columbian' Exchange.
Pueblo	Pueblo is a term used to describe modern (and ancient) communities of Native Americans in the Southwestern United States of America. The first Spanish Explorers of the Southwest used this term to describe communities that consisted of apartment-like structures made from stone, adobe mud, and other local material. These structures were usually multi-storeyed buildings surrounding an open plaza and were occupied by hundreds to thousands of Pueblo People.
Cahokia	Cahokia Mounds State Historic Site is the area of an ancient indigenous city (c. 600-1400 CE) near Collinsville, Illinois. In the American Bottom floodplain, it is across the Mississippi River from St. Louis, Missouri. The 2,200-acre (8.9 km^2) site included 120 human-built earthwork mounds over an area of six square miles, of which 80 remain. Cahokia Mounds is the largest archaeological site related to the Mississippian culture, which developed advanced societies in central and eastern North America, beginning more than five centuries before the arrival of Europeans.
Mississippian culture	The Mississippian culture was a mound-building Native American culture that flourished in what is now the Midwestern, Eastern, and Southeastern United States from approximately 800 CE to 1500 CE, varying regionally. The Mississippian way of life began to develop in the Mississippi River Valley (for which it is named). Cultures in the tributary Tennessee River Valley may have also begun to develop Mississippian characteristics at this point.
Wampum	Wampum are traditional sacred shell beads of the Eastern Woodlands tribes of the indigenous people of North America. Wampum include the white shell beads fashioned from the North Atlantic channeled whelk shell; and the white and purple beads made from the quahog, or Western North Atlantic hard-shelled clam. Woven belts of wampum have been created to commemorate treaties or historical events, and for exchange in personal social transactions, such as marriages. In colonial North America, European colonists often used wampum as currency for trading with Native Americans.

West Africa

West Africa is the westernmost region of the African continent. Geopolitically, the UN definition of Western Africa includes 16 countries and an area of approximately 5 million square miles.

Napoleonic Wars

The Napoleonic Wars were a series of conflicts declared against Napoleon's French Empire and changing sets of European allies by opposing coalitions that ran from 1803 to 1815. As a continuation of the wars sparked by the French Revolution of 1789, they revolutionized European armies and played out on an unprecedented scale, mainly due to the application of modern mass conscription. French power rose quickly, conquering most of Europe, but collapsed rapidly after France's disastrous invasion of Russia in 1812. Napoleon's empire ultimately suffered complete military defeat resulting in the restoration of the Bourbon monarchy in France. The wars resulted in the dissolution of the Holy Roman Empire and sowed the seeds of nascent nationalism in Germany and Italy that would lead to the two nations' consolidation later in the century.

Henry the Navigator

Henry the Navigator was an infante (junior prince) of the Kingdom of Portugal and an important figure in the early days of the Portuguese Empire. He was responsible for the early development of European exploration and maritime trade with other continents.

Henry was the third child of King John I of Portugal, the founder of the Aviz dynasty, and of Philippa of Lancaster, John of Gaunt's daughter.

American Revolution

The American Revolution was the political upheaval during the last half of the 18th century in which thirteen colonies in North America joined together to break free from the British Empire, combining to become the United States of America. They first rejected the authority of the Parliament of Great Britain to govern them from overseas without representation, and then expelled all royal officials. By 1774, each colony had established a Provincial Congress, or an equivalent governmental institution, to govern itself, but still within the empire. The British responded by sending combat troops to re-impose direct rule.

Inca

The Inca was 'the first true five-masted schooner built on the West Coast.'

Inca, 'the second of her rig built on the Pacific, was launched at Port Blakely by Hall Bros. in 1896.'

Launching

'The Inca, because of its size and rig, had attracted considerable attention during the progress of its construction and when the time set for launching arrived a large crowd of people was present in the shipyards. The Port Blakeley schools were closed so that the pupils might attend the exercises incident to launching.

Lucayan

The Lucayan were the original inhabitants of the Bahamas before the arrival of Europeans. They were a branch of the Taínos who inhabited most of the Caribbean islands at the time. The Lucayans were the first inhabitants of the Americas encountered by Christopher Columbus.

Ferdinand Magellan

Ferdinand Magellan was a Portuguese explorer. He was born in Sabrosa, in northern Portugal, but later obtained Spanish nationality in order to serve King Charles I of Spain in search of a westward route to the 'Spice Islands' (modern Maluku Islands in Indonesia).

Magellan's expedition of 1519-1522 became the first expedition to sail from the Atlantic Ocean into the Pacific Ocean , and the first to cross the Pacific.

New Spain

New Spain, formally called the Viceroyalty of New Spain, was a viceroyalty of the Spanish colonial empire, comprising primarily territories in what was known then as 'América Septentrional' or North America. Its capital was Mexico City, formerly Tenochtitlan, capital of the Aztec Empire. New Spain was established following the Spanish conquest of the Aztec Empire in 1521, and at its greatest extent included much of North America south of Canada: all of present-day Mexico and Central America (except Panama), most of the United States west of the Mississippi River and the Floridas.

New Spain also included the Spanish East Indies (Philippine Islands, Mariana Islands, the Caroline Islands, Taiwan, and parts of the Moluccas) and the Spanish West Indies (Cuba, Hispaniola with Haiti and the Dominican Republic, Puerto Rico, Jamaica, Cayman Islands, Trinidad, and the Bay Islands).

Francisco Pizarro	Francisco Pizarro González, Marquess was a Spanish conquistador, conqueror of the Incan Empire, and founder of Lima, the modern-day capital of the Republic of Peru. Early life Pizarro was born in the town of Trujillo, in modern day Extremadura, Spain. Sources differ in the birth year they assign to him: 1471, 1475-1478, or unknown.
Francisco Vasquez de Coronado	Francisco Vasquez de Coronado y Luján (1510 - 22 September 1554) was a Spanish conquistador, who visited New Mexico and other parts of what are now the southwestern United States between 1540 and 1542. Coronado had hoped to conquer the mythical Seven Cities of Gold. Early life Coronado was born into a rich family in Salamanca, Spain, in 1510, the second son of Juan Vásquez de Coronado y Sosa de Ulloa and Isabel de Luján. Juan Vásquez held various positions in the administration of the recently captured Emirate of Granada under Iñigo López de Mendoza, its first Spanish governor.
Pueblo people	The Pueblo people are a Native American people in the Southwestern United States. Their traditional economy is based on agriculture and trade. When first encountered by the Spanish in the 16th century, they were living in villages that the Spanish called pueblos, meaning 'villages'.
Yellow fever	Yellow fever is an acute viral hemorrhagic disease. The virus is a 40 to 50 nm enveloped RNA virus with positive sense of the Flaviviridae family.

The yellow fever virus is transmitted by the bite of female mosquitoes (the yellow fever mosquito, Aedes aegypti, and other species) and is found in tropical and subtropical areas in South America and Africa, but not in Asia. The only known hosts of the virus are primates and several species of mosquito. The origin of the disease is most likely to be Africa, from where it was introduced to South America through the slave trade in the 16th century. Since the 17th century, several major epidemics of the disease have been recorded in the Americas, Africa and Europe. In the 19th century, yellow fever was deemed one of the most dangerous infectious diseases.

Nova Scotia

62°42′W? / ?45.217°N 62.7°W

Nova Scotia is one of Canada's three Maritime provinces and is the most populous province in Atlantic Canada. The provincial capital is Halifax. Nova Scotia is the second-smallest province in Canada with an area of 55,284 square kilometres (21,300 sq mi).

Plains Indians

The Plains Indians are the Indigenous peoples who live on the plains and rolling hills of the Great Plains of North America. Their colorful equestrian culture and resistance to White domination have made the Plains Indians an archetype in literature and art for American Indians everywhere.

Plains Indians are usually divided into two broad classifications which overlap to some degree. The first group were fully nomadic, following the vast herds of buffalo, although some tribes occasionally engaged in agriculture; growing tobacco and corn primarily.

Richard Hakluyt

Richard Hakluyt was an English writer. He is principally remembered for his efforts in promoting and supporting the settlement of North America by the English through his works, notably Divers Voyages Touching the Discoverie of America (1582) and The Principal Navigations, Voiages, Traffiques and Discoueries of the English Nation (1589-1600).

Educated at Westminster School and Christ Church, Oxford, between 1583 and 1588 Hakluyt was chaplain and secretary to Sir Edward Stafford, English ambassador at the French court.

Louisiana

Louisiana was the name of an administrative district of the Viceroyalty of New Spain from 1764 to 1803 that represented territory west of the Mississippi River basin, plus New Orleans. Spain acquired the territory from France: see Louisiana.

History

The area, comprising what is now known as the Louisiana Purchase, was turned over to the French for a few days in 1803 before it, in turn, was turned over to the United States.

Louisiana Purchase

The Louisiana Purchase was the acquisition by the United States of America of 828,800 square miles (2,147,000 km^2) of France's claim to the territory of Louisiana in 1803. The U.S. paid 60 million francs ($11,250,000) plus cancellation of debts worth 18 million francs ($3,750,000), for a total sum of 15 million dollars for the Louisiana territory ($219 million in 2010 dollars). What was purchased was France's claim only, not the actual territory, which belonged to the tribes which inhabited the area. The territory itself was acquired slowly throughout the nineteenth century by purchases to Native American tribes and wars.

Roanoke Colony

The Roanoke Colony on Roanoke Island in Dare County, present-day North Carolina, United States was a late 16th-century attempt to establish a permanent English settlement in what later became the Virginia Colony. The enterprise was financed and organized by Sir Walter Raleigh and carried out by Ralph Lane and Richard Grenville, Raleigh's distant cousin. The final group of colonists disappeared during the Anglo-Spanish War, three years after the last shipment of supplies from England.

Chapter 1. Alien Encounters: Europe in the Americas

Spanish Armada	The Spanish Armada was the Spanish fleet that sailed against England under the command of the Duke of Medina Sidonia in 1588, with the intention of overthrowing Elizabeth I of England to stop English involvement in the Spanish Netherlands and English privateering in the Atlantic and the Pacific. The fleet's mission was to sail to the Gravelines in Flanders and transport an army under the Duke of Parma across the Channel to England. The Armada achieved its first goal and anchored outside Gravelines but while awaiting communications from Parma's army, it was driven from its anchorage by an English fire ship attack, and in the ensuing naval battle at Gravelines the Spanish were forced to abandon their rendezvous.
London Company	The London Company was an English joint stock company established by royal charter by James I of England on April 10, 1606 with the purpose of establishing colonial settlements in North America. The territory granted to the London Company included the coast of North America from the 34th parallel (Cape Fear) north to the 41st parallel (in Long Island Sound), but being part of the Virginia Company and Colony, the London Company owned a large portion of Atlantic and Inland Canada. The company was permitted by its charter to establish a 100-square-mile (260 km^2) settlement within this area. The portion of the company's territory north of the 38th parallel was shared with the Plymouth Company, with the stipulation that neither company found a colony within 100 miles (161 km) of each other.
Pocahontas	Pocahontas was a Virginia Indian notable for her association with the colonial settlement at Jamestown, Virginia. She was the daughter of Chief Powhatan, the head of a network of tributary tribal nations in the Tidewater region of Virginia. In a well-known historical anecdote, she is said to have saved the life of an Indian captive, Englishman John Smith, in 1607 by placing her head upon his own when her father raised his war club to execute him.

John Smith

John Smith also known by the alias John Wilson, was a London housebreaker, most notable for his three evasions of execution. His first evasion granted him the nickname of Half-hanged Smith.

Biography

Early life and career

John Smith was the son of a Malton farmer.

Western

The Western is a genre of art that may be found in film, television, radio, literature, painting and other visual arts. Westerns are devoted to telling stories set primarily in the latter half of the 19th century in the American Old West. Some Westerns are set as early as the Battle of the Alamo in 1836 but most are set between the end of the American Civil War (1865) and the massacre at Wounded Knee in 1890. There are also a number of films about Western-type characters in contemporary settings, such as Junior Bonner set in the 1970s and The Three Burials of Melquiades Estrada in the 21st century.

Powhatan

The Powhatan is the name of a Virginia Indian confederation of tribes. It is estimated that there were about 14,000-21,000 of these native Powhatan people in eastern Virginia when the English settled Jamestown in 1607. They were also known as Virginia Algonquians, as they spoke an eastern-Algonquian language known as Powhatan or Virginia Algonquin.

In the late 16th and early 17th centuries, a mamanatowick (paramount chief) named Wahunsunacawh created a powerful organization by affiliating 30 tributary peoples, whose territory was much of eastern Virginia, called Tsenacommacah ('densely-inhabited Land'), Wahunsunacawh came to be known by the English as 'Chief Powhatan.' Each of the tribes within this organization had its own weroance (chief), but all paid tribute to Chief Powhatan.

England

England is a country that is part of the United Kingdom. It shares land borders with Scotland to the north and Wales to the west; the Irish Sea is to the north west, the Celtic Sea to the south west and the North Sea to the east, with the English Channel to the south separating it from continental Europe. Most of England comprises the central and southern part of the island of Great Britain in the North Atlantic.

Chapter 1. Alien Encounters: Europe in the Americas

William Bradford	William Bradford was an English leader of the settlers of the Plymouth Colony in Massachusetts, and was elected thirty times to be the Governor after John Carver died. His journal (1620-1647) was published as Of Plymouth Plantation. Bradford is credited as the first civil authority to designate what popular American culture now views as Thanksgiving in the United States.
Mayflower	The Mayflower was the ship that transported the English Dissenters, better known as the Pilgrims, from a site near the Mayflower Steps in Plymouth, England, to Plymouth, Massachusetts (which would become the capital of Plymouth Colony), in 1620. There were 102 passengers and a crew of 25-30. The vessel left England on September 6, 1620 (Old Style)/September 16 (New Style), and after a grueling 66-day journey marked by disease, which claimed two lives, the ship dropped anchor inside the hook tip of Cape Cod (Provincetown Harbor) on November 11/November 21. The Mayflower was originally destined for the mouth of the Hudson River, near present-day New York City, at the northern edge of England's Virginia colony, which itself was established with the 1607 Jamestown Settlement. However, the Mayflower went off course as the winter approached, and remained in Cape Cod Bay.
Mayflower Compact	The Mayflower Compact was the first governing document of Plymouth Colony. It was written by the colonists, later together known to history as the Pilgrims, who crossed the Atlantic aboard the Mayflower. Almost half of the colonists were part of a separatist group seeking the freedom to practice Christianity according to their own determination and not the will of the Anglican Church.
New England Colonies	The New England Colonies of British America included the colonies of Massachusetts Bay Colony, Connecticut Colony, Colony of Rhode Island and Providence Plantations and Province of New Hampshire. They were part of the Thirteen Colonies including the Middle Colonies and the Southern Colonies. These were early colonies of what would later be the states in New England.

Pilgrim	Pilgrims (US), or Pilgrim Fathers (UK), is a name commonly applied to early settlers of the Plymouth Colony in present-day Plymouth, Massachusetts, United States. Their leadership came from the religious congregations of English Dissenters who had fled the volatile political environment in the East Midlands of England for the relative calm and tolerance of Holland in the Netherlands. Concerned with losing their cultural identity, the group later arranged with English investors to establish a new colony in North America. The colony, established in 1620, became the oldest continuously inhabited British settlement and the second successful English settlement (after the founding of Jamestown, Virginia in 1607) in what was to become the United States of America. The Pilgrims' story of seeking religious freedom has become a central theme of the history and culture of the United States.
Plymouth Colony	Plymouth Colony was an English colonial venture in North America from 1620 to 1691. The first settlement of the Plymouth Colony was at New Plymouth, a location previously surveyed and named by Captain John Smith. The settlement, which served as the capital of the colony, is today the modern town of Plymouth, Massachusetts. At its height, Plymouth Colony occupied most of the southeastern portion of the modern state of Massachusetts.
Puritan	The Puritans were a significant grouping of English Protestants in the 16th and 17th centuries, including, but not limited to, English Calvinists. Puritanism in this sense was founded by some Marian exiles from the clergy shortly after the accession of Elizabeth I of England in 1558, as an activist movement within the Church of England. The designation 'Puritan' is often incorrectly used, notably based on the assumption that hedonism and puritanism are antonyms: Historically, the word was used pejoratively to characterize the Protestant group as extremists similar to the Cathari of France, and according to Thomas Fuller in his Church History dated back to 1564, Archbishop Matthew Parker of that time used it and 'precisian' with the sense of modern 'stickler'.
John Robinson	John Robinson was a merchant and political figure in the pre-Confederation Province of New Brunswick, Canada. He represented the City of Saint John in the Legislative Assembly of New Brunswick from 1802 to 1809 and from 1810 to 1816. He was born near New York City, the son of Beverley Robinson and Susanna Philipse.

Chapter 1. Alien Encounters: Europe in the Americas

Virginia Company	The Virginia Company refers collectively to a pair of English joint stock companies chartered by James I on 10 April 1606 with the purposes of establishing settlements on the coast of North America. The two companies, called the 'Virginia Company of London' (or the London Company) and the 'Virginia Company of Plymouth' (or Plymouth Company) operated with identical charters but with differing territories. An area of overlapping territory was created within which the two companies were not permitted to establish colonies within one hundred miles of each other. The Plymouth Company never fulfilled its charter, and its territory that later became New England was at that time also claimed by France.
Cape Cod	A Cape Cod cottage is a style of house originating in New England in the 17th century. It is traditionally characterized by a low, broad frame building, generally a story and a half high, with a steep, perfectly pitched roof with end gables, a large central chimney and very little ornamentation. Traditional Cape Cod houses were very simple: symmetrically designed with a central front door surrounded by two multi-paned windows on each side.
John Mason	John Mason was an early American merchant, banker, planter. As a son of George Mason, a Founding Father of the United States, Mason was a scion of the prominent Mason political family. Early life and education Mason was born on 4 April 1766 at Mattawoman plantation, the estate of his maternal grandparents William Eilbeck and Sarah Edgar Eilbeck.
Massachusetts	'Massachusetts', words and music by Arlo Guthrie, was made the official folk song of Massachusetts in July, 1981.
Massachusetts Bay Colony	The Massachusetts Bay Colony was an English settlement on the east coast of North America in the 17th century, in New England, situated around the present-day cities of Salem and Boston. The territory administered by the colony included much of present-day central New England, including portions of the U.S. states of Massachusetts, Maine, New Hampshire, Rhode Island, and Connecticut. Territory claimed but never administered by the colonial government extended as far west as the Pacific Ocean.
Plymouth Company	The Plymouth Company was an English joint stock company founded in 1606 by James I of England with the purpose of establishing settlements on the coast of North America.

The Plymouth Company was one of two companies, along with the London Company, chartered with such a purpose as part of the Virginia Company. In form it was similar to the Company of Merchant Adventurers of London. The territory of the company was the coast of North America from the 38th parallel to the 45th parallel, but being part of the Virginia Company and Colony, The Plymouth Company owned a large portion of Atlantic and Inland Canada.

Squanto

Tisquantum (better known as Squanto) (c. 1580s - November 1622) was a Patuxet. He was the Native American who assisted the Pilgrims after their first winter in the New World and was integral to their survival. The Patuxet tribe was a tributary of the Wampanoag Confederacy.

Border

Border is a 1997 blockbuster Bollywood war film based on the Indo-Pakistani War of 1971. J. P. Dutta directed and produced this war epic which stars Sunny Deol, Jackie Shroff, Sunil Shetty, Akshay Khanna, Pooja Bhatt, Sharbani Mukherjee and Tabu.

Director J.P. Dutta won Best Director at the same award function, while his father O.P. Dutta won for Best Dialogues.

The movie is an adaptation from real life events that happened at the Battle of Longewala fought in Rajasthan (Western Theatre) during the Indo-Pakistani War of 1971 and Bangladesh Liberation War.

Boston

Boston is the capital of and largest city in Massachusetts, and is one of the oldest cities in the United States. The largest city in New England, Boston is regarded as the unofficial 'Capital of New England' for its economic and cultural impact on the entire New England region. The city proper had a 2009 estimated population of 645,169, making it the twentieth largest in the country.

Roger Williams

Roger Williams was an English Protestant theologian who was an early proponent of religious freedom and the separation of church and state. In 1636, he began the colony of Providence Plantation, which provided a refuge for religious minorities. Williams started the first Baptist church in America, the First Baptist Church of Providence, before leaving to become a Seeker.

Chapter 1. Alien Encounters: Europe in the Americas

Anne Hutchinson	Anne Hutchinson was an early-17th century Puritan living in Massachusetts, Rhode Island and New Netherlands who became the leader of a dissident church discussion group. Hutchinson held Bible meetings for women that soon appealed to men as well. Eventually, she went beyond Bible study to proclaim her own theological interpretations of sermons.
Providence Plantations	Providence Plantations was the first permanent European American settlement in present-day Rhode Island. It was established at Providence in 1636 by English clergyman Roger Williams and a small band of followers who had left the repressive atmosphere of the Massachusetts Bay Colony to seek freedom of worship. Narragansett sachems Canonicus and Miantonomi granted Williams a sizable tract of land for his new village.
William Hutchinson	William Hutchinson was a prominent merchant and judge in the Massachusetts Bay Colony and one of the founders of Rhode Island. Hutchinson was born in Alford, Lincolnshire, England. His parents were Edward Hutchinson (1564-1631) and Susanna Wheelright (1564-1645).
Pequot War	The Pequot War was an armed conflict between 1634-1638 between the Pequot tribe against an alliance of the Massachusetts Bay, Plymouth, and Saybrook colonies who were aided by their Native American allies (the Narragansett and Mohegan tribes). Hundreds were killed; hundreds more were captured and sold into slavery to the West Indies. Other survivors were dispersed.
Factory	Factory was the English term for the trading posts system originally established by Europeans in foreign territories, first within different states of medieval Europe, and later in their colonial possessions. Factories served simultaneously as market, warehouse, customs, defense and support to the navigation or exploration, headquarters or de facto government of local communities, with the head of the factory being called a factor. This system was adopted by Americans to exchange goods with local non western societies.
Connecticut	Connecticut is a state in the New England region of the northeastern United States. It is bordered by Rhode Island to the east, Massachusetts to the north, the state of New York to the west, and by the Long Island Sound to the south.

Connecticut Colony	The Connecticut Colony or Colony of Connecticut was an English colony located in British America that became the U.S. state of Connecticut. Originally known as the River Colony, it was organized on March 3, 1636 as a haven for Puritan noblemen. After early struggles with the Dutch, the English gained control of the colony permanently by the late 1630s.
New Netherland	New Netherland, was the 17th-century colonial province of the Republic of the Seven United Netherlands on the East Coast of North America. The claimed territories were the lands from the Delmarva Peninsula to extreme southwestern Cape Cod. The settled areas are now part of the Mid-Atlantic States of New York, New Jersey, Delaware, and Connecticut, with small outposts in Pennsylvania and Rhode Island. The provincial capital, New Amsterdam, was located at the southern tip of the island of Manhattan on upper New York Bay.
North Carolina	North Carolina is a state located in the Southeastern United States. The state borders South Carolina and Georgia to the south, Tennessee to the west and Virginia to the north. North Carolina contains 100 counties.
Albemarle Settlements	The Albemarle Settlements were the first permanent English settlements in what is now North Carolina, founded in the Albemarle Sound and Roanoke River regions, beginning about the middle of the 17th century. The settlers were mainly Virginians migrating south. History In 1653, the Virginia Assembly granted one Roger Green a tract of land on Roanoke River south of Chowan, to be located 'next to those persons who have had a former grant.' In 1662, George Durant purchased lands from the Indians in this region and there is evidence to indicate that others had done the same.
Fur trade	The fur trade is a worldwide industry dealing in the acquisition and sale of animal fur. Since the establishment of world market for in the early modern period furs of boreal, polar and cold temperate mammalian animals have been the most valued. Historically it had a large impact on the exploration and colonization of Siberia, northern North America and the South Shetland and South Sandwich Islands.

Chapter 1. Alien Encounters: Europe in the Americas

New France	New France was the area colonized by France in North America during a period beginning with the exploration of the Saint Lawrence River by Jacques Cartier in 1534 and ending with the cession of New France to Spain and Great Britain in 1763. At its peak in 1712 (before the Treaty of Utrecht), the territory of New France extended from Newfoundland to the Rocky Mountains and from Hudson Bay to the Gulf of Mexico. The territory was then divided into five colonies, each with its own administration: Canada, Acadia, Hudson Bay, Newfoundland (Plaisance), and Louisiana. The Treaty of Utrecht resulted in the relinquishing of French claims to mainland Acadia, the Hudson Bay and Newfoundland, and the establishment of the colony of Île Royale (Cape Breton Island) as the successor to Acadia.
Three-Fifths Compromise	The Three-Fifths Compromise was a compromise between Southern and Northern states reached during the Philadelphia Convention of 1787 in which three-fifths of the enumerated population of slaves would be counted for representation purposes regarding both the distribution of taxes and the apportionment of the members of the United States House of Representatives. It was proposed by delegates James Wilson and Roger Sherman. Delegates opposed to slavery generally wished to count only the free inhabitants of each state.
Berkeley	The Berkeley was one of several ferryboats of the Southern Pacific Railroad that operated on San Francisco Bay between the Oakland Pier and the San Francisco Ferry Building for sixty years. Built in 1898 by the Union Iron Works of San Francisco, she served after the 1906 earthquake, ferrying refugees across the bay to Oakland. The Berkeley was in regular service from 1898 to the spring of 1958, when she was taken out of service for repairs.
Charles Ridgely II	Col. Charles Ridgely II, 'Charles The Merchant' (1702-1772) of 'Ridgely's Whim', a Justice, planter, mechant, ironmaster, and member of the Lower House. Charles II, was the son of Charles Ridgely I, 'Charles The Planter' (ca. 1670-1705) and Deborah Dorsey (ca. 1685-1752).

Charles was born in Prince George's County, and still a minor at the death of his father in 1705. He inherited the estates 'White Wine' and 'Claret' from his grandfather Hon.

Henry E. Hudson

Henry E. Hudson is a United States federal judge on the United States District Court for the Eastern District of Virginia.

Early life and education

Born in Washington, D.C., Hudson was raised in Arlington, Virginia. At the age of 18, he served as a volunteer firefighter and paramedic in Arlington, Virginia.

Land grant

A land grant is a gift of real estate - land or its privileges - made by a government or other authority as a reward for services to an individual, especially in return for military service. Grants of land are also awarded to individuals and companies as incentives to develop unused land in relatively unpopulated countries; the process of awarding land grants are not limited to the countries named below.

Ancient Rome

Roman soldiers were given rewards at the end of their service including cash or land (praemia).

Middle Colonies

The Middle Colonies comprised the middle region of the Thirteen British Colonies in Northern America. Following the American Revolution, the Middle Colonies became the states of New Jersey, Pennsylvania, New York and Delaware.

Much of the area was part of the New Netherland until the British exerted control over the region. The British captured much of the area in its war with the Dutch around 1664, and the majority of the conquered land became the Province of New York.

Chapter 1. Alien Encounters: Europe in the Americas

Peter Minuit	Peter Minuit, Pieter Minuit, Pierre Minuit or Peter Minnewit (1580 - August 5, 1638) was a Walloon from Wesel, in present-day North Rhine-Westphalia, Germany, then part of the Duchy of Clèves. He was the Director-General of the Dutch colony of New Netherland from 1626 until 1633, and he founded the Swedish colony of New Sweden in 1638. According to tradition, Minuit purchased the island of Manhattan from Native Americans on May 24, 1626 for goods to the value of 60 Dutch guilders, which in the 19th century was estimated to be the equivalent of $24 USD. Early life and education Peter Minuit was born in 1580 in Wesel. This was during a period of religious tensions between Protestants and Catholics polities following the Protestant Reformation that culminated in the Thirty Years' War.
New Amsterdam	New Amsterdam was a 17th-century Dutch colonial settlement that served as the capital of New Netherland. It was later renamed to New York City. The settlement, outside of Fort Amsterdam on Manhattan Island in the New Netherland territory (1614-1664), was situated between 38 and 42 degrees latitude and was as a provincial extension of the Dutch Republic as of 1624. Situated on the strategic, fortifiable southern tip of the island of Manhattan, the fort was meant to defend the Dutch East India Company's fur trade operations in the North River (Hudson River).
New Sweden	New Sweden was a Swedish colony along the Delaware River on the Mid-Atlantic coast of North America from 1638 to 1655. Fort Christina, now in Wilmington, Delaware, was the first settlement. New Sweden included parts of the present-day American states of Delaware, New Jersey, and Pennsylvania. Along with Swedes and Finns, a number of the settlers were Dutch.
Patroon	In the United States, a patroon was a landholder with manorial rights to large tracts of land in the 17th century Dutch colony of New Netherland in North America (notably along the Hudson River in New York). Through the Charter of Freedoms and Exemptions of 1629, the Dutch West India Company first started to grant this title and land to some of its invested members. These inducements to foster immigration (also known as the 'Rights and Exemptions'), are the basis for the patroon system.

Quakers	The Religious Society of Friends, or Friends Church, is a Christian movement which stresses the doctrine of the priesthood of all believers. Members are known as Friends, or popularly as Quakers. It is made of independent organisations which have split from one another due to doctrinal differences.
York	York was an African American slave best known for his participation with the Lewis and Clark Expedition. As William Clark's slave, he had to do diffficult manual labour without pay. After the expedition's return he pressed for his freedom, which Clark opposed, he possibly agreed ten years later, though some historians dispute this and say he was never freed.
Delaware Colony	Delaware Colony in the North American Middle Colonies was a region of the Province of Pennsylvania although never legally a separate colony. From 1682 until 1776 it was part of the Penn proprietorship and was known as the lower counties. In 1701 it gained a separate Assembly from the three upper counties but had the same Governor as the rest of Pennsylvania.
Iroquois	The Iroquois, are an association of several tribes of indigenous people of North America. After the Iroquoian-speaking peoples coalesced as distinct tribes, based mostly in present-day central and upstate New York, in the 16th century or earlier they came together in an association known today as the Iroquois League, or the 'League of Peace and Power'. The original Iroquois League was often known as the Five Nations, as it was composed of the Mohawk, Oneida, Onondaga, Cayuga and Seneca nations. After the Tuscarora nation joined the League in 1722, the Iroquois became known as the Six Nations.
William Hepburn Russell	William Hepburn Russell is often credited along with Alexander Majors and William B. Waddell as the founders, owners, and operators of the Pony Express. His public life is one of numerous business ventures, some successful and some failed. While Russell, described as a good-looking man, lived the majority of his life on the edge on the frontier, he was always more at home in the upper class settings of the East coast.

PRACTICE QUIZ
Chapter 1. Alien Encounters: Europe in the Americas

---

1. _________ is a term used to describe modern (and ancient) communities of Native Americans in the Southwestern United States of America. The first Spanish Explorers of the Southwest used this term to describe communities that consisted of apartment-like structures made from stone, adobe mud, and other local material. These structures were usually multi-storeyed buildings surrounding an open plaza and were occupied by hundreds to thousands of _________ People.

   a. Pueblo
   b. Arkansas
   c. Digital Transition Content Security Act
   d. Bangladeshi American

2. 62°42′W? / ?45.217°N 62.7°W

   _________ is one of Canada's three Maritime provinces and is the most populous province in Atlantic Canada. The provincial capital is Halifax. _________ is the second-smallest province in Canada with an area of 55,284 square kilometres (21,300 sq mi).

   a. Arthur Noble
   b. John Taylor Wood
   c. Thomas Gage
   d. Nova Scotia

3. _________ was an infante (junior prince) of the Kingdom of Portugal and an important figure in the early days of the Portuguese Empire. He was responsible for the early development of European exploration and maritime trade with other continents.

   Henry was the third child of King John I of Portugal, the founder of the Aviz dynasty, and of Philippa of Lancaster, John of Gaunt's daughter.

   a. Thomas Gage
   b. Wessagusset Colony
   c. West Jersey
   d. Henry the Navigator

4. _________s (US), or _________ Fathers (UK), is a name commonly applied to early settlers of the Plymouth Colony in present-day Plymouth, Massachusetts, United States. Their leadership came from the religious congregations of English Dissenters who had fled the volatile political environment in the East Midlands of England for the relative calm and tolerance of Holland in the Netherlands. Concerned with losing their cultural identity, the group later arranged with English investors to establish a new colony in North America. The colony, established in 1620, became the oldest continuously inhabited British settlement and the second successful English settlement (after the founding of Jamestown, Virginia in 1607) in what was to become the United States of America. The _________s' story of seeking religious freedom has become a central theme of the history and culture of the United States.

   a. Robert Abell
   b. Pilgrim
   c. Thomas Wellman
   d. Thomas Gage

5. _________ is the central geographic region of the Americas. It is the southernmost, isthmian portion of the North American continent, which connects with South America on the southeast. When considered part of the unified continental model, it is considered a subcontinent.

   a. Digital Transition Content Security Act
   b. Korean American
   c. South Asian American
   d. Central America

ANSWER KEY
Chapter 1. Alien Encounters: Europe in the Americas

---

1. a
2. d
3. d
4. b
5. d

CHAPTER OUTLINE: KEY TERMS, PEOPLE, PLACES, CONCEPTS
Chapter 2
American Society in the Making

______ American Revolution

______ Christianity

______ Fur trade

______ Iroquois

______ Louisiana

______ Natchez

______ New France

______ Plains Indians

______ New Spain

______ Pueblo

______ Pueblo people

______ Washington

______ Chesapeake Colonies

______ Dysentery

______ England

______ Indian American

______ Middle Colonies

______ New England Colonies

______ Headright

______ Lake Erie

______ Land grant

______ Massachusetts

______ Massachusetts Body of Liberties

______ Nathaniel Bacon

______ Berkeley

______ London Company

______ Eliza Lucas

______ North Carolina

______ South Carolina

______ Black Codes

______ Puritan

______ Southern Colonies

______ Great Awakening

______ Border

______ Boston

______ George Corbin Washington

______ John Cotton

______ Half-Way Covenant

Chapter 2. American Society in the Making

_______________ Quakers

_______________ Charles Ridgely II

_______________ Oliver Cromwell

_______________ Glorious Revolution

_______________ Samuel Parris

_______________ Salem witch trials

_______________ Sarah Osborne

_______________ William Phips

_______________ Tituba

_______________ Atlantic slave trade

_______________ Commerce

_______________ Napoleonic Wars

_______________ New Amsterdam

_______________ Diversity

_______________ Benjamin Franklin

_______________ Mennonite

_______________ York

_______________ Jacob Leisler

_______________ Paxton Boys

Pennsylvania Dutch

CHAPTER HIGHLIGHTS: KEY TERMS, PEOPLE, PLACES, CONCEPTS
Chapter 2. American Society in the Making

American Revolution	The American Revolution was the political upheaval during the last half of the 18th century in which thirteen colonies in North America joined together to break free from the British Empire, combining to become the United States of America. They first rejected the authority of the Parliament of Great Britain to govern them from overseas without representation, and then expelled all royal officials. By 1774, each colony had established a Provincial Congress, or an equivalent governmental institution, to govern itself, but still within the empire. The British responded by sending combat troops to re-impose direct rule.
Christianity	Christianity is a monotheistic religion based on the life and teachings of Jesus as presented in canonical gospels and other New Testament writings. Adherents of the Christian faith are known as Christians. Christianity teaches that Jesus is the Son of God, God having become human and the saviour of humanity.
Fur trade	The fur trade is a worldwide industry dealing in the acquisition and sale of animal fur. Since the establishment of world market for in the early modern period furs of boreal, polar and cold temperate mammalian animals have been the most valued. Historically it had a large impact on the exploration and colonization of Siberia, northern North America and the South Shetland and South Sandwich Islands.
Iroquois	The Iroquois, are an association of several tribes of indigenous people of North America. After the Iroquoian-speaking peoples coalesced as distinct tribes, based mostly in present-day central and upstate New York, in the 16th century or earlier they came together in an association known today as the Iroquois League, or the 'League of Peace and Power'. The original Iroquois League was often known as the Five Nations, as it was composed of the Mohawk, Oneida, Onondaga, Cayuga and Seneca nations. After the Tuscarora nation joined the League in 1722, the Iroquois became known as the Six Nations.
Louisiana	Louisiana was the name of an administrative district of the Viceroyalty of New Spain from 1764 to 1803 that represented territory west of the Mississippi River basin, plus New Orleans. Spain acquired the territory from France: see Louisiana. History

The area, comprising what is now known as the Louisiana Purchase, was turned over to the French for a few days in 1803 before it, in turn, was turned over to the United States.

Natchez

Natchez has been the name of several steamboats, and four naval vessels, each named after the city of Natchez, Mississippi or the Natchez people. The current one has been in operation since 1975. The previous Natchez were all operated in the nineteenth century, most by Captain Thomas P. Leathers. Each of the steamboats since Leathers' first had as its ensign a cotton bale between its stacks.

New France

New France was the area colonized by France in North America during a period beginning with the exploration of the Saint Lawrence River by Jacques Cartier in 1534 and ending with the cession of New France to Spain and Great Britain in 1763. At its peak in 1712 (before the Treaty of Utrecht), the territory of New France extended from Newfoundland to the Rocky Mountains and from Hudson Bay to the Gulf of Mexico. The territory was then divided into five colonies, each with its own administration: Canada, Acadia, Hudson Bay, Newfoundland (Plaisance), and Louisiana. The Treaty of Utrecht resulted in the relinquishing of French claims to mainland Acadia, the Hudson Bay and Newfoundland, and the establishment of the colony of Île Royale (Cape Breton Island) as the successor to Acadia.

Plains Indians

The Plains Indians are the Indigenous peoples who live on the plains and rolling hills of the Great Plains of North America. Their colorful equestrian culture and resistance to White domination have made the Plains Indians an archetype in literature and art for American Indians everywhere.

Plains Indians are usually divided into two broad classifications which overlap to some degree. The first group were fully nomadic, following the vast herds of buffalo, although some tribes occasionally engaged in agriculture; growing tobacco and corn primarily.

Chapter 2. American Society in the Making

New Spain	New Spain, formally called the Viceroyalty of New Spain, was a viceroyalty of the Spanish colonial empire, comprising primarily territories in what was known then as 'América Septentrional' or North America. Its capital was Mexico City, formerly Tenochtitlan, capital of the Aztec Empire. New Spain was established following the Spanish conquest of the Aztec Empire in 1521, and at its greatest extent included much of North America south of Canada: all of present-day Mexico and Central America (except Panama), most of the United States west of the Mississippi River and the Floridas. New Spain also included the Spanish East Indies (Philippine Islands, Mariana Islands, the Caroline Islands, Taiwan, and parts of the Moluccas) and the Spanish West Indies (Cuba, Hispaniola with Haiti and the Dominican Republic, Puerto Rico, Jamaica, Cayman Islands, Trinidad, and the Bay Islands).
Pueblo	Pueblo is a term used to describe modern (and ancient) communities of Native Americans in the Southwestern United States of America. The first Spanish Explorers of the Southwest used this term to describe communities that consisted of apartment-like structures made from stone, adobe mud, and other local material. These structures were usually multi-storeyed buildings surrounding an open plaza and were occupied by hundreds to thousands of Pueblo People.
Pueblo people	The Pueblo people are a Native American people in the Southwestern United States. Their traditional economy is based on agriculture and trade. When first encountered by the Spanish in the 16th century, they were living in villages that the Spanish called pueblos, meaning 'villages'.
Washington	Washington was one of the first steamboats to operate in the states of California and Oregon. Operations in California Washington operated in California on the Sacramento River. The vessel was purchased in California in 1851 by pioneer steamboat captain Alexander Sinclair Murray (b.1828).

Chesapeake Colonies	The Chesapeake Colonies were the Colony and Dominion of Virginia, later the Commonwealth of Virginia, and Province of Maryland, later Maryland, both colonies located in British America and centered around the Chesapeake Bay. These colonies were founded in the 17th century and economies were dependent on the Bay's rich fisheries, docking ships, and plantations. The cash crop tobacco was especially important.
Dysentery	Dysentery is an inflammatory disorder of the intestine, especially of the colon, that results in severe diarrhea containing mucus and/or blood in the feces with fever and abdominal pain. If left untreated, dysentery can be fatal.
England	England is a country that is part of the United Kingdom. It shares land borders with Scotland to the north and Wales to the west; the Irish Sea is to the north west, the Celtic Sea to the south west and the North Sea to the east, with the English Channel to the south separating it from continental Europe. Most of England comprises the central and southern part of the island of Great Britain in the North Atlantic.
Indian American	Indian Americans are Americans who are of Asian descent and have ancestors who are born or are native to India. To make a clear distinction and difference between Indians of Asian origin and Indians 'named as' who are Indigenous peoples of the Americas, the U.S. Census Bureau popularized the term Asian Indian to avoid confusion with 'American Indian'. History The term: Indian In North America the term Indian has an ambiguous meaning.
Middle Colonies	The Middle Colonies comprised the middle region of the Thirteen British Colonies in Northern America. Following the American Revolution, the Middle Colonies became the states of New Jersey, Pennsylvania, New York and Delaware.

	Much of the area was part of the New Netherland until the British exerted control over the region. The British captured much of the area in its war with the Dutch around 1664, and the majority of the conquered land became the Province of New York.
New England Colonies	The New England Colonies of British America included the colonies of Massachusetts Bay Colony, Connecticut Colony, Colony of Rhode Island and Providence Plantations and Province of New Hampshire. They were part of the Thirteen Colonies including the Middle Colonies and the Southern Colonies. These were early colonies of what would later be the states in New England.
Headright	A headright is a legal grant of land to settlers. Headrights are most notable for their role in the expansion of the thirteen British colonies in North America; the Virginia Company of London gave headrights to settlers, and the Plymouth Company followed suit. The headright system was used in several colonies, including Maryland, Georgia, North Carolina and South Carolina.
Lake Erie	Lake Erie is the fourth largest lake (by surface area) of the five Great Lakes in North America, and the thirteenth largest globally. It is the southernmost, shallowest, and smallest by volume of the Great Lakes and therefore also has the shortest average water residence time. It is bounded on the north by the Canadian province of Ontario, on the south by the U.S. states of Ohio, Pennsylvania, and New York, and on the west by the state of Michigan.
Land grant	A land grant is a gift of real estate - land or its privileges - made by a government or other authority as a reward for services to an individual, especially in return for military service. Grants of land are also awarded to individuals and companies as incentives to develop unused land in relatively unpopulated countries; the process of awarding land grants are not limited to the countries named below. Ancient Rome Roman soldiers were given rewards at the end of their service including cash or land (praemia).
Massachusetts	'Massachusetts', words and music by Arlo Guthrie, was made the official folk song of Massachusetts in July, 1981.

Massachusetts Body of Liberties	The Massachusetts Body of Liberties was the first legal code to be established by European colonists in New England. Compiled by the Puritan minister Nathaniel Ward, the laws were established by the Massachusetts General Court in 1641. The Body of Liberties begins by establishing the exclusive right of the General Court to legislate and dictate the 'Countenance of Authority'. In 1684 King Charles II revoked the Body of Liberties and reinstated English law over the Commonwealth.
Nathaniel Bacon	Nathaniel Bacon was a wealthy colonist of the Virginia Colony, famous as the instigator of Bacon's Rebellion of 1676, which collapsed when Bacon himself died from dysentery. Early life When he arrived in Virginia, Bacon settled on the frontier near Jamestown, Virginia, and was appointed to the council of Governor William Berkeley.Some sources have claimed that Berkeley's wife, Francis Culpeper was a cousin of Nathaniel Bacon. Bacon's Rebellion Before the 'Virginia Rebellion,' as it was then called, began in earnest, in 1674, a group of so-called 'freeholders' on the Virginia frontier demanded that Native Americans living on treaty-protected lands be driven out or killed.
Berkeley	The Berkeley was one of several ferryboats of the Southern Pacific Railroad that operated on San Francisco Bay between the Oakland Pier and the San Francisco Ferry Building for sixty years. Built in 1898 by the Union Iron Works of San Francisco, she served after the 1906 earthquake, ferrying refugees across the bay to Oakland.

The Berkeley was in regular service from 1898 to the spring of 1958, when she was taken out of service for repairs.

London Company

The London Company was an English joint stock company established by royal charter by James I of England on April 10, 1606 with the purpose of establishing colonial settlements in North America.

The territory granted to the London Company included the coast of North America from the 34th parallel (Cape Fear) north to the 41st parallel (in Long Island Sound), but being part of the Virginia Company and Colony, the London Company owned a large portion of Atlantic and Inland Canada. The company was permitted by its charter to establish a 100-square-mile (260 km^2) settlement within this area. The portion of the company's territory north of the 38th parallel was shared with the Plymouth Company, with the stipulation that neither company found a colony within 100 miles (161 km) of each other.

Eliza Lucas

Eliza Lucas Pinckney (December 27, 1723-1793) changed agriculture in colonial South Carolina, where she developed indigo as one of its most important cash crops. Its cultivation and processing as dye produced one-third the total value of the colony's exports before the Revolutionary War. Manager of three plantations at age seventeen, Pinckney had a major impact on the economy.

North Carolina

North Carolina is a state located in the Southeastern United States. The state borders South Carolina and Georgia to the south, Tennessee to the west and Virginia to the north. North Carolina contains 100 counties.

South Carolina

South Carolina is a state in the Deep South that borders Georgia to the south and North Carolina to the north. Originally part of the Province of Carolina, the Province of South Carolina was one of the 13 colonies that declared independence from the British Crown during the American Revolution. The colony was originally named by King Charles II of England in honor of his father Charles I, as Carolus is Latin for Charles.

Black Codes	The Black Codes were unofficial laws put in place in the United States to limit the basic human rights and civil liberties of blacks. Even though the U.S. constitution originally discriminated against blacks (as 'other persons') and both Northern and Southern states had passed discriminatory legislation from the early 19th century, the term Black Codes is used most often to refer to legislation passed by Southern states at the end of the Civil War to control the labor, migration and other activities of newly-freed slaves. In Texas, the Eleventh Legislature produced these codes in 1866, right after the United States Civil War.
Puritan	The Puritans were a significant grouping of English Protestants in the 16th and 17th centuries, including, but not limited to, English Calvinists. Puritanism in this sense was founded by some Marian exiles from the clergy shortly after the accession of Elizabeth I of England in 1558, as an activist movement within the Church of England. The designation 'Puritan' is often incorrectly used, notably based on the assumption that hedonism and puritanism are antonyms: Historically, the word was used pejoratively to characterize the Protestant group as extremists similar to the Cathari of France, and according to Thomas Fuller in his Church History dated back to 1564, Archbishop Matthew Parker of that time used it and 'precisian' with the sense of modern 'stickler'.
Southern Colonies	The Southern Colonies in North America were established by Europeans during the 16th and 17th centuries and consisted of olden South Carolina, North Carolina, Maryland, Virginia and Georgia. Their historical names were the Colony and Dominion of Virginia, the Province of Carolina, and the Province of Georgia. The colonies were originally instated to compete in the race for colonies in the 15th, 16th, and 17th centuries.
Great Awakening	The Great Awakening was a religious revival in American religious history. Historians and theologians identify three or four waves of Great Awakening occurring from the early 18th century to the late 20th century, each characterized by widespread revivals led by evangelical Protestant ministers, a sharp increase of interest in religion, a profound sense of conviction and redemption on the part of those affected, a jump in evangelical church membership, and the formation of new religious movements and denominations. First Great Awakening

	The First Great Awakening began in 1725 and lasted to about 1750. Ministers from various evangelical Protestant denominations supported the Great Awakening,.
Border	Border is a 1997 blockbuster Bollywood war film based on the Indo-Pakistani War of 1971. J. P. Dutta directed and produced this war epic which stars Sunny Deol, Jackie Shroff, Sunil Shetty, Akshay Khanna, Pooja Bhatt, Sharbani Mukherjee and Tabu. Director J.P. Dutta won Best Director at the same award function, while his father O.P. Dutta won for Best Dialogues. The movie is an adaptation from real life events that happened at the Battle of Longewala fought in Rajasthan (Western Theatre) during the Indo-Pakistani War of 1971 and Bangladesh Liberation War.
Boston	Boston is the capital of and largest city in Massachusetts, and is one of the oldest cities in the United States. The largest city in New England, Boston is regarded as the unofficial 'Capital of New England' for its economic and cultural impact on the entire New England region. The city proper had a 2009 estimated population of 645,169, making it the twentieth largest in the country.
George Corbin Washington	George Corbin Washington was a United States Congressman from the third and fifth districts of Maryland, serving four terms from 1827 to 1833, and 1835 to 1837. He was also a grandnephew of U.S. President George Washington. Washington was born at Haywood Farms near Oak Grove of Westmoreland County, Virginia. He attended Phillips Academy and Harvard University, studied law, but devoted himself to agricultural pursuits on his plantation in Maryland.

John Cotton	John Cotton was an English clergyman and colonist. He was a principal figure among the New England Puritan ministers, who also included Thomas Hooker, Increase Mather (who became his son-in-law), John Davenport, and Thomas Shepard and John Norton, who wrote his first biography. Cotton was the grandfather of Cotton Mather, who was named after him.
Half-Way Covenant	The Half-Way Covenant was a form of partial church membership created by New England in 1662. It was promoted in particular by the Reverend Solomon Stoddard, who felt that the people of the English colonies were drifting away from their original religious purpose. First-generation settlers were beginning to die out, while their children and grandchildren often expressed less religious piety, and more desire for material wealth. Full membership in the tax-supported Puritan church required an account of a conversion experience, and only persons in full membership could have their own children baptized.
Quakers	The Religious Society of Friends, or Friends Church, is a Christian movement which stresses the doctrine of the priesthood of all believers. Members are known as Friends, or popularly as Quakers. It is made of independent organisations which have split from one another due to doctrinal differences.
Charles Ridgely II	Col. Charles Ridgely II, 'Charles The Merchant' (1702-1772) of 'Ridgely's Whim', a Justice, planter, mechant, ironmaster, and member of the Lower House. Charles II, was the son of Charles Ridgely I, 'Charles The Planter' (ca. 1670-1705) and Deborah Dorsey (ca. 1685-1752). Charles was born in Prince George's County, and still a minor at the death of his father in 1705. He inherited the estates 'White Wine' and 'Claret' from his grandfather Hon.
Oliver Cromwell	Oliver Cromwell was an English military and political leader who overthrew the English monarchy and temporarily turned England into a republican Commonwealth, and ruled as Lord Protector of England, Scotland and Ireland. Cromwell was one of the commanders of the New Model Army which defeated the royalists in the English Civil War. After the execution of King Charles I in 1649, Cromwell dominated the short-lived Commonwealth of England, conquered Ireland and Scotland, and ruled as Lord Protector from 1653 until his death in 1658.

Chapter 2. American Society in the Making

Glorious Revolution	The Glorious Revolution, was the overthrow of King James II of England (VII of Scotland and II of Ireland) in 1688 by a union of English Parliamentarians with an invading army led by the Dutch stadtholder William III of Orange-Nassau (William of Orange) who, as a result, ascended the English throne as William III of England together with his wife Mary II of England. The crisis facing King James II came to a head in 1688, when the King fathered a son, James Francis Edward Stuart on 10 June (Julian calendar). Until then the throne would have passed to his daughter Mary, a Protestant, the wife of William.
Samuel Parris	Samuel Parris was the Puritan minister in Salem Village, Massachusetts during the Salem witch trials; he was also the father of one of the afflicted girls, and the uncle of another. He was born in London, England, the son of cloth merchant Thomas Parris. He emigrated to Boston in the early 1660s, where he attended Harvard University.
Salem witch trials	The Salem witch trials were a series of hearings and prosecutions of people accused of witchcraft in colonial Massachusetts, between February 1692 and May 1693. Despite being generally known as the Salem witch trials, the preliminary hearings in 1692 were conducted in a variety of towns across the province: Salem Village (now Danvers), Ipswich, Andover and Salem Town. The most infamous trials were conducted by the Court of Oyer and Terminer in 1692 in Salem Town. One contemporary writer summed the results of the trials thus: At least five more of the accused died in prison.

Sarah Osborne	Sarah Osborne (c. 1643-May 10, 1692) was one of the first three women to be accused of witchcraft in the Salem witch trials of 1692. Osborne is sometimes referred to as 'Goody Osborne', Goody being short for 'Goodwife' and at the time a form of address for old women of lowly social status. Early life and first marriage Sarah Osbourne, born Sarah Warren, married a prominent man by the name of Robert Prince. He was the brother of a woman who married into the prominent Putnam family.
William Phips	Sir William Phips (February 2, 1651 - February 18, 1695) was a colonial governor of Massachusetts. Military career Phips was born the son of James and Mary Phips, at Woolwich, Maine, near the mouth of the Kennebec River, the twenty-sixth child in his family. He was a cousin of Sir Constantine Phipps, Lord Chancellor of Ireland, ancestor of the Marquess of Normanby.
Tituba	Tituba was a 17th-century slave belonging to Samuel Parris of Salem, Massachusetts. Tituba was one of the first three people accused of practicing witchcraft during the Salem witch trials which took place in 1692. Tituba was the third person accused by Betty Parris and Abigail Williams of witchcraft. She was, however, the first person to confess to witchcraft in Salem Village.
Atlantic slave trade	The Atlantic slave trade or trans-atlantic slave trade took place across the Atlantic ocean from the 16th through to the 19th centuries. The vast majority of slaves involved in the Atlantic trade were Africans from the central and western parts of the continent, who were sold by Africans to European slave traders, who transported them across the ocean to the colonies in North and South America. There, the slaves were forced to labor on coffee, tobacco, cocoa, cotton and sugar plantations, toil in gold and silver mines, in rice fields, the construction industry, timber for ships, or in houses to work as servants.

The slave traders were, in order of scale: the Portuguese, the British, the French, the Spanish, the Dutch, and Americans.

Commerce

While business refers to the value-creating activities of an organization for profit, commerce means the whole system of an economy that constitutes an environment for business. The system includes legal, economic, political, social, cultural, and technological systems that are in operation in any country. Thus, commerce is a system or an environment that affects the business prospects of an economy or a nation-state.

Napoleonic Wars

The Napoleonic Wars were a series of conflicts declared against Napoleon's French Empire and changing sets of European allies by opposing coalitions that ran from 1803 to 1815. As a continuation of the wars sparked by the French Revolution of 1789, they revolutionized European armies and played out on an unprecedented scale, mainly due to the application of modern mass conscription. French power rose quickly, conquering most of Europe, but collapsed rapidly after France's disastrous invasion of Russia in 1812. Napoleon's empire ultimately suffered complete military defeat resulting in the restoration of the Bourbon monarchy in France. The wars resulted in the dissolution of the Holy Roman Empire and sowed the seeds of nascent nationalism in Germany and Italy that would lead to the two nations' consolidation later in the century.

New Amsterdam

New Amsterdam was a 17th-century Dutch colonial settlement that served as the capital of New Netherland. It was later renamed to New York City.

The settlement, outside of Fort Amsterdam on Manhattan Island in the New Netherland territory (1614-1664), was situated between 38 and 42 degrees latitude and was as a provincial extension of the Dutch Republic as of 1624. Situated on the strategic, fortifiable southern tip of the island of Manhattan, the fort was meant to defend the Dutch East India Company's fur trade operations in the North River (Hudson River).

Diversity

The 'business case for diversity' theorizes that, in a global marketplace, a company that employs a diverse workforce (both men and women, people of many generations, people from ethnically and racially diverse backgrounds etc). is better able to understand the demographics of the marketplace it serves and is thus better equipped to thrive in that marketplace than a company that has a more limited range of employee demographics.

An additional corollary suggests that a company that supports the diversity of its workforce can also improve employee satisfaction, productivity, and retention.

Benjamin Franklin

Benjamin Franklin was one of the Founding Fathers of the United States. A noted polymath, Franklin was a leading author and printer, political theorist, politician, postmaster, scientist, inventor, satirist, civic activist, statesman, and diplomat. As a scientist, he was a major figure in the American Enlightenment and the history of physics for his discoveries and theories regarding electricity.

Mennonite

The Mennonites are a group of Christian Anabaptist denominations named after the Frisian Menno Simons (1496-1561), who, through his writings, articulated and thereby formalized the teachings of earlier Swiss founders. The teachings of the Mennonites were founded on their belief in both the mission and ministry of Jesus Christ, which they held to with great conviction despite persecution by the various Roman Catholic and Protestant states. Rather than fight, the majority survived by fleeing to neighboring states where ruling families were tolerant of their radical belief in adult baptism.

York

York was an African American slave best known for his participation with the Lewis and Clark Expedition. As William Clark's slave, he had to do diffficult manual labour without pay. After the expedition's return he pressed for his freedom, which Clark opposed, he possibly agreed ten years later, though some historians dispute this and say he was never freed.

Jacob Leisler

Jacob Leisler was a German-born American colonist. He helped create the Huguenot settlement of New Rochelle in 1688 and later served as the acting Lieutenant Governor of New York. Beginning in 1689, he led an insurrection dubbed Leisler's Rebellion in colonial New York, seizing control of the colony until he was captured and executed in New York City for treason against William and Mary.

Paxton Boys

The Paxton Boys were a vigilante group who murdered 20 Susquehannock in events collectively called the Conestoga Massacre. Scots-Irish frontiersmen from central Pennsylvania along the Susquehanna River formed a vigilante group to retaliate against local American Indians in the aftermath of the French and Indian War and Pontiac's Rebellion.

Attack on Susquehannock

In the aftermath of the French and Indian War, the frontier of Pennsylvania remained unsettled.

Pennsylvania Dutch	The Pennsylvania Dutch are the descendants of Germanic peoples who emigrated to the U.S. (primarily to Pennsylvania), from Southwestern Germany and Switzerland. The origin of the word 'Dutch' is a 'folk-rendering' of the Pennsylvania Dutch's own self-designation Deitsch. There is also some speculation among scholars that 'Dutch' is actually an archaic term that was used to refer to all people of Germanic descent, and that is the term that stuck in the English-speaking community.

1. The Religious Society of Friends, or Friends Church, is a Christian movement which stresses the doctrine of the priesthood of all believers. Members are known as Friends, or popularly as _________. It is made of independent organisations which have split from one another due to doctrinal differences.

   a. Respect for America's Fallen Heroes Act
   b. Jessica's Law
   c. Quakers
   d. Adelbert Ames, Jr.

2. The _________ are the descendants of Germanic peoples who emigrated to the U.S. (primarily to Pennsylvania), from Southwestern Germany and Switzerland. The origin of the word 'Dutch' is a 'folk-rendering' of the _________'s own self-designation Deitsch. There is also some speculation among scholars that 'Dutch' is actually an archaic term that was used to refer to all people of Germanic descent, and that is the term that stuck in the English-speaking community.

   a. Digital Transition Content Security Act
   b. Dutch West India Company
   c. Pennsylvania Dutch
   d. Pinkster

3. The _________ was one of several ferryboats of the Southern Pacific Railroad that operated on San Francisco Bay between the Oakland Pier and the San Francisco Ferry Building for sixty years. Built in 1898 by the Union Iron Works of San Francisco, she served after the 1906 earthquake, ferrying refugees across the bay to Oakland.

   The _________ was in regular service from 1898 to the spring of 1958, when she was taken out of service for repairs.

   a. Digital Transition Content Security Act
   b. Peregrine Bland
   c. Berkeley
   d. John Casor

4. _________ was the area colonized by France in North America during a period beginning with the exploration of the Saint Lawrence River by Jacques Cartier in 1534 and ending with the cession of _________ to Spain and Great Britain in 1763. At its peak in 1712 (before the Treaty of Utrecht), the territory of _________ extended from Newfoundland to the Rocky Mountains and from Hudson Bay to the Gulf of Mexico. The territory was then divided into five colonies, each with its own administration: Canada, Acadia, Hudson Bay, Newfoundland (Plaisance), and Louisiana. The Treaty of Utrecht resulted in the relinquishing of French claims to mainland Acadia, the Hudson Bay and Newfoundland, and the establishment of the colony of Île Royale (Cape Breton Island) as the successor to Acadia.

a. New Netherland
b. New Sweden
c. New France
d. Treaty of Whitehall

5. The _________ was the political upheaval during the last half of the 18th century in which thirteen colonies in North America joined together to break free from the British Empire, combining to become the United States of America. They first rejected the authority of the Parliament of Great Britain to govern them from overseas without representation, and then expelled all royal officials. By 1774, each colony had established a Provincial Congress, or an equivalent governmental institution, to govern itself, but still within the empire. The British responded by sending combat troops to re-impose direct rule.

a. American Revolution
b. Apology Resolution
c. Appointments Clause
d. Army Appropriations Act of 1916

ANSWER KEY
Chapter 2. American Society in the Making

1. c
2. c
3. c
4. c
5. a

CHAPTER OUTLINE: KEY TERMS, PEOPLE, PLACES, CONCEPTS
Chapter 3

America in the British Empire

_______ John G. Adams

_______ Delaware Colony

_______ England

_______ Gettysburg Campaign

_______ Glorious Revolution

_______ Albany Plan

_______ Commerce

_______ PLANS

_______ Colonial agent

_______ Iron Act

_______ Navigation Acts

_______ Christianity

_______ Great Awakening

_______ Molasses Act

_______ Benjamin Franklin

_______ Theodore Frelinghuysen

_______ South Carolina

_______ William Tennent

_______ Brown University

Chapter 3. America in the British Empire

- Timothy Cutler
- Jonathan Edwards
- Joseph Hawley
- Solomon Stoddard
- Columbia
- Deism
- Union
- American Philosophical Society
- Fur trade
- Paxton Boys
- American Revolution
- Iroquois
- Massachusetts
- Nation
- New Amsterdam
- Nova Scotia
- Ohio Company
- War of the Austrian Succession
- War of the Spanish Succession

______________ Constitutional Convention

______________ Fort Duquesne

______________ Fort Moultrie

______________ French and Indian War

______________ Alabama

______________ CSS Alabama

______________ Fort Pitt

______________ George Mason II

______________ Aztec

______________ George Mason III

______________ Early American currency

______________ Continental Congress

______________ Salutary neglect

______________ Roy Lichtenstein

______________ East Florida

______________ Sugar Act

______________ West Florida

______________ Patrick Henry

______________ House of Burgesses

Chapter 3. America in the British Empire

________ Thomas Hutchinson

________ Sons of Liberty

________ Stamp Act Congress

________ Quartering Acts

________ Samuel Adams

________ John Dickinson

________ Townshend Acts

________ Boston

________ Boston Massacre

________ Tea Act

________ Boston Tea Party

________ Boston Port Act

________ First Continental Congress

________ Joseph Galloway

________ Massachusetts Government Act

John G. Adams	John G. Adams was the US Army's counsel in the Army-McCarthy Hearings. He was an Army veteran of World War II, and he worked in Washington, DC for the Defense Department before he became the US Army general counsel in 1953. From 1953 to 1955 he was the chief legal adviser to Army Secretary Robert Ten Broeck Stevens. Publications • Adams, John G. (1983).
Delaware Colony	Delaware Colony in the North American Middle Colonies was a region of the Province of Pennsylvania although never legally a separate colony. From 1682 until 1776 it was part of the Penn proprietorship and was known as the lower counties. In 1701 it gained a separate Assembly from the three upper counties but had the same Governor as the rest of Pennsylvania.
England	England is a country that is part of the United Kingdom. It shares land borders with Scotland to the north and Wales to the west; the Irish Sea is to the north west, the Celtic Sea to the south west and the North Sea to the east, with the English Channel to the south separating it from continental Europe. Most of England comprises the central and southern part of the island of Great Britain in the North Atlantic.
Gettysburg Campaign	The Gettysburg Campaign was a series of battles fought in June and July 1863, during the American Civil War. After his victory in the Battle of Chancellorsville, Confederate General Robert E. Lee's Army of Northern Virginia moved north for offensive operations in Maryland and Pennsylvania. The Union Army of the Potomac, commanded by Maj.
Glorious Revolution	The Glorious Revolution, was the overthrow of King James II of England (VII of Scotland and II of Ireland) in 1688 by a union of English Parliamentarians with an invading army led by the Dutch stadtholder William III of Orange-Nassau (William of Orange) who, as a result, ascended the English throne as William III of England together with his wife Mary II of England. The crisis facing King James II came to a head in 1688, when the King fathered a son, James Francis Edward Stuart on 10 June (Julian calendar). Until then the throne would have passed to his daughter Mary, a Protestant, the wife of William.

Chapter 3. America in the British Empire

Albany Plan	The Albany Plan of Union was proposed by Benjamin Franklin at the Albany Congress in 1754 in Albany, New York. It was an early attempt at forming a union of the colonies 'under one government as far as might be necessary for defense and other general important purposes' luring the French and Indian War. Franklin's plan of union was one of several put forth by various delegates of the Albany Congress.
Commerce	While business refers to the value-creating activities of an organization for profit, commerce means the whole system of an economy that constitutes an environment for business. The system includes legal, economic, political, social, cultural, and technological systems that are in operation in any country. Thus, commerce is a system or an environment that affects the business prospects of an economy or a nation-state.
PLANS	People for Legal and Non-Sectarian Schools (PLANS) is an organization based in California in the United States which campaigns against the public funding of Waldorf methods charter schools alleging they violate the United States Constitution's separation of church and state. The group claims independent Waldorf schools and public Waldorf methods charter schools teach anthroposophical content, that this content is religious in nature, and that the schools disguise the anthroposophical content from the public. PLANS filed federal suit in 1998 against two California public school districts, Sacramento City Unified School District and Twin Ridges Elementary School District, to halt the Waldorf methods educational programs implemented in two of their schools.
Colonial agent	A colonial agent was the official representative of one of the Thirteen American Colonies in London in the period before 1775. About 200 men served. They were selected and paid a fixed salary by the colonial government, and given the long delays in communication, they played a major role in negotiating with royal officials, and explaining colonial needs and resources. Their main business was with the Board of Trade, where the agent dealt with land problems, border disputes, military affairs, and Indian affairs.
Iron Act	In American Colonial history, the Iron Act, strictly Importation, etc. Act 1750 (Statute 23 Geo. II c. 29) was one of the legislative measures introduced by the British Parliament, seeking to restrict manufacturing activities in British colonies, particularly in North America, and encourage manufacture to take place in Great Britain.

Navigation Acts

The English Navigation Acts were a series of laws that restricted the use of foreign shipping for trade between England (after 1707 Great Britain) and its colonies, a process which had started in 1651. Their goal was to force colonial development into lines favourable to England, and stop direct colonial trade with the Netherlands, France and other European countries. The original ordinance of 1651 was renewed at the Restoration by Acts of 1660 and 1663, and subsequently subject to minor amendment. These Acts also formed the basis for British overseas trade for nearly 200 years.

Christianity

Christianity is a monotheistic religion based on the life and teachings of Jesus as presented in canonical gospels and other New Testament writings. Adherents of the Christian faith are known as Christians. Christianity teaches that Jesus is the Son of God, God having become human and the saviour of humanity.

Great Awakening

The Great Awakening was a religious revival in American religious history. Historians and theologians identify three or four waves of Great Awakening occurring from the early 18th century to the late 20th century, each characterized by widespread revivals led by evangelical Protestant ministers, a sharp increase of interest in religion, a profound sense of conviction and redemption on the part of those affected, a jump in evangelical church membership, and the formation of new religious movements and denominations.

First Great Awakening

The First Great Awakening began in 1725 and lasted to about 1750. Ministers from various evangelical Protestant denominations supported the Great Awakening,.

Molasses Act

The Molasses Act of March 1733 was an Act of the Parliament of Great Britain (citation 6 Geo II. c. 13), which imposed a tax of six pence per gallon on imports of molasses from non-British colonies. Parliament created the act largely at the insistence of large plantation owners in the British West Indies. The Act was not passed for the purpose of raising revenue, but rather to regulate trade by making British products cheaper than those from the French West Indies.

Chapter 3. America in the British Empire

Benjamin Franklin	Benjamin Franklin was one of the Founding Fathers of the United States. A noted polymath, Franklin was a leading author and printer, political theorist, politician, postmaster, scientist, inventor, satirist, civic activist, statesman, and diplomat. As a scientist, he was a major figure in the American Enlightenment and the history of physics for his discoveries and theories regarding electricity.
Theodore Frelinghuysen	Theodore Frelinghuysen was an American politician, serving as New Jersey Attorney General, United States Senator, and Mayor of Newark, New Jersey before running as a candidate for Vice President with Henry Clay on the Whig ticket in the election of 1844. Upon its incorporation in 1848, Frelinghuysen Township, New Jersey was named after him. Biography He was born in 1787 in Millstone, New Jersey, to Frederick Frelinghuysen. His siblings include: Catharine Frelinghuysen; John Frelinghuysen (1776-1833) the General who married Louisa Mercer and after her death married Elizabeth Mercereau Van Vechten; Maria Frelinghuysen (1778-?); and Frederick Frelinghuysen (1788-1820) the lawyer who married Jane Dumont.
South Carolina	South Carolina is a state in the Deep South that borders Georgia to the south and North Carolina to the north. Originally part of the Province of Carolina, the Province of South Carolina was one of the 13 colonies that declared independence from the British Crown during the American Revolution. The colony was originally named by King Charles II of England in honor of his father Charles I, as Carolus is Latin for Charles.
William Tennent	William Tennent was an early American religious leader and educator in British North America. Early life

Tennent was born in Mid Calder, Linlithgowshire, Scotland, in 1673. He graduated from the University of Edinburgh in 1695 and was ordained in the Church of Ireland in 1706. He migrated to the Thirteen Colonies in 1718, arriving in the colony of Pennsylvania at the urging of his wife's cousin James Logan, an Irish Quaker and close friend of William Penn. In 1726 he was called to a pastorate at the Neshaminy-Warwick Presbyterian Church in present-day Warminster, where he stayed for the remainder of his life.

The Log College

In 1727 Tennent established a religious school in a log cabin that became famous as the Log College.

Brown University

Brown University is a private, Ivy League university located in Providence, Rhode Island, United States. Founded in 1764 prior to American independence from the British Empire as the College in the English Colony of Rhode Island and Providence Plantations early in the reign of King George III (1760-1820), Brown is the third oldest institution of higher education in New England and seventh oldest in the United States.

Several of the buildings on the Brown campus from its founding 18th century period through the 20th century offer fine representation of the Georgian style of American colonial era architecture.

Timothy Cutler

Timothy Cutler was an American Episcopal clergyman and rector of Yale College.

Family background

Cutler was born in Charlestown, Massachusetts, a descendant of Robert Cutler who settled there prior to October 28, 1636. His father was Major John Cutler, an anchorsmith, and his mother, Martha Wiswall. Both his father and grandfather opposed the government formed after the overthrow of Edmund Andros, an early colonial governor in North America, and head of the short-lived Dominion of New England in 1689. Although severely penalized, they refused to subscribe to the government until it had received royal sanction.

Chapter 3. America in the British Empire

Jonathan Edwards	Jonathan Edwards was a preacher, theologian, and missionary to Native Americans. Edwards 'is widely acknowledged to be America's most important and original philosophical theologian,' and one of America's greatest intellectuals. Edwards's theological work is very broad in scope, but he is often associated with his defense of Reformed theology, the metaphysics of theological determinism, and the Puritan heritage.
Joseph Hawley	Joseph Hawley born in Parwich, Derbyshire, England, was the first of the Hawley name to come to America in 1629 . He settled at Stratford, Connecticut in 1650, becoming the town's first town clerk or record keeper, tavern (ordinary) keeper and a shipbuilder . Biography The Hawley Record of 1890 states that Joseph arrived in Boston, Massachusetts around 1629 or 1630 along with Thomas and Robert, who spelled their last name Haule.
Solomon Stoddard	Solomon Stoddard was the American colonial minister who succeeded Rev. Eleazer Mather as pastor at Northampton, Massachusetts, where he died, after Mather's death. Stoddard significantly liberalized church policy while promoting more power for the clergy, decrying drinking and extravagance, and urging the preaching of hellfire and the Judgment. Religious leader Stoddard was a puritan religious leader in the colonial period and the grandfather of the prominent theologian Rev. Jonathan Edwards.
Columbia	The Columbia was a 310 ton, 6 gun barque in the service of the Columbia District of the Hudson's Bay Company on the Columbia River and elsewhere in the Pacific Northwest in the 1830s and 1840s. The vessel's complement of crew was 24 men.

Deism	Deism in the philosophy of religion is the standpoint that reason and observation of the natural world, without the need for organized religion, can determine that the universe is a creation and has a creator. Further the term often implies that this supreme being does not intervene in human affairs or suspend the natural laws of the universe. Deists typically reject supernatural events such as prophecy and miracles, tending to assert that a god (or 'the Supreme Architect') has a plan for the universe that this god does not alter by (regularly or ever) intervening in the affairs of human life.
Union	During the American Civil War, the Union was a name used to refer to the federal government of the United States, which was supported by the twenty free states and five border slave states. It was opposed by 11 Southern slave states that had declared a secession to join together to form the Confederacy. Although the Union states included the Western states of California, Oregon, and (after 1864) Nevada, as well as states generally considered to be part of the Midwest, the Union has been also often loosely referred to as 'the North', both then and now.
American Philosophical Society	The American Philosophical Society, founded in 1741 and located in Philadelphia, Pa., is an eminent scholarly organization of international reputation, that promotes useful knowledge in the sciences and humanities through excellence in scholarly research, professional meetings, publications, library resources, and community outreach. Considered the country's first learned society, it has played an important role in American cultural and intellectual life for over 270 years. Through research grants, published journals, the upkeep of the American Philosophical Society Museum, an extensive library, and regular meetings, the society continues to advance careful study in a wide variety of disciplines in the humanities and the sciences.
Fur trade	The fur trade is a worldwide industry dealing in the acquisition and sale of animal fur. Since the establishment of world market for in the early modern period furs of boreal, polar and cold temperate mammalian animals have been the most valued. Historically it had a large impact on the exploration and colonization of Siberia, northern North America and the South Shetland and South Sandwich Islands.
Paxton Boys	The Paxton Boys were a vigilante group who murdered 20 Susquehannock in events collectively called the Conestoga Massacre. Scots-Irish frontiersmen from central Pennsylvania along the Susquehanna River formed a vigilante group to retaliate against local American Indians in the aftermath of the French and Indian War and Pontiac's Rebellion. Attack on Susquehannock

Chapter 3. America in the British Empire

	In the aftermath of the French and Indian War, the frontier of Pennsylvania remained unsettled.
American Revolution	The American Revolution was the political upheaval during the last half of the 18th century in which thirteen colonies in North America joined together to break free from the British Empire, combining to become the United States of America. They first rejected the authority of the Parliament of Great Britain to govern them from overseas without representation, and then expelled all royal officials. By 1774, each colony had established a Provincial Congress, or an equivalent governmental institution, to govern itself, but still within the empire. The British responded by sending combat troops to re-impose direct rule.
Iroquois	The Iroquois, are an association of several tribes of indigenous people of North America. After the Iroquoian-speaking peoples coalesced as distinct tribes, based mostly in present-day central and upstate New York, in the 16th century or earlier they came together in an association known today as the Iroquois League, or the 'League of Peace and Power'. The original Iroquois League was often known as the Five Nations, as it was composed of the Mohawk, Oneida, Onondaga, Cayuga and Seneca nations. After the Tuscarora nation joined the League in 1722, the Iroquois became known as the Six Nations.
Massachusetts	'Massachusetts', words and music by Arlo Guthrie, was made the official folk song of Massachusetts in July, 1981.
Nation	Nation has different meanings in different contexts. In worldwide diplomacy, nation can mean country or sovereign state. The United Nations, for instance, speaks of how it was founded after the Second World War with '51 countries' and currently has '192 member states'.
New Amsterdam	New Amsterdam was a 17th-century Dutch colonial settlement that served as the capital of New Netherland. It was later renamed to New York City. The settlement, outside of Fort Amsterdam on Manhattan Island in the New Netherland territory (1614-1664), was situated between 38 and 42 degrees latitude and was as a provincial extension of the Dutch Republic as of 1624. Situated on the strategic, fortifiable southern tip of the island of Manhattan, the fort was meant to defend the Dutch East India Company's fur trade operations in the North River (Hudson River).

Nova Scotia	62°42′W? / ?45.217°N 62.7°W Nova Scotia is one of Canada's three Maritime provinces and is the most populous province in Atlantic Canada. The provincial capital is Halifax. Nova Scotia is the second-smallest province in Canada with an area of 55,284 square kilometres (21,300 sq mi).
Ohio Company	The Ohio Company, formally known as the Ohio Company of Virginia, was a land speculation company organized for the settlement by Virginians of the Ohio Country (approximately the present state of Ohio) and to trade with the Indians there. The Company had a land grant from Britain and a treaty with Indians, but France also claimed the area, and the conflict helped provoke the outbreak of the French and Indian War. No lands were actually settled, and the company ended operations by 1776.
War of the Austrian Succession	The War of the Austrian Succession - also known as King George's War in North America, and incorporating the War of Jenkins' Ear with Spain and two of the three Silesian wars - involved nearly all the powers of Europe, except for the Polish-Lithuanian Commonwealth, the Portuguese Empire and the Ottoman Empire. The war began under the pretext that Maria Theresa of Austria was ineligible to succeed to the Habsburg thrones of her father, Charles VI, because Salic law precluded royal inheritance by a woman, though in reality this was a convenient excuse put forward by Prussia and France to challenge Habsburg power. Austria was supported by Great Britain and the Dutch Republic, the traditional enemies of France, as well as the Kingdom of Sardinia and Saxony.
War of the Spanish Succession	The War of the Spanish Succession was fought among several European powers, principally the Spanish loyal to Archduke Charles, the Holy Roman Empire, Great Britain, the Dutch Republic, Portugal and the Duchy of Savoy against the Spanish loyal to Philip V, France and the Electorate of Bavaria over a possible unification of the Kingdoms of Spain and France under one Bourbon monarch. Such a unification would have drastically changed the European balance of power. The war was fought mostly in Europe but included Queen Anne's War in North America and it was marked by the military leadership of notable generals including the Duc de Villars, the Jacobite Duke of Berwick, the Duke of Marlborough and Prince Eugene of Savoy.

Chapter 3. America in the British Empire

Constitutional Convention	The United States Constitutional Convention took place from May 25 to September 17, 1787, in Philadelphia, Pennsylvania, to address problems in governing the United States of America, which had been operating under the Articles of Confederation following independence from Great Britain. Although the Convention was purportedly intended only to revise the Articles of Confederation, the intention from the outset of many of its proponents, chief among them James Madison and Alexander Hamilton, was to create a new government rather than fix the existing one. The delegates elected George Washington to preside over the convention.
Fort Duquesne	Fort Duquesne was a fort established by the French in 1754, at the junction of the Allegheny and Monongahela rivers in what is now downtown Pittsburgh in the state of Pennsylvania. It was destroyed and replaced by Fort Pitt in 1758; over two centuries later, the site formerly occupied by Fort Duquesne is now Point State Park. Fort Duquesne, built at a point where the Allegheny and Monongahela rivers come together to form the Ohio River, was long seen as important for controlling the Ohio Country, both for settlement and for trade.
Fort Moultrie	Fort Moultrie is the name of a series of citadels on Sullivan's Island, South Carolina, built to protect the city of Charleston, South Carolina. The first fort, built of palmetto logs, inspired the flag and nickname (Palmetto State) of South Carolina. It is named in honour of the commander in the Battle of Sullivan's Island, General William Moultrie.
French and Indian War	The French and Indian War is the common American name for the war between Great Britain and France in North America from 1754 to 1763. In 1756, the war erupted into the world-wide conflict known as the Seven Years' War and thus came to be regarded as the North American theater of that war. In Canada, it is usually just referred to as the Seven Years' War, although French Canadians often call it La guerre de la Conquête ('The War of Conquest'). In Europe, there is no specific name for the North American part of the war.
Alabama	Alabama is a state located in the southeastern region of the United States of America. It is bordered by Tennessee to the north, Georgia to the east, Florida and the Gulf of Mexico to the south, and Mississippi to the west. Alabama ranks 30th in total land area and ranks second in the size of its inland waterways. The state ranks 23rd in population with 4.7 million residents in 2009.

CSS Alabama	CSS Alabama was a screw sloop-of-war built for the Confederate States Navy at Birkenhead, United Kingdom, in 1862 by John Laird Sons and Company. Alabama served as a commerce raider, attacking Union merchant and naval ships over the course of her two-year career, during which she never anchored in a Southern port. She was sunk in battle by the USS Kearsarge in 1864 near the Port of Cherbourg, France.
Fort Pitt	Fort Pitt was a fort built at the location of Pittsburgh, Allegheny County, Pennsylvania. French and Indian War The fort was built from 1759 to 1761 during the French and Indian War (Seven Years War), next to the site of former Fort Duquesne. The French built Fort Duquesne in 1754, at the beginning of that war, and it became a focal point due to its strategic river location.
George Mason II	George Mason II was an early American planter and statesman. Mason was the grandfather of George Mason IV, a Founding Father of the United States. Early life Mason was born in 1660 at Accokeek plantation in Stafford County, Virginia.
Aztec	The Aztec people were certain ethnic groups of central Mexico, particularly those groups who spoke the Nahuatl language and who dominated large parts of Mesoamerica in the 14th, 15th and 16th centuries, a period referred to as the late post-classic period in Mesoamerican chronology.

Aztec (Aztecatl) is the Nahuatl word for 'people from Aztlan', a mythological place for the Nahuatl-speaking culture of the time, and later adopted as the word to define the Mexica people. Often the term 'Aztec' refers exclusively to the Mexica people of Tenochtitlan (now the location of Mexico City), situated on an island in Lake Texcoco, who referred to themselves as Mexica Tenochca or Colhua-Mexica. Sometimes the term also includes the inhabitants of Tenochtitlan's two principal allied city-states, the Acolhuas of Texcoco and the Tepanecs of Tlacopan, who together with the Mexica formed the Aztec Triple Alliance which has also become known as the 'Aztec Empire'.

George Mason III

George Mason III was an early American planter, businessman, and statesman. Mason was the father of George Mason IV, a Founding Father of the United States.

Early life

Mason was born in 1690 at Chopawamsic plantation in Stafford County, Virginia.

Early American currency

Early American currency went through several stages of development in the colonial and post-Revolutionary history of the United States. Because few coins were minted in the thirteen colonies that became the United States in 1776, foreign coins like the Spanish dollar were widely circulated. Colonial governments sometimes issued paper money to facilitate economic activity.

Continental Congress

The Continental Congress was a convention of delegates called together from the Thirteen Colonies that became the governing body of the United States during the American Revolution.

The Congress met from 1774 to 1789 in three incarnations. The first call for a convention was made over issues of mounting taxation without representation in Parliament and because of the British blockade.

Salutary neglect	Salutary neglect was an undocumented, though long-lasting, British policy of avoiding strict enforcement of parliamentary laws, meant to keep the American colonies obedient to Great Britain. Prime Minister Robert Walpole stated that 'If no restrictions were placed on the colonies, they would flourish'. This policy, which lasted from about 1607 to 1763, allowed the enforcement of trade relations laws to be lenient.
Roy Lichtenstein	Roy Lichtenstein was a prominent American pop artist. During the 1960s his paintings were exhibited at the Leo Castelli Gallery in New York City and along with Andy Warhol, Jasper Johns, James Rosenquist and others he became a leading figure in the new art movement. His work defined the basic premise of pop art better than any other through parody. Favoring the old-fashioned comic strip as subject matter, Lichtenstein produced hard-edged, precise compositions that documented while it parodied often in a tongue-in-cheek humorous manner. His work was heavily influenced by both popular advertising and the comic book style. He himself described Pop Art as, 'not 'American' painting but actually industrial painting'.
East Florida	East Florida was a colony of Great Britain from 1763-1783 and of Spain from 1783-1822. East Florida was established by the British colonial government in 1763; as its name implies it consisted of the eastern part of the region of Florida, with West Florida comprising the western parts. Its capital was St. Augustine, which had been the capital of Spanish Florida. Britain formed East and West Florida out of territory it had received from France and Spain following the Seven Years' War .
Sugar Act	The Sugar Act, was a revenue-raising act passed by the Parliament of Great Britain on April 5, 1764. The preamble to the act stated: 'it is expedient that new provisions and regulations should be established for improving the revenue of this Kingdom ... and ... it is just and necessary that a revenue should be raised ... for defraying the expenses of defending, protecting, and securing the same.' The earlier Molasses Act of 1733, which had imposed a tax of six pence per gallon of molasses, had never been effectively collected due to colonial evasion. By reducing the rate by half and increasing measures to enforce the tax, the British hoped that the tax would actually be collected. These incidents increased the colonists' concerns about the intent of the British Parliament and helped the growing movement that became the American Revolution.

Chapter 3. America in the British Empire

West Florida	West Florida was a region on the north shore of the Gulf of Mexico, which underwent several boundary and sovereignty changes during its history. West Florida was first established in 1763 by the British government; as its name suggests it largely consisted of the western portion of the region called Florida by Spain, with East Florida comprising the eastern part. It included most of what is now the Florida Panhandle, plus parts of the modern U.S. states of Louisiana, Mississippi, and Alabama.
Patrick Henry	Patrick Henry was an orator and politician who led the movement for independence in Virginia in the 1770s. A Founding Father, he served as the first and sixth post-colonial Governor of Virginia from 1776 to 1779 and subsequently, from 1784 to 1786. Henry led the opposition to the Stamp Act of 1765 and is well remembered for his 'Give me Liberty, or give me Death!' speech. Along with Samuel Adams and Thomas Paine, he is remembered as one of the most influential exponents of Republicanism, promoters of the American Revolution and Independence, especially in his denunciations of corruption in government officials and his defense of historic rights.
House of Burgesses	The House of Burgesses was the first assembly of elected representatives of English colonists in North America. The House was established by the Virginia Company, who created the body as part of an effort to encourage English craftsmen to settle in North America. Its first meeting was held in Jamestown, Virginia, on June 30, 1619. The word 'Burgess' originally referred to a freeman of a borough or burgh. It later came to mean an elected or appointed official of a municipality, or the representative of a borough in the English House of Commons.
Thomas Hutchinson	Thomas Hutchinson was the British royal governor of colonial Massachusetts from 1771 to 1774 and a prominent Loyalist in the years before the American Revolution. Early life Hutchinson was born in Boston. He showed remarkable aptitude for business early on, and by the time he was 24 had accumulated considerable property in trading ventures on his own account.

Sons of Liberty

The Sons of Liberty was a political group made up of American patriots that originated in the pre-independence North American British colonies. The group was formed to protect the rights of the colonists from the usurpations by the British government after 1766. They are best known for undertaking the Boston Tea Party in 1773, which led to the Intolerable Acts (an intense crackdown by the British government), and a counter-mobilization by the Patriots that led directly to the American Revolutionary War in 1775.

Origin

After 1765 the major American cities saw the formation of secret groups set up to defend their rights.

Stamp Act Congress

The Stamp Act Congress was a meeting held between October 7 and 25, 1765 in New York City, consisting of representatives from some British colonies of North America; it was the first gathering of elected representatives from several of the American colonies to devise a unified protest against new British taxation. Parliament had passed the Stamp Act, which governed all its overseas colonies and was coming into effect November 1. The Congress discussed and united against the act, because Parliament did not include any representation from the colonies. The Congress consisted of delegates from nine of the 19 British colonies in North America; all nine would be from the Thirteen Colonies that eventually formed the United States of America.

The Congress met in the building that became Federal Hall in the city, and was held at a a time of widespread protests in the colonies against the Stamp Act's implementation (including some violence).

Quartering Acts

The Quartering Act is the name of at least two 18th-century Acts of the Parliament of Great Britain. These Quartering Acts ordered the local governments of the American colonies to provide housing and provisions for British soldiers. They were amendments to the Mutiny Act, which had to be renewed annually by Parliament.

Samuel Adams

Samuel Adams was an American statesman, political philosopher, and one of the Founding Fathers of the United States. As a politician in colonial Massachusetts, Adams was a leader of the movement that became the American Revolution, and was one of the architects of the principles of American republicanism that shaped the political culture of the United States. He was a second cousin to President John Adams.

Chapter 3. America in the British Empire

John Dickinson	John Dickinson was an American lawyer and politician from Philadelphia, Pennsylvania and Wilmington, Delaware. He was a militia officer during the American Revolution, a Continental Congressman from Pennsylvania and Delaware, a delegate to the U.S. Constitutional Convention of 1787, President of Delaware and President of Pennsylvania. Among the wealthiest men in the British American colonies, he is known as the 'Penman of the Revolution' for his Letters from a Farmer in Pennsylvania; upon receiving news of his death, President Thomas Jefferson recognized him as being 'among the first of the advocates for the rights of his country when assailed by Great Britain' whose 'name will be consecrated in history as one of the great worthies of the revolution.' He is the namesake of Dickinson College.
Townshend Acts	The Townshend Acts were a series of laws passed beginning in 1767 by the Parliament of Great Britain relating to the British colonies in North America. The acts are named for Charles Townshend, the Chancellor of the Exchequer, who proposed the program. Historians vary slightly in which acts they include under the heading 'Townshend Acts', but five laws are frequently mentioned: the Revenue Act of 1767, the Indemnity Act, the Commissioners of Customs Act, the Vice Admiralty Court Act, and the New York Restraining Act.
Boston	Boston is the capital of and largest city in Massachusetts, and is one of the oldest cities in the United States. The largest city in New England, Boston is regarded as the unofficial 'Capital of New England' for its economic and cultural impact on the entire New England region. The city proper had a 2009 estimated population of 645,169, making it the twentieth largest in the country.
Boston Massacre	The Boston Massacre, called The Incident on King Street by the British, was an incident on March 5, 1770, in which British Army soldiers killed five civilian men. British troops had been stationed in Boston, capital of the Province of Massachusetts Bay, since 1768 in order to protect and support crown-appointed colonial officials attempting to enforce unpopular Parliamentary legislation. Amid ongoing tense relations between the population and the soldiers, a mob formed around a British sentry, who was subjected to verbal abuse and harassment.
Tea Act	The Tea Act was an Act of the Parliament of Great Britain. Its principal overt objective was to reduce the massive surplus of tea held by the financially troubled British East India Company in its London warehouses. A related objective was to undercut the price of tea smuggled into Britain's North American colonies.
Boston Tea Party	

The Boston Tea Party was a direct action by colonists in Boston, a town in the British colony of Massachusetts, against the British government and the monopolistic East India Company that controlled all the tea imported into the colonies. On December 16, 1773, after officials in Boston refused to return three shiploads of taxed tea to Britain, a group of colonists boarded the ships and destroyed the tea by throwing it into Boston Harbor. The incident remains an iconic event of American history, and other political protests often refer to it.

Boston Port Act

The Boston Port Act is an Act of the Parliament of Great Britain which became law on March 30, 1774, and is one of the measures (variously called the Intolerable Acts, the Punitive Acts or the Coercive Acts) that were designed to secure Great Britain's jurisdictions over her American dominions.

A response to the Boston Tea Party, it outlawed the use of the Port of Boston (by setting up a barricade/blockade) for 'landing and discharging, loading or shipping, of goods, wares, and merchandise' until such time as restitution was made to the King's treasury (for customs duty lost) and to the East India Company for damages suffered. In other words, it closed Boston Port to all ships, no matter what business the ship had.

First Continental Congress

The First Continental Congress was a convention of delegates from twelve British North American colonies that met on September 5, 1774, at Carpenters' Hall in Philadelphia, Pennsylvania, early in the American Revolution. It was called in response to the passage of the Coercive Acts (also known as Intolerable Acts by the Colonial Americans) by the British Parliament. The Intolerable Acts had punished Boston for the Boston Tea Party.

Joseph Galloway

Joseph Galloway was an American Loyalist during the American Revolution, after serving as delegate to the First Continental Congress from Pennsylvania.

Early life

He was born near West River, Anne Arundel County, Maryland, and moved with his father to Pennsylvania in 1749, where he received a liberal schooling. He studied law, was admitted to the bar and began practice in Philadelphia.

Massachusetts Government Act	The Massachusetts Government Act was passed by the Parliament of Great Britain and became a law on May 20, 1774. This act gave the British Governor complete control of the town meetings, and taking control out of the hands of the colonialists.The Act is one of the Intolerable Acts (also Repressive Acts and/or the Coercive Acts), designed to suppress dissent and restore order in the Province of Massachusetts Bay. In the wake of the Boston Tea Party, Parliament launched a legislative offensive against Massachusetts to control its errant behavior. British officials realized part of their inability to control the colony was rooted in the highly independent nature of local government there.

1. _________ was the US Army's counsel in the Army-McCarthy Hearings. He was an Army veteran of World War II, and he worked in Washington, DC for the Defense Department before he became the US Army general counsel in 1953. From 1953 to 1955 he was the chief legal adviser to Army Secretary Robert Ten Broeck Stevens.

   Publications

   - Adams, John G. (1983).

   a. John G. Adams
   b. George Mason Lovering
   c. Heinrich Hoffman
   d. Simone Holcomb

2. The Quartering Act is the name of at least two 18th-century Acts of the Parliament of Great Britain. These _________ ordered the local governments of the American colonies to provide housing and provisions for British soldiers. They were amendments to the Mutiny Act, which had to be renewed annually by Parliament.

   a. Digital Transition Content Security Act
   b. Quartering Acts
   c. Phrygian cap
   d. Pine Tree Riot

3. The _________ was a meeting held between October 7 and 25, 1765 in New York City, consisting of representatives from some British colonies of North America; it was the first gathering of elected representatives from several of the American colonies to devise a unified protest against new British taxation. Parliament had passed the Stamp Act, which governed all its overseas colonies and was coming into effect November 1. The Congress discussed and united against the act, because Parliament did not include any representation from the colonies. The Congress consisted of delegates from nine of the 19 British colonies in North America; all nine would be from the Thirteen Colonies that eventually formed the United States of America.

   The Congress met in the building that became Federal Hall in the city, and was held at a a time of widespread protests in the colonies against the Stamp Act's implementation (including some violence).

---

a. Virginia Declaration of Rights
b. Philipsburg Proclamation
c. Stamp Act Congress
d. Pine Tree Riot

4. _________ in the North American Middle Colonies was a region of the Province of Pennsylvania although never legally a separate colony. From 1682 until 1776 it was part of the Penn proprietorship and was known as the lower counties. In 1701 it gained a separate Assembly from the three upper counties but had the same Governor as the rest of Pennsylvania.

a. Dominion of New England
b. Loyal Company of Virginia
c. Province of Maine
d. Delaware Colony

5. _________ is a state in the Deep South that borders Georgia to the south and North Carolina to the north. Originally part of the Province of Carolina, the Province of _________ was one of the 13 colonies that declared independence from the British Crown during the American Revolution. The colony was originally named by King Charles II of England in honor of his father Charles I, as Carolus is Latin for Charles.

a. Tennessee
b. Arkansas
c. Thomas Gage
d. South Carolina

ANSWER KEY
Chapter 3. America in the British Empire

---

1. a
2. b
3. c
4. d
5. d

Samuel Adams

William Bradford

American Revolution

Boston

Boston Tea Party

Early American currency

Continental Congress

First Continental Congress

Massachusetts

Militia

Patriot

Paul Revere

Continental Army

Fort Ticonderoga

Patrick Henry

Second Continental Congress

Ticonderoga

John Dickinson

Tea Act

Chapter 4. The American Revolution

________ Common Sense

________ Louisiana

________ Louisiana Purchase

________ Roger Sherman

________ Benedict Arnold

________ Loyalist

________ Montgomery

________ Long Island

________ Silas Deane

________ Benjamin Franklin

________ Arthur Lee

________ Fort Sumter

________ Thomas Sumter

________ Daniel Morgan

________ John Jay

________ Paxton Boys

________ John Trumbull

________ Northwest Territory

________ Articles of Confederation

______ Gettysburg Campaign

______ Robert Morris

______ Washington

______ George Corbin Washington

______ African American

______ Erie Canal

______ George Mason III

______ Middle Colonies

______ South Carolina

______ Abigail Adams

______ John Marshall

______ Northwest Ordinance

______ Western

______ Deism

______ John Carroll

______ Columbia

______ England

______ Wampum

Samuel Adams	Samuel Adams was an American statesman, political philosopher, and one of the Founding Fathers of the United States. As a politician in colonial Massachusetts, Adams was a leader of the movement that became the American Revolution, and was one of the architects of the principles of American republicanism that shaped the political culture of the United States. He was a second cousin to President John Adams.
William Bradford	William Bradford was an English leader of the settlers of the Plymouth Colony in Massachusetts, and was elected thirty times to be the Governor after John Carver died. His journal (1620-1647) was published as Of Plymouth Plantation. Bradford is credited as the first civil authority to designate what popular American culture now views as Thanksgiving in the United States.
American Revolution	The American Revolution was the political upheaval during the last half of the 18th century in which thirteen colonies in North America joined together to break free from the British Empire, combining to become the United States of America. They first rejected the authority of the Parliament of Great Britain to govern them from overseas without representation, and then expelled all royal officials. By 1774, each colony had established a Provincial Congress, or an equivalent governmental institution, to govern itself, but still within the empire. The British responded by sending combat troops to re-impose direct rule.
Boston	Boston is the capital of and largest city in Massachusetts, and is one of the oldest cities in the United States. The largest city in New England, Boston is regarded as the unofficial 'Capital of New England' for its economic and cultural impact on the entire New England region. The city proper had a 2009 estimated population of 645,169, making it the twentieth largest in the country.
Boston Tea Party	The Boston Tea Party was a direct action by colonists in Boston, a town in the British colony of Massachusetts, against the British government and the monopolistic East India Company that controlled all the tea imported into the colonies. On December 16, 1773, after officials in Boston refused to return three shiploads of taxed tea to Britain, a group of colonists boarded the ships and destroyed the tea by throwing it into Boston Harbor. The incident remains an iconic event of American history, and other political protests often refer to it.

Early American currency: Early American currency went through several stages of development in the colonial and post-Revolutionary history of the United States. Because few coins were minted in the thirteen colonies that became the United States in 1776, foreign coins like the Spanish dollar were widely circulated. Colonial governments sometimes issued paper money to facilitate economic activity.

Continental Congress: The Continental Congress was a convention of delegates called together from the Thirteen Colonies that became the governing body of the United States during the American Revolution.

The Congress met from 1774 to 1789 in three incarnations. The first call for a convention was made over issues of mounting taxation without representation in Parliament and because of the British blockade.

First Continental Congress: The First Continental Congress was a convention of delegates from twelve British North American colonies that met on September 5, 1774, at Carpenters' Hall in Philadelphia, Pennsylvania, early in the American Revolution. It was called in response to the passage of the Coercive Acts (also known as Intolerable Acts by the Colonial Americans) by the British Parliament. The Intolerable Acts had punished Boston for the Boston Tea Party.

Massachusetts: 'Massachusetts', words and music by Arlo Guthrie, was made the official folk song of Massachusetts in July, 1981.

Militia: The role of militia, in the United States is complex and has transformed over time. The term militia can be used to describe any number of groups within the United States. Primarily, these fall into:

- The organized militia created by the Militia Act of 1903, which split from the 1792 Uniform Militia forces, and consist of State militia forces, notably the National Guard and the Naval Militia.

Chapter 4. The American Revolution

Patriot	Patriots (also known as American Whigs, Revolutionaries, Congress-Men or Rebels) was the name that the colonists of the British Thirteen United Colonies, who rebelled against British control during the American Revolution, called themselves. It was their leading figures who, in July 1776, declared the United States of America an independent nation. Their rebellion was based on the political philosophy of republicanism, as expressed by pamphleteers, such as Thomas Jefferson, Alexander Hamilton, and Thomas Paine.
Paul Revere	Paul Revere was an American silversmith and a patriot in the American Revolution. He was celebrated after his death for his role as a messenger in the battles of Lexington and Concord, and Revere's name and his 'midnight ride' are well-known in the United States as a patriotic symbol.
Continental Army	**American Revolutionary War** The Continental Army was formed after the outbreak of the American Revolutionary War by the colonies that became the United States of America. Established by a resolution of the Continental Congress on June 14, 1775, it was created to coordinate the military efforts of the Thirteen Colonies in their revolt against the rule of Great Britain. The Continental Army was supplemented by local militias and other troops that remained under control of the individual states. General George Washington was the Commander-in-Chief of the army throughout the war.
Fort Ticonderoga	Fort Ticonderoga, formerly Fort Carillon, is a large 18th-century fort built by the French at a narrows near the south end of Lake Champlain in upstate New York in the United States. It was constructed by Michel Chartier de Lotbinière, Marquis de Lotbinière between 1754 and 1757 during the Seven Years' War, often referred to as the French and Indian War in the USA, and was of strategic importance during the 18th-century colonial conflicts between Great Britain and France, and again to a lesser extent during the American Revolutionary War.

The site controlled a river portage alongside the mouth of the rapids-infested La Chute River in the 3.5 miles (6 kilometers) between Lake Champlain and Lake George and was strategically placed in conflicts over trade routes between the British-controlled Hudson River Valley and the French-controlled Saint Lawrence River Valley.

Patrick Henry

Patrick Henry was an orator and politician who led the movement for independence in Virginia in the 1770s. A Founding Father, he served as the first and sixth post-colonial Governor of Virginia from 1776 to 1779 and subsequently, from 1784 to 1786. Henry led the opposition to the Stamp Act of 1765 and is well remembered for his 'Give me Liberty, or give me Death!' speech. Along with Samuel Adams and Thomas Paine, he is remembered as one of the most influential exponents of Republicanism, promoters of the American Revolution and Independence, especially in his denunciations of corruption in government officials and his defense of historic rights.

Second Continental Congress

The Second Continental Congress was a convention of delegates from the Thirteen Colonies that started meeting on May 10, 1775, in Philadelphia, Pennsylvania, soon after warfare in the American Revolutionary War had begun. It succeeded the First Continental Congress, which met between September 5, 1774 and October 26, 1774, also in Philadelphia. The second Congress managed the colonial war effort, and moved incrementally towards independence, adopting the United States Declaration of Independence on July 4, 1776. By raising armies, directing strategy, appointing diplomats, and making formal treaties, the Congress acted as the de facto national government of what became the United States.

Ticonderoga

The steamboat Ticonderoga is America's last remaining side-paddle-wheel passenger steamer with a vertical beam engine of the type that provided freight and passenger service on America's lakes and rivers from the early 19th to the mid-20th centuries. Commissioned by the Champlain Transportation Company, the Ticonderoga was built in 1906 at the Shelburne Shipyard in Shelburne, Vermont on Lake Champlain.

The Ti measures 220 feet in length and 59 feet in beam, with a displacement of 892 tons.

Chapter 4. The American Revolution

John Dickinson

John Dickinson was an American lawyer and politician from Philadelphia, Pennsylvania and Wilmington, Delaware. He was a militia officer during the American Revolution, a Continental Congressman from Pennsylvania and Delaware, a delegate to the U.S. Constitutional Convention of 1787, President of Delaware and President of Pennsylvania. Among the wealthiest men in the British American colonies, he is known as the 'Penman of the Revolution' for his Letters from a Farmer in Pennsylvania; upon receiving news of his death, President Thomas Jefferson recognized him as being 'among the first of the advocates for the rights of his country when assailed by Great Britain' whose 'name will be consecrated in history as one of the great worthies of the revolution.' He is the namesake of Dickinson College.

Tea Act

The Tea Act was an Act of the Parliament of Great Britain. Its principal overt objective was to reduce the massive surplus of tea held by the financially troubled British East India Company in its London warehouses. A related objective was to undercut the price of tea smuggled into Britain's North American colonies.

Common Sense

Common Sense is a pamphlet written by Thomas Paine. It was first published anonymously on January 10, 1776, during the American Revolution. Common Sense, signed 'Written by an Englishman', became an immediate success.

Louisiana

Louisiana was the name of an administrative district of the Viceroyalty of New Spain from 1764 to 1803 that represented territory west of the Mississippi River basin, plus New Orleans. Spain acquired the territory from France: see Louisiana.

History

The area, comprising what is now known as the Louisiana Purchase, was turned over to the French for a few days in 1803 before it, in turn, was turned over to the United States.

Louisiana Purchase

The Louisiana Purchase was the acquisition by the United States of America of 828,800 square miles (2,147,000 km^2) of France's claim to the territory of Louisiana in 1803. The U.S. paid 60 million francs ($11,250,000) plus cancellation of debts worth 18 million francs ($3,750,000), for a total sum of 15 million dollars for the Louisiana territory ($219 million in 2010 dollars). What was purchased was France's claim only, not the actual territory, which belonged to the tribes which inhabited the area. The territory itself was acquired slowly throughout the nineteenth century by purchases to Native American tribes and wars.

Roger Sherman	Roger Sherman was an early American lawyer and politician. He served as the first mayor of New Haven, Connecticut, and served on the Committee of Five that drafted the Declaration of Independence, and was also a representative and senator in the new republic. He was the only person to sign all four great state papers of the U.S.: the Continental Association, the Declaration of Independence, the Articles of Confederation and the Constitution.
Benedict Arnold	Benedict Arnold was president and then governor of the Colony of Rhode Island and Providence Plantations. He served four and a half years as the President of the colony under the Patent of 1643/44, and then under the royal charter of 1663 became the colony's first governor, subsequently serving for an additional six and a half years in this capacity. Arnold learned the language of the Narragansett people, frequently acting as an interpreter, and like his father was able to acquire a significant amount of land from them.
Loyalist	In general, a loyalist is someone who maintains loyalty to an established government, political party, or sovereign, especially during war or revolutionary change such as the Republicans in the Spanish Civil War in the late 1930s. In modern English usage, the most common application is to loyalty to the British Crown.
Montgomery	The Montgomery is a steam-powered sternwheel-propelled snagboat built in 1925 by the Charleston Dry Dock and Machine Company of Charleston, South Carolina, and operated by the United States Army Corps of Engineers. The Montgomery cleared snags and obstructions from the Coosa, Alabama, Apalachicola, Chattahoochee, Flint, Black Warrior, and Tombigbee Rivers until her retirement from the Corps of Engineers on 8 November 1982. She was restored in 1984 and again in 2004, declared a National Historic Landmark in 1989. The Montgomery now operates as a museum boat in Carrollton, Alabama.
Long Island	The secession of Long Island from New York was proposed as early as 1896, but talk was revived towards the latter part of the 20th century. On March 28, 2008 Suffolk County, New York Comptroller Joseph Sawicki and Keith Durgan proposed a plan that would make Long Island the 51st state of the United States of America. Sawicki says that all the Long Island taxpayers' money would stay on Long Island, rather than the funds being dispersed all over the entire state of New York. The state of Long Island would include over 2.7 million people.

Chapter 4. The American Revolution

Silas Deane	Silas Deane was an American merchant, politician and diplomat. Originally a supporter of American independence Deane served as a delegate to the Continental Congress and then as the United States' first foreign diplomat when he travelled to France to lobby the French government for aid. Deane was drawn into a major political row over his actions in Paris, and subsequently endorsed Loyalist criticisms of American independence.
Benjamin Franklin	Benjamin Franklin was one of the Founding Fathers of the United States. A noted polymath, Franklin was a leading author and printer, political theorist, politician, postmaster, scientist, inventor, satirist, civic activist, statesman, and diplomat. As a scientist, he was a major figure in the American Enlightenment and the history of physics for his discoveries and theories regarding electricity.
Arthur Lee	Dr. Arthur Lee was an American diplomat during the American Revolutionary War. He was the son of Hon. Thomas Lee (1690-1750) and Hannah Harrison Ludwell (1701-1750).
Fort Sumter	Fort Sumter is a Third System masonry coastal fortification located in Charleston harbor, South Carolina. The fort is best known as the site upon which the shots initiating the American Civil War were fired, at the Battle of Fort Sumter. Construction Named after General Thomas Sumter, Revolutionary War hero, Fort Sumter was built following the War of 1812, as one of a series of fortifications on the southern U.S. coast.
Thomas Sumter	Thomas Sumter nicknamed the Carolina Gamecock, was a hero of the American Revolution and went on to become a longtime member of the Congress of the United States. Sumter was born in Virginia in 1734. His father was an emigrant from Wales. Timberlake Expedition On November 19, 1761, as the construction of Fort Robinson was nearing completion, a 400-man Cherokee force led by Chief Kanagatucko (sometimes called 'Old Hop') arrived at the camp and asked for peace, which was immediately granted by Colonel Adam Stephen.

Daniel Morgan	Daniel Morgan was an American pioneer, soldier, and United States Representative from Virginia. One of the most gifted battlefield tacticians of the American Revolutionary War, he later commanded the troops that suppressed the Whiskey Rebellion. Early years Most authorities believe that Morgan was born in Hunterdon County, New Jersey.
John Jay	John Jay was an American lawyer and diplomat, son of William Jay and a grandson of Chief Justice John Jay. He was born in New York City, graduated at Columbia College in 1836, and was admitted to the bar three years later. He early became intensely interested in the antislavery movement, and while still in college (1834) was president of the New York Young Men's Antislavery Society.
Paxton Boys	The Paxton Boys were a vigilante group who murdered 20 Susquehannock in events collectively called the Conestoga Massacre. Scots-Irish frontiersmen from central Pennsylvania along the Susquehanna River formed a vigilante group to retaliate against local American Indians in the aftermath of the French and Indian War and Pontiac's Rebellion. Attack on Susquehannock In the aftermath of the French and Indian War, the frontier of Pennsylvania remained unsettled.
John Trumbull	John Trumbull was an American artist during the period of the American Revolutionary War and was notable for his historical paintings. His Declaration of Independence was used on the reverse of the two-dollar bill. Early years Trumbull was born in Lebanon, Connecticut in 1756, to Jonathan Trumbull, who was Governor of Connecticut from 1769 to 1784, and his wife Faith {Robinson} Trumbull.

Chapter 4. The American Revolution

Northwest Territory	The Territory Northwest of the River Ohio, more commonly known as the Northwest Territory, was an organized incorporated territory of the United States that existed from July 13, 1787, until March 1, 1803, when the southeastern portion of the territory was admitted to the Union as the state of Ohio. Previously, it was part of the Indian Reserve, a territory under British rule set aside in the Royal Proclamation of 1763 for use by American Indians, which was assigned to the United States in the Treaty of Paris (1783). The Congress of the Confederation enacted the Northwest Ordinance in 1787 to provide for the administration of the territories and set rules for admission as a state.
Articles of Confederation	The Articles of Confederation, formally the Articles of Confederation and Perpetual Union, was an agreement among the 13 founding states that legally established the United States of America as a confederation of sovereign states and served as its first constitution. Its drafting by the Continental Congress began in mid 1776 and an approved version was sent to the states for ratification in late 1777. The formal ratification by all 13 states was completed in early 1781. Even if not yet ratified, the Articles provided domestic and international legitimacy for the Continental Congress to direct the American Revolutionary War, conduct diplomacy with Europe and deal with territorial issues and Indian relations. Nevertheless, a perceived weak government created by the Articles became a matter of concern for key nationalists and in 1789 the Articles were replaced with the U.S. Constitution.
Gettysburg Campaign	The Gettysburg Campaign was a series of battles fought in June and July 1863, during the American Civil War. After his victory in the Battle of Chancellorsville, Confederate General Robert E. Lee's Army of Northern Virginia moved north for offensive operations in Maryland and Pennsylvania. The Union Army of the Potomac, commanded by Maj.
Robert Morris	Robert Morris, Jr. (January 20, 1734 - May 9, 1806) was an American merchant, and signer of the Declaration of Independence, the Articles of Confederation, and the United States Constitution. He was elected to the Pennsylvania Assembly and became the Chairman of the Pennsylvania Committee of Safety and a member of the Second Continental Congress where he served as chairman of the 'Secret Committee of Trade' and as a member of the Committee of Correspondence.
Washington	Washington was one of the first steamboats to operate in the states of California and Oregon. Operations in California

Washington operated in California on the Sacramento River. The vessel was purchased in California in 1851 by pioneer steamboat captain Alexander Sinclair Murray (b.1828).

George Corbin Washington

George Corbin Washington was a United States Congressman from the third and fifth districts of Maryland, serving four terms from 1827 to 1833, and 1835 to 1837. He was also a grandnephew of U.S. President George Washington.

Washington was born at Haywood Farms near Oak Grove of Westmoreland County, Virginia. He attended Phillips Academy and Harvard University, studied law, but devoted himself to agricultural pursuits on his plantation in Maryland.

African American

African Americans (also referred to as Black Americans or Afro-Americans, and formerly as American Negroes) are citizens or residents of the United States who have origins in any of the black populations of Africa. In the United States, the terms are generally used for Americans with at least partial Sub-Saharan African ancestry. Most African Americans are the direct descendants of captive Africans who survived the slavery era within the boundaries of the present United States, although some are--or are descended from--immigrants from African, Caribbean, Central American or South American nations. As an adjective, the term is usually written as African-American.

Erie Canal

The Erie Canal is a waterway in New York that runs about 363 miles (584 km) from Albany, New York, on the Hudson River to Buffalo, New York, at Lake Erie, completing a navigable water route from the Atlantic Ocean to the Great Lakes. The canal contains 36 locks and encompasses a total elevation differential of around 565 ft. (169 m).

George Mason III

George Mason III was an early American planter, businessman, and statesman. Mason was the father of George Mason IV, a Founding Father of the United States.

Early life

Mason was born in 1690 at Chopawamsic plantation in Stafford County, Virginia.

Chapter 4. The American Revolution

Middle Colonies	The Middle Colonies comprised the middle region of the Thirteen British Colonies in Northern America. Following the American Revolution, the Middle Colonies became the states of New Jersey, Pennsylvania, New York and Delaware. Much of the area was part of the New Netherland until the British exerted control over the region. The British captured much of the area in its war with the Dutch around 1664, and the majority of the conquered land became the Province of New York.
South Carolina	South Carolina is a state in the Deep South that borders Georgia to the south and North Carolina to the north. Originally part of the Province of Carolina, the Province of South Carolina was one of the 13 colonies that declared independence from the British Crown during the American Revolution. The colony was originally named by King Charles II of England in honor of his father Charles I, as Carolus is Latin for Charles.
Abigail Adams	Abigail Adams was the wife of John Adams, who was the second President of the United States, and the mother of John Quincy Adams, the sixth. She was the first Second Lady of the United States, and the second First Lady of the United States. Adams is remembered for the many letters she wrote to her husband while he stayed in Philadelphia, Pennsylvania, during the Continental Congresses.
John Marshall	John Marshall was the Chief Justice of the United States (1801-1835) whose court opinions helped lay the basis for American constitutional law while promoting nationalism and making the Supreme Court of the United States a center of power with the capability of overruling Congress. Previously Marshall had been a leader of the Federalist Party in Virginia. and served in the United States House of Representatives from 1799 to 1800. He was Secretary of State under President John Adams from 1800 to 1801.
Northwest Ordinance	The Northwest Ordinance was an act of the Congress of the Confederation of the United States. The primary effect of the ordinance was the creation of the Northwest Territory as the first organized territory of the United States out of the region south of the Great Lakes, north and west of the Ohio River, and east of the Mississippi River. On August 7, 1789, the U.S. Congress affirmed the Ordinance with slight modifications under the Constitution.

Western	The Western is a genre of art that may be found in film, television, radio, literature, painting and other visual arts. Westerns are devoted to telling stories set primarily in the latter half of the 19th century in the American Old West. Some Westerns are set as early as the Battle of the Alamo in 1836 but most are set between the end of the American Civil War (1865) and the massacre at Wounded Knee in 1890. There are also a number of films about Western-type characters in contemporary settings, such as Junior Bonner set in the 1970s and The Three Burials of Melquiades Estrada in the 21st century.
Deism	Deism in the philosophy of religion is the standpoint that reason and observation of the natural world, without the need for organized religion, can determine that the universe is a creation and has a creator. Further the term often implies that this supreme being does not intervene in human affairs or suspend the natural laws of the universe. Deists typically reject supernatural events such as prophecy and miracles, tending to assert that a god (or 'the Supreme Architect') has a plan for the universe that this god does not alter by (regularly or ever) intervening in the affairs of human life.
John Carroll	John Carroll, (January 8, 1735 - December 3, 1815) was the first Roman Catholic bishop and archbishop in the United States -- serving as the ordinary of the Archdiocese of Baltimore. He is also known as the founder of Georgetown University, the oldest Catholic university in the United States, and the Georgetown Preparatory School, the oldest Catholic day and boarding school in the United States. Early life and education John Carroll was born to Daniel Carroll, a native of Ireland, and Eleanor Darnall Carroll, of English descent, at the large plantation which Eleanor Darnall had inherited from her family.
Columbia	The Columbia was a 310 ton, 6 gun barque in the service of the Columbia District of the Hudson's Bay Company on the Columbia River and elsewhere in the Pacific Northwest in the 1830s and 1840s. The vessel's complement of crew was 24 men.
England	England is a country that is part of the United Kingdom. It shares land borders with Scotland to the north and Wales to the west; the Irish Sea is to the north west, the Celtic Sea to the south west and the North Sea to the east, with the English Channel to the south separating it from continental Europe. Most of England comprises the central and southern part of the island of Great Britain in the North Atlantic.

Wampum	Wampum are traditional sacred shell beads of the Eastern Woodlands tribes of the indigenous people of North America. Wampum include the white shell beads fashioned from the North Atlantic channeled whelk shell; and the white and purple beads made from the quahog, or Western North Atlantic hard-shelled clam. Woven belts of wampum have been created to commemorate treaties or historical events, and for exchange in personal social transactions, such as marriages. In colonial North America, European colonists often used wampum as currency for trading with Native Americans.

1. _________ are traditional sacred shell beads of the Eastern Woodlands tribes of the indigenous people of North America. _________ include the white shell beads fashioned from the North Atlantic channeled whelk shell; and the white and purple beads made from the quahog, or Western North Atlantic hard-shelled clam. Woven belts of _________ have been created to commemorate treaties or historical events, and for exchange in personal social transactions, such as marriages. In colonial North America, European colonists often used _________ as currency for trading with Native Americans.

   a. Warning out of town
   b. Wessagusset Colony
   c. West Jersey
   d. Wampum

2. _________ was a United States Congressman from the third and fifth districts of Maryland, serving four terms from 1827 to 1833, and 1835 to 1837. He was also a grandnephew of U.S. President George Washington.

   Washington was born at Haywood Farms near Oak Grove of Westmoreland County, Virginia. He attended Phillips Academy and Harvard University, studied law, but devoted himself to agricultural pursuits on his plantation in Maryland.

   a. George Corbin Washington
   b. Francisco de Montejo
   c. Juan de Grijalva
   d. Marc Lescarbot

3. _________ was an American lawyer and politician from Philadelphia, Pennsylvania and Wilmington, Delaware. He was a militia officer during the American Revolution, a Continental Congressman from Pennsylvania and Delaware, a delegate to the U.S. Constitutional Convention of 1787, President of Delaware and President of Pennsylvania. Among the wealthiest men in the British American colonies, he is known as the 'Penman of the Revolution' for his Letters from a Farmer in Pennsylvania; upon receiving news of his death, President Thomas Jefferson recognized him as being 'among the first of the advocates for the rights of his country when assailed by Great Britain' whose 'name will be consecrated in history as one of the great worthies of the revolution.' He is the namesake of Dickinson College.

   a. John McKinly
   b. John Dickinson
   c. Francisco de Montejo
   d. Papers of the Continental Congress

---

4. The _________ is a waterway in New York that runs about 363 miles (584 km) from Albany, New York, on the Hudson River to Buffalo, New York, at Lake Erie, completing a navigable water route from the Atlantic Ocean to the Great Lakes. The canal contains 36 locks and encompasses a total elevation differential of around 565 ft. (169 m).

   a. Executive Branch Reform Act
   b. Erie Canal
   c. America's Affordable Health Choices Act of 2009
   d. Edgar Allan Poe Museum

5. _________ was the Chief Justice of the United States (1801-1835) whose court opinions helped lay the basis for American constitutional law while promoting nationalism and making the Supreme Court of the United States a center of power with the capability of overruling Congress. Previously Marshall had been a leader of the Federalist Party in Virginia. and served in the United States House of Representatives from 1799 to 1800. He was Secretary of State under President John Adams from 1800 to 1801.

   a. Leonidas Polk
   b. Mary Lee Fitzhugh Custis
   c. John Henry Hobart
   d. John Marshall

ANSWER KEY
Chapter 4. The American Revolution

1. d
2. a
3. b
4. b
5. d

________ Articles of Confederation

________ Burr conspiracy

________ James Madison

________ Loyalist

________ York

________ Race riot

________ Constitutional Convention

________ Early American currency

________ Continental Congress

________ Alexander Hamilton

________ New Jersey Plan

________ PLANS

________ Roger Sherman

________ Virginia Plan

________ Commerce

________ Electoral College

________ President

________ State of the Union address

________ Three-Fifths Compromise

Chapter 5. The Federalist Era: Nationalism Triumphant

Union

John Jay

David Ramsay

Nathaniel Bacon

Paxton Boys

Turners

Samuel Adams

Boston

Connecticut

Connecticut Colony

Delaware Colony

Patrick Henry

Massachusetts

South Carolina

Erie Canal

Louisiana

Louisiana Purchase

North Carolina

England

______ American Revolution

______ Continental Army

______ Revenue Act of 1913

______ Report on Manufactures

______ Washington

______ Napoleonic Wars

______ Yellow fever

______ Gazette of the United States

______ Whiskey Rebellion

______ Indian Territory

______ Farewell

______ Mississippi Territory

______ Tennessee

______ Alien and Sedition Acts

______ XYZ Affair

______ Virginia Resolves

CHAPTER HIGHLIGHTS: KEY TERMS, PEOPLE, PLACES, CONCEPTS
Chapter 5. The Federalist Era: Nationalism Triumphant

Articles of Confederation	The Articles of Confederation, formally the Articles of Confederation and Perpetual Union, was an agreement among the 13 founding states that legally established the United States of America as a confederation of sovereign states and served as its first constitution. Its drafting by the Continental Congress began in mid 1776 and an approved version was sent to the states for ratification in late 1777. The formal ratification by all 13 states was completed in early 1781. Even if not yet ratified, the Articles provided domestic and international legitimacy for the Continental Congress to direct the American Revolutionary War, conduct diplomacy with Europe and deal with territorial issues and Indian relations. Nevertheless, a perceived weak government created by the Articles became a matter of concern for key nationalists and in 1789 the Articles were replaced with the U.S. Constitution.
Burr conspiracy	The Burr conspiracy in the beginning of the 19th century was a suspected treasonous cabal of planters, politicians, and army officers led by former U.S. Vice President Aaron Burr. According to the accusations against him, Burr's goal was to create an independent nation in the center of North America and/or the Southwest and parts of Mexico. Burr's explanation: To take possession of, and farm, 40,000 acres (160 km²) in the Texas Territory leased to him by the Spanish.
James Madison	James Madison, Jr. (March 16, 1751 - June 28, 1836) was an American politician and political philosopher who served as the fourth President of the United States (1809-1817) and is considered one of the Founding Fathers of the United States. He was the principal author of the United States Constitution, and is often called the 'Father of the Constitution'.
Loyalist	In general, a loyalist is someone who maintains loyalty to an established government, political party, or sovereign, especially during war or revolutionary change such as the Republicans in the Spanish Civil War in the late 1930s. In modern English usage, the most common application is to loyalty to the British Crown.
York	York was an African American slave best known for his participation with the Lewis and Clark Expedition. As William Clark's slave, he had to do diffficult manual labour without pay. After the expedition's return he pressed for his freedom, which Clark opposed, he possibly agreed ten years later, though some historians dispute this and say he was never freed.

Race riot	A race riot is an outbreak of violent civil disorder in which race is a key factor. A phenomenon frequently confused with the concept of 'race riot' is sectarian violence, which involves public mass violence or conflict over non-racial factors.
Constitutional Convention	The United States Constitutional Convention took place from May 25 to September 17, 1787, in Philadelphia, Pennsylvania, to address problems in governing the United States of America, which had been operating under the Articles of Confederation following independence from Great Britain. Although the Convention was purportedly intended only to revise the Articles of Confederation, the intention from the outset of many of its proponents, chief among them James Madison and Alexander Hamilton, was to create a new government rather than fix the existing one. The delegates elected George Washington to preside over the convention.
Early American currency	Early American currency went through several stages of development in the colonial and post-Revolutionary history of the United States. Because few coins were minted in the thirteen colonies that became the United States in 1776, foreign coins like the Spanish dollar were widely circulated. Colonial governments sometimes issued paper money to facilitate economic activity.
Continental Congress	The Continental Congress was a convention of delegates called together from the Thirteen Colonies that became the governing body of the United States during the American Revolution. The Congress met from 1774 to 1789 in three incarnations. The first call for a convention was made over issues of mounting taxation without representation in Parliament and because of the British blockade.
Alexander Hamilton	Alexander Hamilton was the first United States Secretary of the Treasury, a Founding Father, economist, and political philosopher.

Aide-de-camp to General George Washington during the American Revolutionary War, he was a leader of American nationalists calling for a new Constitution; he was one of America's first constitutional lawyers, and wrote most of the Federalist Papers, a primary source for Constitutional interpretation. Hamilton was the primary author of the economic policies of the George Washington Administration, especially the funding of the state debts by the Federal government, the establishment of a national bank, a system of tariffs, and friendly trade relations with Britain.

New Jersey Plan

The New Jersey Plan was a proposal for the structure of the United States Government presented by William Paterson at the Constitutional Convention on June 15, 1787. The plan was created in response to the Virginia Plan, which called for two houses of Congress, both elected with apportionment according to population. The less populous states were adamantly opposed to giving most of the control of the national government to the more populous states, and so proposed an alternative plan that would have kept the one-vote-per-state representation under one legislative body from the Articles of Confederation. The New Jersey Plan was opposed by James Madison and Edmund Randolph (the proponents of the Virginia Plan).

PLANS

People for Legal and Non-Sectarian Schools (PLANS) is an organization based in California in the United States which campaigns against the public funding of Waldorf methods charter schools alleging they violate the United States Constitution's separation of church and state. The group claims independent Waldorf schools and public Waldorf methods charter schools teach anthroposophical content, that this content is religious in nature, and that the schools disguise the anthroposophical content from the public. PLANS filed federal suit in 1998 against two California public school districts, Sacramento City Unified School District and Twin Ridges Elementary School District, to halt the Waldorf methods educational programs implemented in two of their schools.

Roger Sherman

Roger Sherman was an early American lawyer and politician. He served as the first mayor of New Haven, Connecticut, and served on the Committee of Five that drafted the Declaration of Independence, and was also a representative and senator in the new republic.

He was the only person to sign all four great state papers of the U.S.: the Continental Association, the Declaration of Independence, the Articles of Confederation and the Constitution.

Virginia Plan	The Virginia Plan was a proposal by Virginia delegates for a bicameral legislative branch. The plan was drafted by James Madison while he waited for a quorum to assemble at the Constitutional Convention of 1787. The Virginia Plan was notable for its role in setting the overall agenda for debate in the convention and, in particular, for setting forth the idea of population-weighted representation in the proposed national legislature. Background The Constitutional Convention gathered in Philadelphia to revise the Articles of Confederation.
Commerce	While business refers to the value-creating activities of an organization for profit, commerce means the whole system of an economy that constitutes an environment for business. The system includes legal, economic, political, social, cultural, and technological systems that are in operation in any country. Thus, commerce is a system or an environment that affects the business prospects of an economy or a nation-state.
Electoral College	The Electoral College consists of the popularly elected representatives (electors) who formally elect the President and Vice President of the United States.
President	President was a steamboat which currently lies dismantled in St. Elmo, Illinois. Originally named Cincinnati, it was built in 1924, and is the only remaining 'Western Rivers' style sidewheel river excursion steamboat in the United States. She was listed on the National Register of Historic Places and declared a National Historic Landmark in 1989. Her home ports have been Cincinnati, Ohio, New Orleans, Louisiana, Vicksburg, Mississippi, St. Louis, Missouri and Davenport, Iowa.
State of the Union address	The State of the Union is an annual address presented by the President of the United States to the United States Congress. The address not only reports on the condition of the nation but also allows the president to outline his legislative agenda (for which he needs the cooperation of Congress) and his national priorities. The practice arises from a command given to the president in the Constitution of the United States: Although the language of the Constitution is not specific, by tradition, the President makes this report annually in late January.

While not required to deliver a speech, every president since Woodrow Wilson has made the State of the Union report as a speech delivered before a joint session of Congress. Before that time, most presidents delivered the State of the Union as a written report.

Since Wilson, the State of the Union is given typically each January before a joint session of the United States Congress and is held in the House of Representatives chamber of the United States Capitol.

What began as a communication between president and Congress has become a communication between the president and the people of the United States. Since the advent of radio, and then television, the speech has been broadcast live on most networks, preempting scheduled programming. To reach the largest television audience, the speech, once given during the day, is now typically given in the evening, after 9 p.m. ET.

Also, in recent decades, newly inaugurated presidents have chosen to deliver speeches to joint sessions of Congress in the early months of their presidencies, but have not officially considered them State of the Union addresses.

Three-Fifths Compromise

The Three-Fifths Compromise was a compromise between Southern and Northern states reached during the Philadelphia Convention of 1787 in which three-fifths of the enumerated population of slaves would be counted for representation purposes regarding both the distribution of taxes and the apportionment of the members of the United States House of Representatives. It was proposed by delegates James Wilson and Roger Sherman.

Delegates opposed to slavery generally wished to count only the free inhabitants of each state.

Union

During the American Civil War, the Union was a name used to refer to the federal government of the United States, which was supported by the twenty free states and five border slave states. It was opposed by 11 Southern slave states that had declared a secession to join together to form the Confederacy. Although the Union states included the Western states of California, Oregon, and (after 1864) Nevada, as well as states generally considered to be part of the Midwest, the Union has been also often loosely referred to as 'the North', both then and now.

John Jay	John Jay was an American lawyer and diplomat, son of William Jay and a grandson of Chief Justice John Jay. He was born in New York City, graduated at Columbia College in 1836, and was admitted to the bar three years later. He early became intensely interested in the antislavery movement, and while still in college (1834) was president of the New York Young Men's Antislavery Society.
David Ramsay	David Ramsay was an American physician and historian from Charleston, South Carolina. He served as a South Carolina delegate to the Continental Congress in 1782-1783 and again in 1785-1786. He was one of the first major historians of the American Revolution. The son of an Irish emigrant, he was born in Lancaster County, Pennsylvania.
Nathaniel Bacon	Nathaniel Bacon was a wealthy colonist of the Virginia Colony, famous as the instigator of Bacon's Rebellion of 1676, which collapsed when Bacon himself died from dysentery. Early life When he arrived in Virginia, Bacon settled on the frontier near Jamestown, Virginia, and was appointed to the council of Governor William Berkeley.Some sources have claimed that Berkeley's wife, Francis Culpeper was a cousin of Nathaniel Bacon. Bacon's Rebellion Before the 'Virginia Rebellion,' as it was then called, began in earnest, in 1674, a group of so-called 'freeholders' on the Virginia frontier demanded that Native Americans living on treaty-protected lands be driven out or killed.
Paxton Boys	The Paxton Boys were a vigilante group who murdered 20 Susquehannock in events collectively called the Conestoga Massacre. Scots-Irish frontiersmen from central Pennsylvania along the Susquehanna River formed a vigilante group to retaliate against local American Indians in the aftermath of the French and Indian War and Pontiac's Rebellion. Attack on Susquehannock

	In the aftermath of the French and Indian War, the frontier of Pennsylvania remained unsettled.
Turners	Turners are members of German-American gymnastic clubs. A German gymnastic movement was started by Turnvater (turners' father) Friedrich Ludwig Jahn in the early 19th century when Germany was occupied by Napoleon. The Turnvereine ('gymnastic unions') were not only athletic, but also political, reflecting their origin in similar 'nationalistic gymnastic' organizations in Europe.
Samuel Adams	Samuel Adams was an American statesman, political philosopher, and one of the Founding Fathers of the United States. As a politician in colonial Massachusetts, Adams was a leader of the movement that became the American Revolution, and was one of the architects of the principles of American republicanism that shaped the political culture of the United States. He was a second cousin to President John Adams.
Boston	Boston is the capital of and largest city in Massachusetts, and is one of the oldest cities in the United States. The largest city in New England, Boston is regarded as the unofficial 'Capital of New England' for its economic and cultural impact on the entire New England region. The city proper had a 2009 estimated population of 645,169, making it the twentieth largest in the country.
Connecticut	Connecticut is a state in the New England region of the northeastern United States. It is bordered by Rhode Island to the east, Massachusetts to the north, the state of New York to the west, and by the Long Island Sound to the south.
Connecticut Colony	The Connecticut Colony or Colony of Connecticut was an English colony located in British America that became the U.S. state of Connecticut. Originally known as the River Colony, it was organized on March 3, 1636 as a haven for Puritan noblemen. After early struggles with the Dutch, the English gained control of the colony permanently by the late 1630s.
Delaware Colony	Delaware Colony in the North American Middle Colonies was a region of the Province of Pennsylvania although never legally a separate colony. From 1682 until 1776 it was part of the Penn proprietorship and was known as the lower counties. In 1701 it gained a separate Assembly from the three upper counties but had the same Governor as the rest of Pennsylvania.

Patrick Henry	Patrick Henry was an orator and politician who led the movement for independence in Virginia in the 1770s. A Founding Father, he served as the first and sixth post-colonial Governor of Virginia from 1776 to 1779 and subsequently, from 1784 to 1786. Henry led the opposition to the Stamp Act of 1765 and is well remembered for his 'Give me Liberty, or give me Death!' speech. Along with Samuel Adams and Thomas Paine, he is remembered as one of the most influential exponents of Republicanism, promoters of the American Revolution and Independence, especially in his denunciations of corruption in government officials and his defense of historic rights.
Massachusetts	'Massachusetts', words and music by Arlo Guthrie, was made the official folk song of Massachusetts in July, 1981.
South Carolina	South Carolina is a state in the Deep South that borders Georgia to the south and North Carolina to the north. Originally part of the Province of Carolina, the Province of South Carolina was one of the 13 colonies that declared independence from the British Crown during the American Revolution. The colony was originally named by King Charles II of England in honor of his father Charles I, as Carolus is Latin for Charles.
Erie Canal	The Erie Canal is a waterway in New York that runs about 363 miles (584 km) from Albany, New York, on the Hudson River to Buffalo, New York, at Lake Erie, completing a navigable water route from the Atlantic Ocean to the Great Lakes. The canal contains 36 locks and encompasses a total elevation differential of around 565 ft. (169 m).
Louisiana	Louisiana was the name of an administrative district of the Viceroyalty of New Spain from 1764 to 1803 that represented territory west of the Mississippi River basin, plus New Orleans. Spain acquired the territory from France: see Louisiana. History The area, comprising what is now known as the Louisiana Purchase, was turned over to the French for a few days in 1803 before it, in turn, was turned over to the United States.

Louisiana Purchase	The Louisiana Purchase was the acquisition by the United States of America of 828,800 square miles (2,147,000 km^2) of France's claim to the territory of Louisiana in 1803. The U.S. paid 60 million francs ($11,250,000) plus cancellation of debts worth 18 million francs ($3,750,000), for a total sum of 15 million dollars for the Louisiana territory ($219 million in 2010 dollars). What was purchased was France's claim only, not the actual territory, which belonged to the tribes which inhabited the area. The territory itself was acquired slowly throughout the nineteenth century by purchases to Native American tribes and wars.
North Carolina	North Carolina is a state located in the Southeastern United States. The state borders South Carolina and Georgia to the south, Tennessee to the west and Virginia to the north. North Carolina contains 100 counties.
England	England is a country that is part of the United Kingdom. It shares land borders with Scotland to the north and Wales to the west; the Irish Sea is to the north west, the Celtic Sea to the south west and the North Sea to the east, with the English Channel to the south separating it from continental Europe. Most of England comprises the central and southern part of the island of Great Britain in the North Atlantic.
American Revolution	The American Revolution was the political upheaval during the last half of the 18th century in which thirteen colonies in North America joined together to break free from the British Empire, combining to become the United States of America. They first rejected the authority of the Parliament of Great Britain to govern them from overseas without representation, and then expelled all royal officials. By 1774, each colony had established a Provincial Congress, or an equivalent governmental institution, to govern itself, but still within the empire. The British responded by sending combat troops to re-impose direct rule.
Continental Army	**American Revolutionary War** The Continental Army was formed after the outbreak of the American Revolutionary War by the colonies that became the United States of America. Established by a resolution of the Continental Congress on June 14, 1775, it was created to coordinate the military efforts of the Thirteen Colonies in their revolt against the rule of Great Britain. The Continental Army was supplemented by local militias and other troops that remained under control of the individual states. General George Washington was the Commander-in-Chief of the army throughout the war.

Revenue Act of 1913	The United States Revenue Act of 1913, Underwood Tariff, Underwood Tariff Act, or Underwood-Simmons Act (ch. 16, 38 Stat. 114, October 3, 1913), re-imposed the federal income tax following the ratification of the Sixteenth Amendment and lowered basic tariff rates from 40% to 25%, well below the Payne-Aldrich Tariff Act of 1909. It was signed into law by President Woodrow Wilson on October 3, 1913, and was sponsored by Alabama Representative Oscar Underwood. Tariffs President Woodrow Wilson summoned a special session of Congress in April 1913. His immediate objective was to confront the perennial tariff question, and he brought special attention to the matter by deciding to appear in person before Congress to make his appeal. He was the first president since John Adams to do so.
Report on Manufactures	The Report on Manufactures is the third report, and magnum opus, of American Founding Father and 1st U.S. Treasury Secretary Alexander Hamilton. It was presented to Congress on December 5, 1791 and recommended economic policies to stimulate the new republic's economy and ensure the independence won with the conclusion of the Revolutionary War in 1783. Hamilton's 'Report on Manufactures' laid forth economic principles rooted in both the Mercantilist System of Elizabeth I's England and the practices of Jean-Baptiste Colbert of France.
Washington	Washington was one of the first steamboats to operate in the states of California and Oregon. Operations in California Washington operated in California on the Sacramento River. The vessel was purchased in California in 1851 by pioneer steamboat captain Alexander Sinclair Murray (b.1828).

Chapter 5. The Federalist Era: Nationalism Triumphant

Napoleonic Wars	The Napoleonic Wars were a series of conflicts declared against Napoleon's French Empire and changing sets of European allies by opposing coalitions that ran from 1803 to 1815. As a continuation of the wars sparked by the French Revolution of 1789, they revolutionized European armies and played out on an unprecedented scale, mainly due to the application of modern mass conscription. French power rose quickly, conquering most of Europe, but collapsed rapidly after France's disastrous invasion of Russia in 1812. Napoleon's empire ultimately suffered complete military defeat resulting in the restoration of the Bourbon monarchy in France. The wars resulted in the dissolution of the Holy Roman Empire and sowed the seeds of nascent nationalism in Germany and Italy that would lead to the two nations' consolidation later in the century.
Yellow fever	Yellow fever is an acute viral hemorrhagic disease. The virus is a 40 to 50 nm enveloped RNA virus with positive sense of the Flaviviridae family. The yellow fever virus is transmitted by the bite of female mosquitoes (the yellow fever mosquito, Aedes aegypti, and other species) and is found in tropical and subtropical areas in South America and Africa, but not in Asia. The only known hosts of the virus are primates and several species of mosquito. The origin of the disease is most likely to be Africa, from where it was introduced to South America through the slave trade in the 16th century. Since the 17th century, several major epidemics of the disease have been recorded in the Americas, Africa and Europe. In the 19th century, yellow fever was deemed one of the most dangerous infectious diseases.
Gazette of the United States	The Gazette of the United States was an early American partisan newspaper first issued on April 15, 1789, as a biweekly publication friendly to the administration of George Washington, and to the policies and members of the emerging Federalist Party. The Gazette was originally published in New York City by editor John Fenno, but followed the United States Government in 1790 to its new temporary seat and capital in Philadelphia, Pennsylvania. There the editorship was taken over by Joseph Dennie until he founded Port Folio.
Whiskey Rebellion	The Whiskey Rebellion, was a tax protest in the United States in 1789, during the presidency of George Washington. Farmers who sold their grain in the form of whiskey had to pay a new tax which they strongly resented. The tax was a part of treasury secretary Alexander Hamilton's program to pay off the national debt.

Indian Territory	The Indian Territory, was land set aside within the United States for the use of American Indians. The general borders were set by the Indian Intercourse Act of 1834. The Indian Territory had its roots in the British Royal Proclamation of 1763, which limited white settlement to Crown lands east of the Appalachian Mountains.
Farewell	Farewell, is a song by American singer-songwriter Bob Dylan. Dylan wrote the song in January 1963. He considered it for his third album, The Times They Are a-Changin', but only attempted a few takes during the album's first studio session. Dylan's earlier recordings of 'Farewell' found their way onto various bootlegs, and a collection of demos that included the song was released in October 2010 on The Bootleg Series Vol. 9 - The Witmark Demos: 1962-1964.
Mississippi Territory	The Territory of Mississippi was an organized incorporated territory of the United States that existed from April 7, 1798, until December 10, 1817, when the final extent of the territory was admitted to the Union as the state of Mississippi. The Mississippi Territory was expanded in 1804 and again in 1812 until it extended from the Gulf of Mexico to the southern border of Tennessee. (Georgia gave up the northern portion in 1802, and the Gulf Coast region was acquired from Spain).
Tennessee	Tennessee is a U.S. state located in the Southeastern United States. It has a population of 6,214,888, making it the nation's 17th-largest state by population, and covers 42,169 square miles (109,220 km^2), making it the 36th-largest by total land area. Tennessee is bordered by Kentucky and Virginia to the north, North Carolina to the east, Georgia, Alabama, and Mississippi to the south, and Arkansas and Missouri to the west.
Alien and Sedition Acts	The Alien and Sedition Acts were four bills passed in 1798 by the Federalists in the 5th United States Congress in the aftermath of the French Revolution's reign of terror and during an undeclared naval war with France, later known as the Quasi-War. They were signed into law by President John Adams. Opposition to Federalists among Democratic-Republicans reached new heights at this time since the Democratic-Republicans had supported France.

Chapter 5. The Federalist Era: Nationalism Triumphant

XYZ Affair	The XYZ Affair was a 1798 diplomatic episode during the administration of John Adams that Americans interpreted as an insult from France. It led to an undeclared naval war called the Quasi-War, which raged at sea from 1798 to 1800. The Federalist Party took advantage of the national anger to build an army and pass the Alien and Sedition Acts to damage the rival Democratic-Republican Party. History In the wake of the [French Revolution]], relations between the new French Republic and the United States became ever more strained.
Virginia Resolves	The Virginia Resolves were a series of resolutions passed by the Virginia General Assembly in response to the Stamp Act of 1765. The Stamp Act had been passed by the British Parliament to help pay off some of its debt from its various wars, including the French and Indian War fought in part to protect the American colonies. The resolves claimed that in accordance with long established British law, Virginia was subject to taxation only by a parliamentary assembly to which Virginians themselves elected representatives. Since no colonial representatives were elected to the Parliament the only assembly legally allowed to raise taxes would be the Virginia General Assembly.

1. The _________, was a tax protest in the United States in 1789, during the presidency of George Washington. Farmers who sold their grain in the form of whiskey had to pay a new tax which they strongly resented. The tax was a part of treasury secretary Alexander Hamilton's program to pay off the national debt.

   a. Wounded Knee incident
   b. Digital Transition Content Security Act
   c. Whiskey Rebellion
   d. Yankee traders

2. _________ was an African American slave best known for his participation with the Lewis and Clark Expedition. As William Clark's slave, he had to do diffficult manual labour without pay. After the expedition's return he pressed for his freedom, which Clark opposed, he possibly agreed ten years later, though some historians dispute this and say he was never freed.

   a. York
   b. George Thomson Mason
   c. Carter Bassett Harrison
   d. Philip Pendleton Barbour

3. The _________ was the political upheaval during the last half of the 18th century in which thirteen colonies in North America joined together to break free from the British Empire, combining to become the United States of America. They first rejected the authority of the Parliament of Great Britain to govern them from overseas without representation, and then expelled all royal officials. By 1774, each colony had established a Provincial Congress, or an equivalent governmental institution, to govern itself, but still within the empire. The British responded by sending combat troops to re-impose direct rule.

   a. American Revolution
   b. Apology Resolution
   c. Appointments Clause
   d. Army Appropriations Act of 1916

4. The _________, formally the _________ and Perpetual Union, was an agreement among the 13 founding states that legally established the United States of America as a confederation of sovereign states and served as its first constitution. Its drafting by the Continental Congress began in mid 1776 and an approved version was sent to the states for ratification in late 1777. The formal ratification by all 13 states was completed in early 1781. Even if not yet ratified, the Articles provided domestic and international legitimacy for the Continental Congress to direct the American Revolutionary War, conduct diplomacy with Europe and deal with territorial issues and Indian relations. Nevertheless, a perceived weak government created by the Articles became a matter of concern for key nationalists and in 1789 the Articles were replaced with the U.S. Constitution.

a. Aviation Service Act
b. Edmunds Act
c. Electronic Surveillance Modernization Act
d. Articles of Confederation

5. The _________ were four bills passed in 1798 by the Federalists in the 5th United States Congress in the aftermath of the French Revolution's reign of terror and during an undeclared naval war with France, later known as the Quasi-War. They were signed into law by President John Adams. Opposition to Federalists among Democratic-Republicans reached new heights at this time since the Democratic-Republicans had supported France.

a. Respect for America's Fallen Heroes Act
b. Alien and Sedition Acts
c. Digital Transition Content Security Act
d. Nevada Territory

ANSWER KEY
Chapter 5. The Federalist Era: Nationalism Triumphant

---

1. c
2. a
3. a
4. d
5. b

______ Burr conspiracy

______ Monticello

______ Robert Morris

______ President

______ Northwest Ordinance

______ Eston Hemings

______ Madison Hemings

______ Randolph Jefferson

______ Louisiana

______ Louisiana Purchase

______ Marbury v. Madison

______ Decatur

______ Sons of Liberty

______ Tripoli

______ Toussaint Louverture

______ West Florida

______ Henry Adams

______ Constitutional Convention

______ Jonathan Edwards

Chapter 6. Jeffersonian Democracy

________ Essex

________ Essex Junto

________ Lewis and Clark Expedition

________ Fort Mandan

________ Alexander Slidell MacKenzie

________ Mandan

________ Peter Pond

________ Milan Decree

________ Napoleonic Wars

________ Order-in-Council

________ Impressment

________ Massachusetts

________ John Randolph

Burr conspiracy	The Burr conspiracy in the beginning of the 19th century was a suspected treasonous cabal of planters, politicians, and army officers led by former U.S. Vice President Aaron Burr. According to the accusations against him, Burr's goal was to create an independent nation in the center of North America and/or the Southwest and parts of Mexico. Burr's explanation: To take possession of, and farm, 40,000 acres (160 km^2) in the Texas Territory leased to him by the Spanish.
Monticello	The Monticello was a Confederate blockade runner during the American Civil War. She was a two-masted schooner out of Havana, Cuba and of unknown nationality. She ran ashore about 6 to 8 miles east of Fort Morgan and the main inlet to Mobile Bay in Alabama on June 26, 1862, after sailing from Havana, and was then set on fire by the crew to prevent her capture.
Robert Morris	Robert Morris, Jr. (January 20, 1734 - May 9, 1806) was an American merchant, and signer of the Declaration of Independence, the Articles of Confederation, and the United States Constitution. He was elected to the Pennsylvania Assembly and became the Chairman of the Pennsylvania Committee of Safety and a member of the Second Continental Congress where he served as chairman of the 'Secret Committee of Trade' and as a member of the Committee of Correspondence.
President	President was a steamboat which currently lies dismantled in St. Elmo, Illinois. Originally named Cincinnati, it was built in 1924, and is the only remaining 'Western Rivers' style sidewheel river excursion steamboat in the United States. She was listed on the National Register of Historic Places and declared a National Historic Landmark in 1989. Her home ports have been Cincinnati, Ohio, New Orleans, Louisiana, Vicksburg, Mississippi, St. Louis, Missouri and Davenport, Iowa.
Northwest Ordinance	The Northwest Ordinance was an act of the Congress of the Confederation of the United States. The primary effect of the ordinance was the creation of the Northwest Territory as the first organized territory of the United States out of the region south of the Great Lakes, north and west of the Ohio River, and east of the Mississippi River. On August 7, 1789, the U.S. Congress affirmed the Ordinance with slight modifications under the Constitution.
Eston Hemings	Eston Hemings Jefferson (1808-1856) was born a slave at Monticello, the youngest child of Thomas Jefferson and Sally Hemings, a slave in the household of Thomas Jefferson. Family tradition and oral history hold that he was one of the sons of President Thomas Jefferson. Evidence from a 1998 DNA test showed that Eston's descendants are indeed descendants of the male Jefferson line, but because Jefferson had no confirmed male descendants, the tests cannot show conclusively whether they are descended from Thomas Jefferson.

Chapter 6. Jeffersonian Democracy

Madison Hemings

Madison Hemings was a putative son of president Thomas Jefferson by his slave Sally Hemings, with whom he developed a liaison while he was on diplomatic service in Paris. Hemings claimed the connection in his memoir, published in a newspaper interview in 1873. It is supported by the weight of historical evidence, as well as circumstantial evidence, including DNA tests linking his brother Eston Hemings to the male Jefferson line. Hemings' memoir attracted national and international attention.

Randolph Jefferson

Randolph Jefferson was the younger brother of Thomas Jefferson. He was Thomas' only brother to survive infancy, and was a twin to Anna Scott, Thomas' youngest sister. Randolph was 12 years younger than Thomas and lived at Monticello for many years.

Louisiana

Louisiana was the name of an administrative district of the Viceroyalty of New Spain from 1764 to 1803 that represented territory west of the Mississippi River basin, plus New Orleans. Spain acquired the territory from France: see Louisiana.

History

The area, comprising what is now known as the Louisiana Purchase, was turned over to the French for a few days in 1803 before it, in turn, was turned over to the United States.

Louisiana Purchase

The Louisiana Purchase was the acquisition by the United States of America of 828,800 square miles (2,147,000 km^2) of France's claim to the territory of Louisiana in 1803. The U.S. paid 60 million francs ($11,250,000) plus cancellation of debts worth 18 million francs ($3,750,000), for a total sum of 15 million dollars for the Louisiana territory ($219 million in 2010 dollars). What was purchased was France's claim only, not the actual territory, which belonged to the tribes which inhabited the area. The territory itself was acquired slowly throughout the nineteenth century by purchases to Native American tribes and wars.

Marbury v. Madison

Marbury v. Madison, 5 U.S. (1 Cranch) 137 (1803) is a landmark case in United States law and in the history of law worldwide It was also the first time in Western history a court invalidated a law by declaring it 'unconstitutional'. The landmark decision helped define the boundary between the constitutionally separate executive and judicial branches of the American form of government.

The case resulted from a petition to the Supreme Court by William Marbury, who had been appointed by President John Adams as Justice of the Peace in the District of Columbia but whose commission was not subsequently delivered. Marbury petitioned the Supreme Court to force the new Secretary of State James Madison to deliver the documents. The Court, with John Marshall as Chief Justice, found firstly that Madison's refusal to deliver the commission was both illegal and remediable The petition was therefore denied.

Background of the case

In the presidential election of 1800, Thomas Jefferson defeated John Adams, becoming the third President of the United States. Although the election was decided on February 17, 1801, Jefferson did not take office until March 4, 1801. Until that time, outgoing president Adams and the Federalist-controlled 6th Congress were still in power. During this lame-duck session, Congress passed the Judiciary Act of 1801. This Act modified the Judiciary Act of 1789 in establishing ten new district courts, expanding the number of circuit courts from three to six, and adding additional judges to each circuit, giving the President the authority to appoint Federal judges and justices of the peace. The act also reduced the number of Supreme Court justices from six to five, effective upon the next vacancy in the Court.

On March 3, just before his term was to end, Adams, in an attempt to stymie the incoming Democratic-Republican Congress and administration, appointed 16 Federalist circuit judges and 42 Federalist justices of the peace to offices created by the Judiciary Act of 1801. These appointees, the infamous 'Midnight Judges', were all located in the Washington and Alexandria area. One of them was William Marbury, a native of Maryland and a prosperous financier. An ardent Federalist, Marbury was active in Maryland politics and a vigorous supporter of the Adams presidency. He had been appointed to the position of justice of the peace in the District of Columbia. The term for a justice of the peace was five years, and they were 'authorized to hold courts and cognizance of personal demands of the value of 20 dollars.'

On the following day, the appointments were approved en masse by the Senate; however, to go into effect, the commissions had to be delivered to those appointed. This task fell to John Marshall, who, even though recently appointed Chief Justice of the United States, continued as the acting Secretary of State at President Adams's personal request.

While a majority of the commissions were delivered, it proved impossible for all of them to be delivered before Adams's term as president expired. As these appointments were routine in nature, Marshall assumed the new Secretary of State James Madison would see they were delivered, since 'they had been properly submitted and approved, and were, therefore, legally valid appointments.' On March 4, 1801, Thomas Jefferson was sworn in as President. As soon as he was able, President Jefferson ordered Levi Lincoln, who was the new administration's Attorney General and acting Secretary of State until the arrival of James Madison, not to deliver the remaining appointments. Without the commissions, the appointees were unable to assume the offices and duties to which they had been appointed. In Jefferson's opinion, the undelivered commissions, not having been delivered on time, were void.

The newly sworn-in Democratic-Republican 7th Congress immediately set about voiding the Judiciary Act of 1801 with their own Judiciary Act of 1802 which reversed the act of 1801 so that the Judicial branch once again operated under the dictates of the original Judiciary Act of 1789. In addition, it replaced the Court's two annual sessions with one session to begin on the first Monday in February, and 'canceled the Supreme Court term scheduled for June of that year [1802] ... seeking to delay a ruling on the constitutionality of the repeal act until months after the new judicial system was in operation.'

Status of the judicial power before Marbury

Although the power of judicial review is sometimes said to have originated with Marbury, the concept of judicial review has ancient roots. The idea that courts could nullify statutes originated in England with Chief Justice Edward Coke's 1610 opinion in Dr. Bonham's Case, 8 Co. Rep. 107a. That decision arose under a statute of Parliament enabling the London College of Physicians to levy fines against anyone who violated their rules. The College accused a doctor of practicing without a license and fined him accordingly. Coke found that their statutory powers violated 'common right or reason' because 'no person should be a judge in his own case.'

The U.S. Supreme Court stated Bonham's Case did not set a precedent in the United States to make common law supreme over statutory law:

The idea that courts could declare statutes void was defeated in England with the Glorious Revolution of 1688, when King James II was removed and the elected Parliament declared itself supreme. However, it continued to be known in the American colonies and in the bars of young states, where Coke's books were very influential. The doctrine was specifically enshrined in some state constitutions, and by 1803 it had been employed in both State and Federal courts in actions dealing with state statutes, but only insofar as the statutes conflicted with the language of state constitutions.

A number of legal scholars argue that the power of judicial review in the United States predated Marbury, and that Marbury was merely the first Supreme Court case to exercise a power that already existed and was acknowledged. These scholars point to statements about judicial review made in the Constitutional Convention and the state ratifying conventions, statements about judicial review in publications debating ratification, and court cases before Marbury that involved judicial review.

At the Constitutional Convention in 1787, there were a number of references to judicial review. Fifteen delegates made statements about the power of the federal courts to review the constitutionality of laws, with all but two of them supporting the idea.

Likewise, at the state ratifying conventions, over two dozen delegates in at least seven states indicated that under the Constitution, the federal courts would have the power to declare statutes unconstitutional. Professors Saikrishna Prakash and John Yoo point out, with respect to the ratification of the Constitution, that 'no scholar to date has identified even one participant in the ratification fight who argued that the Constitution did not authorize judicial review of Federal statutes. This silence in the face of the numerous comments on the other side is revealing.'

The concept of judicial review was discussed in the Federalist Papers. Alexander Hamilton asserted in Federalist No. 78 that under the Constitution, the federal courts would have not just the power, but the duty, to examine the constitutionality of statutes:

The opponents to ratification, known as Anti-federalists, agreed that the federal courts would have the power to declare statutes unconstitutional, but were concerned that this would give the federal courts too much power. Robert Yates argued: 'The supreme court then have a right, independent of the legislature, to give a construction to the constitution and every part of it, and there is no power provided in this system to correct their construction or do it away. If, therefore, the legislature pass any laws, inconsistent with the sense the judges put upon the constitution, they will declare it void.'

A number of courts engaged in judicial review before Marbury was decided. At the time of the Constitutional Convention, there had been cases in the state courts of at least seven states involving judicial review of state statutes. Between the ratification of the Constitution in 1788 and the Supreme Court's decision in Marbury in 1803, judicial review was used a number of times in both state and federal courts. One scholar counted thirty-one cases during this period in which courts found statutes unconstitutional, concluding: 'The sheer number of these decisions not only belies the notion that the institution of judicial review was created by Chief Justice Marshall in Marbury, it also reflects widespread acceptance and application of the doctrine.'

Scholars have pointed out the Supreme Court itself already had engaged in judicial review before Marbury, although it had not struck down the statute in question because it concluded that the statute was constitutional. In Hylton v. United States, 3 U.S. (3 Dall). 171 (1796), the Court upheld a federal tax on carriages against a claim that the tax violated the 'direct tax' provision of the Constitution. Therefore, the concept of judicial review was familiar before Marbury.

However, it is important to note that nothing in the text of the Constitution explicitly authorized the power of judicial review, despite persistent fears voiced by Anti-federalists over the power of the new Federal court system.

Relevant law

The issue

There are three ways a case can be heard in the Supreme Court: (1) filing directly in the Supreme Court; (2) filing in a lower federal court, such as a district court, and appealing all the way up to the Supreme Court; (3) filing in a state court, appealing all the way up through the state's highest courts, and then appealing to the Supreme Court on an issue of federal law. The first is an exercise of the Court's original jurisdiction; the second and third are exercises of the Supreme Court's appellate jurisdiction.

Because Marbury filed his petition for the writ of mandamus directly in the Supreme Court, the Court needed to be able to exercise original jurisdiction over the case in order to have the power to hear it.

Marbury's argument is that in the Judiciary Act of 1789, Congress granted the Supreme Court original jurisdiction over petitions for writs of mandamus In short, the constitutional issue on which Marbury v. Madison was decided was whether Congress could expand the original jurisdiction of the Supreme Court.

The decision

On February 24, 1803, the Court rendered a unanimous (4-0) decision, that Marbury had the right to his commission but the court did not have the power to force Madison to deliver the commission. Chief Justice Marshall wrote the opinion of the court. Marshall presented the case as raising three distinct questions:

- Did Marbury have a right to the commission?
- Do the laws of the country give Marbury a legal remedy?
- Is asking the Supreme Court for a writ of mandamus the correct legal remedy?

Marshall quickly answered the first two questions affirmatively. He found that the failure to deliver the commission was 'violative of a vested legal right.'

In deciding whether Marbury had a remedy, Marshall stated: 'The Government of the United States has been emphatically termed a government of laws, and not of men. It will certainly cease to deserve this high appellation if the laws furnish no remedy for the violation of a vested legal right.' One of the key legal principles on which Marbury relies is the notion that for every violation of a vested legal right, there must be a legal remedy. Marshall next described two distinct types of Executive actions: political actions, where the official can exercise discretion, and purely ministerial functions, where the official is legally required to do something. Marshall found that delivering the appointment to Marbury was a purely ministerial function required by law, and therefore the law provided him a remedy.

A federal court has a 'special obligation to 'satisfy itself not only of its own jurisdiction, but also that of the lower courts in a cause under review." If a court does not have the power to hear a case, it will not issue dicta. Consequently, with exceptions not applicable here, a federal court must decide whether it has jurisdiction before discussing the merits of the case. Chief Justice Marshall, however, did not address jurisdictional issues until addressing the first two questions presented above. Because of the canon of constitutional avoidance (i.e., where a statute can fairly be interpreted so as to avoid a constitutional issue, it should be so interpreted), courts generally deal with the constitutional issues only if necessary. In this case, the jurisdictional issue was a constitutional one.

In analyzing the third question, Marshall divided the question further, asking if a writ of mandamus was the correct means by which to restore Marbury to his right, and if so, whether the writ Marbury sought could issue from the Supreme Court. Concluding quickly that since a writ of mandamus, by definition, was the correct judicial means to order an official of the United States (in this case, the Secretary of State) to do something required of him (in this case, deliver a commission), Marshall devotes the remainder of his inquiry at the second part of the question: 'Whether it [the writ] can issue from this court.'

Marshall first examined the Judiciary Act of 1789 and determined that the Act purported to give the Supreme Court original jurisdiction over writs of mandamus Marbury had argued that the Constitution was only intended to set a floor for original jurisdiction that Congress could add to. Marshall disagreed and held that Congress does not have the power to modify the Supreme Court's original jurisdiction. Consequently, Marshall found that the Constitution and the Judiciary Act conflict.

This conflict raised the important question of what happens when an Act of Congress conflicts with the Constitution. Marshall answered that Acts of Congress that conflict with the Constitution are not law and the Courts are bound instead to follow the Constitution, affirming the principle of judicial review. In support of this position Marshall looked to the nature of the written Constitution--there would be no point of having a written Constitution if the courts could just ignore it. 'To what purpose are powers limited, and to what purpose is that limitation committed to writing, if these limits may, at any time, be passed by those intended to be restrained?' Marshall also argued that the very nature of the judicial function requires courts to make this determination. Since it is a court's duty to decide cases, courts have to be able to decide what law applies to each case. Therefore, if two laws conflict with each other, a court must decide which law applies. Finally, Marshall pointed to the judge's oath requiring them to uphold the Constitution, and to the Supremacy Clause of the Constitution, which lists the 'Constitution' before the 'laws of the United States.' Part of the core of this reasoning is found in the following statements from the decision:

'In denying his request, the Court held that it lacked jurisdiction because Section 13 of the Judiciary Act passed by Congress in 1789, which authorized the Court to issue such a writ, was unconstitutional and thus invalid.' Marbury never became a Justice of the Peace in the District of Columbia.

Criticism

At the time, Jefferson disagreed with Marshall's reasoning in this case, saying that if this view of judicial power became accepted, it would be 'placing us under the despotism of an oligarchy.' Jefferson expanded on this in a letter he wrote some 20 years later to Justice William Johnson, whom he had appointed to the court in 1804.

Some legal scholars have questioned the legal reasoning of Marshall's opinion. They argue that Marshall selectively quoted the Judiciary Act of 1789, interpreting it to grant the Supreme Court the power to hear writs of mandamus on original jurisdiction. These scholars argue that there is little connection between the notion of original jurisdiction and the Supreme Court, and note that the Act seems to affirm the Court's power to exercise only appellate jurisdiction'

Questions have also frequently been raised about the logic of Marshall's argument for judicial review, for example by Alexander Bickel in his book The Least Dangerous Branch. Bickel argues that Marshall's argument implies an unrealistically mechanical view of jurisprudence, one which suggests that the Court has an absolute duty to strike down every law it finds violative of the Constitution. Under Marshall's conception of the judicial process in Marbury, judges themselves have no independent agency and can never take into account the consequences of their actions when deciding cases.

Marbury can also be criticized on grounds that it was improper for the Court to consider any issues beyond jurisdiction. After concluding that the Court lacked jurisdiction in the case, the further review regarding the substantive issues presented was arguably improper. Also, it has been argued that Justice Marshall should have recused himself on the grounds that he was still acting Secretary of State at the time the commissions were to be delivered and it was his brother, James Marshall, who was charged with delivering a number of the commissions.

Because the Constitution lacks a clear statement authorizing the Federal courts to nullify the acts of coequal branches, critics contend that the argument for judicial review must rely on a significant gloss on the Constitution's terms. Despite such criticisms of Marbury v. Madison, judicial review has been accepted in the American legal community.

Decatur

The Decatur was an American schooner built for privateering during the Atlantic Ocean theater of the War of 1812. She was named for the United States Navy Commodore Stephen Decatur who served with distinction in many of America's earliest conflicts. Decatur is best known for being commanded by Captain Dominique Diron who captured several British ships in the Napoleonic Wars and the War of 1812. Captain Diron, defeated the the stronger Royal Navy schooner HMS Dominica in a battle off Bermuda on August 5, 1813. After a long engagement the Americans chased down the Dominca and boarded, forcing down her colors and killing her commander in the process.

See Also

- Lynx (1812 privateer)
- Lady Washington

Sons of Liberty

The Sons of Liberty was a political group made up of American patriots that originated in the pre-independence North American British colonies. The group was formed to protect the rights of the colonists from the usurpations by the British government after 1766. They are best known for undertaking the Boston Tea Party in 1773, which led to the Intolerable Acts (an intense crackdown by the British government), and a counter-mobilization by the Patriots that led directly to the American Revolutionary War in 1775.

Origin

After 1765 the major American cities saw the formation of secret groups set up to defend their rights.

Tripoli

Tripoli is the capital and largest city in Libya. It is also known as Western Tripoli, to distinguish it from Tripoli, Lebanon. It is affectionately called The Mermaid of the Mediterranean, describing its turquoise waters and its whitewashed buildings.

Toussaint Louverture

François-Dominique Toussaint Louverture, also Toussaint Bréda, Toussaint-Louverture (May 20, 1743 - April 7, 1803) was the leader of the Haitian Revolution. His military genius and political acumen led to the establishment of the independent black state of Haiti, transforming an entire society of slaves into a free, self-governing people. The success of the Haitian Revolution shook the institution of slavery throughout the New World.

West Florida

West Florida was a region on the north shore of the Gulf of Mexico, which underwent several boundary and sovereignty changes during its history. West Florida was first established in 1763 by the British government; as its name suggests it largely consisted of the western portion of the region called Florida by Spain, with East Florida comprising the eastern part. It included most of what is now the Florida Panhandle, plus parts of the modern U.S. states of Louisiana, Mississippi, and Alabama.

Henry Adams

Henry Brooks Adams (February 16, 1838 - March 27, 1918; normally called Henry Adams) was an American journalist, historian, academic and novelist. He is best-known for his autobiographical book, The Education of Henry Adams. He was a member of the Adams political family.

Chapter 6. Jeffersonian Democracy

Constitutional Convention	The United States Constitutional Convention took place from May 25 to September 17, 1787, in Philadelphia, Pennsylvania, to address problems in governing the United States of America, which had been operating under the Articles of Confederation following independence from Great Britain. Although the Convention was purportedly intended only to revise the Articles of Confederation, the intention from the outset of many of its proponents, chief among them James Madison and Alexander Hamilton, was to create a new government rather than fix the existing one. The delegates elected George Washington to preside over the convention.
Jonathan Edwards	Jonathan Edwards was a preacher, theologian, and missionary to Native Americans. Edwards 'is widely acknowledged to be America's most important and original philosophical theologian,' and one of America's greatest intellectuals. Edwards's theological work is very broad in scope, but he is often associated with his defense of Reformed theology, the metaphysics of theological determinism, and the Puritan heritage.
Essex	The Essex was an American whaleship from Nantucket, Massachusetts. She was 87 feet (27 m) long, measured 238 tons, and was captained by the 28-year-old George Pollard, Jr. She is best known for being attacked and sunk by a sperm whale in the Pacific Ocean in 1820. The incident was an inspiration for Herman Melville's 1851 classic novel Moby-Dick.
Essex Junto	The Essex Junto was a group of lawyers and merchants from Essex County, Massachusetts. These Federalists supported Alexander Hamilton and the Massachusetts radicals. When Hamilton was offered a place in the plot to secede New England from the Union, he denied the offer.
Lewis and Clark Expedition	The Lewis and Clark Expedition, or 'Corps of Discovery Expedition' (1804-1806) was the first transcontinental expedition to the Pacific Coast by the United States. Commissioned by President Thomas Jefferson and led by two Virginia-born veterans of Indian wars in the Ohio Valley, Meriwether Lewis and William Clark, the expedition had several goals. Their objects were both scientific and commercial - to study the area's plants, animal life, and geography, and to discover how the region could be exploited economically.
Fort Mandan	Fort Mandan was the name of the encampment at which the Lewis and Clark Expedition wintered in 1804-1805. The encampment was located on the Missouri River approximately twelve miles from Washburn, North Dakota, though the precise location is not known for certain and may be under the nearby river.

The fort was built of cottonwood lumber cut from the riverbanks. It was triangular in shape, with high walls on all sides and a gate facing the riverbank.

Alexander Slidell MacKenzie

Alexander Slidell MacKenzie was an officer in the United States Navy during the American Civil War.

Biography

Born in New York City, MacKenzie was appointed midshipman September 29, 1855. Serving in USS Hartford on the China Station at the outbreak of the Civil War, he returned to the United States and joined Kineo, in which he served during Farragut's daring dash past Forts Jackson and St. Philip on the lower Mississippi to capture New Orleans in 1862.

During 1863 and 1864 he participated in the blockade of Charleston and the attacks on Fort Sumter and Morris Island.

Mandan

The Mandan are a tribe in the United States that historically lived along the banks of the Missouri River and two of its tributaries--the Heart and Knife Rivers--in present-day North and South Dakota. Speakers of Mandan, a Siouan language, the people developed a settled culture in contrast to that of more nomadic tribes in the Great Plains region. They established permanent villages featuring large, round, earthen lodges some 40 feet in diameter, surrounding a central plaza.

Peter Pond

Peter Pond was born in Milford, Connecticut. He was a soldier with a Connecticut regiment, a fur trader, a founding member of the North West Company, an explorer and a cartographer.

Biography

Pond began his fur trading career with his father out of Detroit Michigan.

Chapter 6. Jeffersonian Democracy

Milan Decree	The Milan Decree was issued on December 17, 1807 by Napoleon I of France to enforce the Berlin Decree of 1806 which had initiated the Continental System. This system was the basis for his plan to defeat the British by waging economic warfare. The Milan Decree stated that no European country was to trade with the United Kingdom.
Napoleonic Wars	The Napoleonic Wars were a series of conflicts declared against Napoleon's French Empire and changing sets of European allies by opposing coalitions that ran from 1803 to 1815. As a continuation of the wars sparked by the French Revolution of 1789, they revolutionized European armies and played out on an unprecedented scale, mainly due to the application of modern mass conscription. French power rose quickly, conquering most of Europe, but collapsed rapidly after France's disastrous invasion of Russia in 1812. Napoleon's empire ultimately suffered complete military defeat resulting in the restoration of the Bourbon monarchy in France. The wars resulted in the dissolution of the Holy Roman Empire and sowed the seeds of nascent nationalism in Germany and Italy that would lead to the two nations' consolidation later in the century.
Order-in-Council	An Order-in-Council is a type of legislation in many countries, typically those in the Commonwealth of Nations. In the United Kingdom this legislation is formally made in the name of the Queen by the Privy Council (Queen-in-Council), but in other countries the terminology may vary. Assent Although the Orders are nominally made by the Queen, in practice, royal assent is a formality only.
Impressment	Impressment, colloquially, 'the Press', refers to the act of taking men into a navy by force and without notice. It was used by the Royal Navy, beginning in 1664 and during the 18th and early 19th centuries, in wartime, as a means of crewing warships, although legal sanction for the practice goes back to the time of Edward I of England. The Royal Navy impressed many British merchant sailors, as well as some sailors from other nations.
Massachusetts	'Massachusetts', words and music by Arlo Guthrie, was made the official folk song of Massachusetts in July, 1981.

John Randolph	John Randolph was an American film, television and stage actor. Early life Randolph was born Emanuel Hirsch Cohen in New York City, the son of Jewish immigrants Dorothy (née Shore), an insurance agent, and Louis Cohen, a hat manufacturer. His stepfather was Joseph Lippman, and as a result Randolph was briefly known as Mortimer Lippman during his childhood.

PRACTICE QUIZ
Chapter 6. Jeffersonian Democracy

1. _________ was a putative son of president Thomas Jefferson by his slave Sally Hemings, with whom he developed a liaison while he was on diplomatic service in Paris. Hemings claimed the connection in his memoir, published in a newspaper interview in 1873. It is supported by the weight of historical evidence, as well as circumstantial evidence, including DNA tests linking his brother Eston Hemings to the male Jefferson line. Hemings' memoir attracted national and international attention.

   a. Isaac Jefferson
   b. Thomas Gage
   c. Madison Hemings
   d. Juan de Grijalva

2. The _________ was a group of lawyers and merchants from Essex County, Massachusetts. These Federalists supported Alexander Hamilton and the Massachusetts radicals. When Hamilton was offered a place in the plot to secede New England from the Union, he denied the offer.

   a. Executive Branch Reform Act
   b. Three-fifths compromise
   c. Connecticut Compromise
   d. Essex Junto

3. The _________ was an American whaleship from Nantucket, Massachusetts. She was 87 feet (27 m) long, measured 238 tons, and was captained by the 28-year-old George Pollard, Jr. She is best known for being attacked and sunk by a sperm whale in the Pacific Ocean in 1820. The incident was an inspiration for Herman Melville's 1851 classic novel Moby-Dick.

   a. Executive Branch Reform Act
   b. Essex
   c. Connecticut Compromise
   d. Iraq War De-Escalation Act of 2007

4. _________ was the name of the encampment at which the Lewis and Clark Expedition wintered in 1804-1805. The encampment was located on the Missouri River approximately twelve miles from Washburn, North Dakota, though the precise location is not known for certain and may be under the nearby river.

   The fort was built of cottonwood lumber cut from the riverbanks. It was triangular in shape, with high walls on all sides and a gate facing the riverbank.

a. Bonanzaville, USA
b. Fort Mandan
c. Digital Transition Content Security Act
d. Mexican Cession

5. _________, colloquially, 'the Press', refers to the act of taking men into a navy by force and without notice. It was used by the Royal Navy, beginning in 1664 and during the 18th and early 19th centuries, in wartime, as a means of crewing warships, although legal sanction for the practice goes back to the time of Edward I of England. The Royal Navy impressed many British merchant sailors, as well as some sailors from other nations.

a. Executive Branch Reform Act
b. Battle of Friedland
c. Impressment
d. Iraq War De-Escalation Act of 2007

---

1. c
2. d
3. b
4. b
5. c

CHAPTER OUTLINE: KEY TERMS, PEOPLE, PLACES, CONCEPTS
Chapter 7
National Growing Pains

______ Democratic Party

______ Louisiana

______ Louisiana Purchase

______ Order-in-Council

______ Robert E. Gould

______ Tecumseh

______ Tenskwatawa

______ Early American currency

______ Continental System

______ Monticello

______ War Hawk

______ William G. Bainbridge

______ Decatur

______ Fort Niagara

______ Niagara

______ Washington

______ Hartford Convention

______ Treaty of Ghent

______ Massachusetts

__________ American Revolution

__________ Border

__________ Napoleonic Wars

__________ East Florida

__________ Monroe Doctrine

__________ West Florida

__________ John Quincy

__________ Declaration of Neutrality

__________ Era of Good Feelings

__________ Constitutional Convention

__________ Missouri Compromise

__________ National Road

__________ Albany Regency

__________ American System

__________ Black Codes

__________ Boston

__________ Boston Massacre

__________ Northwest Ordinance

__________ Arkansas

Chapter 7. National Growing Pains

_______________ Arkansas Territory

_______________ Three-Fifths Compromise

_______________ South Carolina

_______________ Burr conspiracy

Democratic Party	The Democratic Party is one of two major contemporary political parties in the United States, along with the Republican Party. The party's social liberal and progressive platform is largely considered center-left in the U.S. political spectrum. The party has the lengthiest record of continuous operation in the United States.
Louisiana	Louisiana was the name of an administrative district of the Viceroyalty of New Spain from 1764 to 1803 that represented territory west of the Mississippi River basin, plus New Orleans. Spain acquired the territory from France: see Louisiana. History The area, comprising what is now known as the Louisiana Purchase, was turned over to the French for a few days in 1803 before it, in turn, was turned over to the United States.
Louisiana Purchase	The Louisiana Purchase was the acquisition by the United States of America of 828,800 square miles (2,147,000 km^2) of France's claim to the territory of Louisiana in 1803. The U.S. paid 60 million francs ($11,250,000) plus cancellation of debts worth 18 million francs ($3,750,000), for a total sum of 15 million dollars for the Louisiana territory ($219 million in 2010 dollars). What was purchased was France's claim only, not the actual territory, which belonged to the tribes which inhabited the area. The territory itself was acquired slowly throughout the nineteenth century by purchases to Native American tribes and wars.
Order-in-Council	An Order-in-Council is a type of legislation in many countries, typically those in the Commonwealth of Nations. In the United Kingdom this legislation is formally made in the name of the Queen by the Privy Council (Queen-in-Council), but in other countries the terminology may vary. Assent Although the Orders are nominally made by the Queen, in practice, royal assent is a formality only.

Chapter 7. National Growing Pains

Robert E. Gould

Robert Emery Gould (March 20, 1924 - February 25, 1998) was clinical professor of psychiatry at New York Medical College, and chief of adolescent services at Bellevue Hospital. Gould was known as outspoken advocate on social issues, including psychiatric treatment of homeless people, violence on television (he was the president of lobbying group National Coalition on Television Violence), homosexuality and AIDS The Chicago Tribune summarized: 'There's almost no danger of getting AIDS from ordinary sexual intercourse, and the irrational fear of AIDS that stifles guilt-free enjoyment of sex may prove more destructive in the long run than the AIDS virus itself, Dr. Robert E. Gould, a professor of psychiatry and of obstetrics and gynecology at New York Medical College, said in the January Cosmopolitan.

Tecumseh

Tecumseh also known as Tecumtha or Tekamthi, was a Native American leader of the Shawnee and a large tribal confederacy that opposed the United States during Tecumseh's War and the War of 1812. He grew up in the Ohio country during the American Revolutionary War and the Northwest Indian War, where he was constantly exposed to warfare.

His brother Tenskwatawa was a religious leader who advocated a return to the ancestral lifestyle of the tribes. A large following and a confederacy grew around his prophetic teachings.

Tenskwatawa

Tenskwatawa, (also called Tenskatawa, Tenskwatawah, Tensquatawa or Lalawethika) (1775 - November 1836) was a Native American religious and political leader of the Shawnee tribe, known as The Prophet or the Shawnee Prophet. He was the brother of Tecumseh, leader of the Shawnee. He was originally given the name Lalawethika (He Makes a Loud Noise or The Noise Maker).

Early American currency

Early American currency went through several stages of development in the colonial and post-Revolutionary history of the United States. Because few coins were minted in the thirteen colonies that became the United States in 1776, foreign coins like the Spanish dollar were widely circulated. Colonial governments sometimes issued paper money to facilitate economic activity.

Continental System

The Continental System or Continental Blockade was the foreign policy of Napoleon I of France in his struggle against the United Kingdom of Great Britain and Ireland during the Napoleonic Wars. It was a large-scale embargo against British trade, inaugurated on November 21, 1806. This embargo ended in April 11, 1814 after Napoleon's first abdication.

	The United Kingdom was an important force in encouraging and financing alliances against Napoleonic France.
Monticello	The Monticello was a Confederate blockade runner during the American Civil War. She was a two-masted schooner out of Havana, Cuba and of unknown nationality. She ran ashore about 6 to 8 miles east of Fort Morgan and the main inlet to Mobile Bay in Alabama on June 26, 1862, after sailing from Havana, and was then set on fire by the crew to prevent her capture.
War Hawk	The term war hawk, in modern use, describes one who seeks war on a country or region and is used in contrast to the more peaceful dove. Historical War Hawks The War Hawks were Democratic-Republicans and were primarily from southern and western states. (The American West then consisted of Kentucky, Tennessee, and Ohio, as well as territories in the Old Northwest that did not yet have votes in Congress.
William G. Bainbridge	William G. Bainbridge was the fifth Sergeant Major of the Army, was sworn in on July 1, 1975 and served until June, 1979. He was born in Galesburg, Illinois, on April 17, 1925 and died on November 29, 2008. He entered the Army in June 1943 from Williamsfield, Illinois. He was captured during the Battle of the Bulge.

Chapter 7. National Growing Pains

Decatur	The Decatur was an American schooner built for privateering during the Atlantic Ocean theater of the War of 1812. She was named for the United States Navy Commodore Stephen Decatur who served with distinction in many of America's earliest conflicts. Decatur is best known for being commanded by Captain Dominique Diron who captured several British ships in the Napoleonic Wars and the War of 1812. Captain Diron, defeated the the stronger Royal Navy schooner HMS Dominica in a battle off Bermuda on August 5, 1813. After a long engagement the Americans chased down the Dominca and boarded, forcing down her colors and killing her commander in the process. See Also • Lynx (1812 privateer) • Lady Washington .
Fort Niagara	Fort Niagara is a fortification originally built to protect the interests of New France in North America. It is located near Youngstown, New York, on the eastern bank of the Niagara River at its mouth, on Lake Ontario. Origin René-Robert Cavelier, Sieur de La Salle built the first structure, called Fort Conti, in 1678. In 1687, the Governor of New France, the Marquis de Denonville, constructed a new fort at the former site of Fort Conti. He named it Fort Denonville and posted a hundred men under the command of Capt.
Niagara	The Niagara was a 245-foot (75 m) long sidewheel palace steamer launched in 1846. Like the others of its kind, it carried passengers and cargo around the North American Great Lakes. It was owned by the Collingwood Line. On September 23, 1856, the Niagara left Sheboygan, Wisconsin headed for Port Washington, Wisconsin, on Lake Michigan, carrying 170 passengers and a heavy load of cargo.

Washington	Washington was one of the first steamboats to operate in the states of California and Oregon. Operations in California Washington operated in California on the Sacramento River. The vessel was purchased in California in 1851 by pioneer steamboat captain Alexander Sinclair Murray (b.1828).
Hartford Convention	The Hartford Convention was an event in 1814-1815 in the United States in which New England Federalists met to discuss their grievances concerning the ongoing War of 1812 and the political problems arising from the domination of the Federal Government by Presidents from Virginia. Despite many outcries in the Federalist press for New England secession and a separate peace with Great Britain, moderates dominated the Convention and such extreme proposals were not a major focus of the convention's debate. The convention discussed removing the Three-fifths compromise which gave slave states more power in Congress and requiring a 2/3 super majority in Congress for the admission of new states, declarations of war, and laws restricting trade.
Treaty of Ghent	The Treaty of Ghent signed on 24 December 1814, in Ghent, was the peace treaty that ended the War of 1812 between the United States of America and the United Kingdom of Great Britain and Ireland. The treaty largely restored relations between the two nations to status quo ante bellum. Because of the era's slow communications, it took weeks for news of the peace treaty to reach the United States, and the Battle of New Orleans was fought after it was signed though before it was ratified.
Massachusetts	'Massachusetts', words and music by Arlo Guthrie, was made the official folk song of Massachusetts in July, 1981.

Chapter 7. National Growing Pains

American Revolution	The American Revolution was the political upheaval during the last half of the 18th century in which thirteen colonies in North America joined together to break free from the British Empire, combining to become the United States of America. They first rejected the authority of the Parliament of Great Britain to govern them from overseas without representation, and then expelled all royal officials. By 1774, each colony had established a Provincial Congress, or an equivalent governmental institution, to govern itself, but still within the empire. The British responded by sending combat troops to re-impose direct rule.
Border	Border is a 1997 blockbuster Bollywood war film based on the Indo-Pakistani War of 1971. J. P. Dutta directed and produced this war epic which stars Sunny Deol, Jackie Shroff, Sunil Shetty, Akshay Khanna, Pooja Bhatt, Sharbani Mukherjee and Tabu. Director J.P. Dutta won Best Director at the same award function, while his father O.P. Dutta won for Best Dialogues. The movie is an adaptation from real life events that happened at the Battle of Longewala fought in Rajasthan (Western Theatre) during the Indo-Pakistani War of 1971 and Bangladesh Liberation War.
Napoleonic Wars	The Napoleonic Wars were a series of conflicts declared against Napoleon's French Empire and changing sets of European allies by opposing coalitions that ran from 1803 to 1815. As a continuation of the wars sparked by the French Revolution of 1789, they revolutionized European armies and played out on an unprecedented scale, mainly due to the application of modern mass conscription. French power rose quickly, conquering most of Europe, but collapsed rapidly after France's disastrous invasion of Russia in 1812. Napoleon's empire ultimately suffered complete military defeat resulting in the restoration of the Bourbon monarchy in France. The wars resulted in the dissolution of the Holy Roman Empire and sowed the seeds of nascent nationalism in Germany and Italy that would lead to the two nations' consolidation later in the century.
East Florida	East Florida was a colony of Great Britain from 1763-1783 and of Spain from 1783-1822. East Florida was established by the British colonial government in 1763; as its name implies it consisted of the eastern part of the region of Florida, with West Florida comprising the western parts. Its capital was St. Augustine, which had been the capital of Spanish Florida.

Britain formed East and West Florida out of territory it had received from France and Spain following the Seven Years' War .

Monroe Doctrine

The Monroe Doctrine is a policy of the United States introduced on December 2, 1823. It stated that further efforts by European nations to colonize land or interfere with states in North or South America would be viewed as acts of aggression requiring U.S. intervention. The Doctrine noted that the United States would neither interfere with existing European colonies nor meddle in the internal concerns of European countries. The Doctrine was issued at a time when nearly all Latin American colonies of Spain and Portugal had achieved independence from the Spanish Empire (except Peru and Bolivia, which became independent in 1823 and 1825 respectively, and Cuba and Puerto Rico).

West Florida

West Florida was a region on the north shore of the Gulf of Mexico, which underwent several boundary and sovereignty changes during its history. West Florida was first established in 1763 by the British government; as its name suggests it largely consisted of the western portion of the region called Florida by Spain, with East Florida comprising the eastern part. It included most of what is now the Florida Panhandle, plus parts of the modern U.S. states of Louisiana, Mississippi, and Alabama.

John Quincy

Colonel John Quincy was an American soldier, politician and member of the Quincy political family. His granddaughter Abigail Adams named her son, John Quincy Adams, in his honor. The city of Quincy, Massachusetts is named in his honor, as well.

Declaration of Neutrality

The Declaration of Neutrality was a declaration by the Austrian Parliament declaring the country permanently neutral. It was enacted on 26 October 1955 as a constitutional act of parliament, i.e., as part of the Constitution of Austria.

Formally, the declaration was promulgated voluntarily by the Republic of Austria.

Era of Good Feelings

The Era of Good Feelings marked a period in the political history of the United States that reflected a sense of national purpose and a desire for unity among Americans in the aftermath of the Napoleonic Wars. The era saw a brief lull in the bitter partisan disputes that had plagued the Democratic-Republican and Federalist parties during the First Party System. President James Monroe endeavored to consolidate the Republican and Federalist parties through 'amalgamation', with the ultimate goal of eliminating parties altogether from national politics.

Chapter 7. National Growing Pains

Constitutional Convention

The United States Constitutional Convention took place from May 25 to September 17, 1787, in Philadelphia, Pennsylvania, to address problems in governing the United States of America, which had been operating under the Articles of Confederation following independence from Great Britain. Although the Convention was purportedly intended only to revise the Articles of Confederation, the intention from the outset of many of its proponents, chief among them James Madison and Alexander Hamilton, was to create a new government rather than fix the existing one. The delegates elected George Washington to preside over the convention.

Missouri Compromise

The Missouri Compromise was an agreement passed in 1820 between the pro-slavery and anti-slavery factions in the United States Congress, involving primarily the regulation of slavery in the western territories. It prohibited slavery in the former Louisiana Territory north of the parallel 36° 30′ north except within the boundaries of the proposed state of Missouri. Prior to the agreement, the House of Representatives had refused to accept this compromise, and a conference committee was appointed.

National Road

The National Road or Cumberland Road was one of the first major improved highways in the United States to be built by the federal government. Construction began in 1811 at Cumberland, Maryland, on the Potomac River. It crossed the Allegheny Mountains and southwestern Pennsylvania, reaching Wheeling, Virginia (now West Virginia), on the Ohio River in 1818. Plans were made to continue through St. Louis, Missouri, on the Mississippi River to Jefferson City, Missouri, but funding ran out and construction stopped at Vandalia, Illinois, in 1838.

Albany Regency

The Albany Regency was a group of politicians who controlled the New York state government between 1822 and 1838. The group was among the first American political machines. In the beginning they were the leading figures of the Bucktails faction of the Democratic-Republican Party, later the Jacksonian Democrats and finally became the Hunkers faction of the Democratic Party.

History

The Albany Regency was a loosely organized group of politicians with similar views and goals who resided in or near Albany, New York, the state capital.

American System	The American System, was a mercantilist economic plan based on the 'American School' ideas of Alexander Hamilton, expanded upon later by Friedrich List, consisting of a high tariff to support internal improvements such as road-building, and a national bank to encourage productive enterprise and form a national currency. This program was intended to allow the United States to grow and prosper, by providing a defense against the dumping of cheap foreign products, mainly at the time from the British Empire. History A plan to strengthen and unify the nation, the American System was advanced by the Whig Party and a number of leading politicians including Henry Clay, John C. Calhoun and John Quincy Adams.
Black Codes	The Black Codes were unofficial laws put in place in the United States to limit the basic human rights and civil liberties of blacks. Even though the U.S. constitution originally discriminated against blacks (as 'other persons') and both Northern and Southern states had passed discriminatory legislation from the early 19th century, the term Black Codes is used most often to refer to legislation passed by Southern states at the end of the Civil War to control the labor, migration and other activities of newly-freed slaves. In Texas, the Eleventh Legislature produced these codes in 1866, right after the United States Civil War.
Boston	Boston is the capital of and largest city in Massachusetts, and is one of the oldest cities in the United States. The largest city in New England, Boston is regarded as the unofficial 'Capital of New England' for its economic and cultural impact on the entire New England region. The city proper had a 2009 estimated population of 645,169, making it the twentieth largest in the country.

Chapter 7. National Growing Pains

Boston Massacre	The Boston Massacre, called The Incident on King Street by the British, was an incident on March 5, 1770, in which British Army soldiers killed five civilian men. British troops had been stationed in Boston, capital of the Province of Massachusetts Bay, since 1768 in order to protect and support crown-appointed colonial officials attempting to enforce unpopular Parliamentary legislation. Amid ongoing tense relations between the population and the soldiers, a mob formed around a British sentry, who was subjected to verbal abuse and harassment.
Northwest Ordinance	The Northwest Ordinance was an act of the Congress of the Confederation of the United States. The primary effect of the ordinance was the creation of the Northwest Territory as the first organized territory of the United States out of the region south of the Great Lakes, north and west of the Ohio River, and east of the Mississippi River. On August 7, 1789, the U.S. Congress affirmed the Ordinance with slight modifications under the Constitution.
Arkansas	Arkansas is a state located in the southern region of the United States. Its name is an Algonquian name of the Quapaw Indians. Arkansas shares a border with six states with its eastern border largely defined by the Mississippi River.
Arkansas Territory	The Territory of Arkansas, initially organized as the Territory of Arkansaw, was an organized incorporated territory of the United States that existed from July 4, 1819 until June 15, 1836, when the final extent of the territory was admitted to the Union as the State of Arkansas. History The Arkansas Territory was created from the portion of the Missouri Territory lying south of a point on the Mississippi River at 36 degrees north latitude running west to the St. Francois River, then followed the river to 36 degrees 30 minutes north latitude, then west to the territorial boundary. This included all of the present state of Oklahoma south of the parallel 36°30' north.
Three-Fifths Compromise	The Three-Fifths Compromise was a compromise between Southern and Northern states reached during the Philadelphia Convention of 1787 in which three-fifths of the enumerated population of slaves would be counted for representation purposes regarding both the distribution of taxes and the apportionment of the members of the United States House of Representatives. It was proposed by delegates James Wilson and Roger Sherman.

	Delegates opposed to slavery generally wished to count only the free inhabitants of each state.
South Carolina	South Carolina is a state in the Deep South that borders Georgia to the south and North Carolina to the north. Originally part of the Province of Carolina, the Province of South Carolina was one of the 13 colonies that declared independence from the British Crown during the American Revolution. The colony was originally named by King Charles II of England in honor of his father Charles I, as Carolus is Latin for Charles.
Burr conspiracy	The Burr conspiracy in the beginning of the 19th century was a suspected treasonous cabal of planters, politicians, and army officers led by former U.S. Vice President Aaron Burr. According to the accusations against him, Burr's goal was to create an independent nation in the center of North America and/or the Southwest and parts of Mexico. Burr's explanation: To take possession of, and farm, 40,000 acres (160 km^2) in the Texas Territory leased to him by the Spanish.

PRACTICE QUIZ
Chapter 7. National Growing Pains

---

1. The _________, was a mercantilist economic plan based on the 'American School' ideas of Alexander Hamilton, expanded upon later by Friedrich List, consisting of a high tariff to support internal improvements such as road-building, and a national bank to encourage productive enterprise and form a national currency. This program was intended to allow the United States to grow and prosper, by providing a defense against the dumping of cheap foreign products, mainly at the time from the British Empire.

   History

   A plan to strengthen and unify the nation, the _________ was advanced by the Whig Party and a number of leading politicians including Henry Clay, John C. Calhoun and John Quincy Adams.

   a. Executive Branch Reform Act
   b. American System
   c. Ellis W. Hawley Prize
   d. Impeachment of Andrew Johnson

2. The _________ is one of two major contemporary political parties in the United States, along with the Republican Party. The party's social liberal and progressive platform is largely considered center-left in the U.S. political spectrum. The party has the lengthiest record of continuous operation in the United States.

   a. Democratic Party
   b. Federal Funding Accountability and Transparency Act of 2006
   c. Jessica's Law
   d. Respect for America's Fallen Heroes Act

3. An _________ is a type of legislation in many countries, typically those in the Commonwealth of Nations. In the United Kingdom this legislation is formally made in the name of the Queen by the Privy Council (Queen-in-Council), but in other countries the terminology may vary.

   Assent

   Although the Orders are nominally made by the Queen, in practice, royal assent is a formality only.

a. Order-in-Council
b. Chiaha
c. Iraq War De-Escalation Act of 2007
d. America's Affordable Health Choices Act of 2009

4. The _________ or Continental Blockade was the foreign policy of Napoleon I of France in his struggle against the United Kingdom of Great Britain and Ireland during the Napoleonic Wars. It was a large-scale embargo against British trade, inaugurated on November 21, 1806. This embargo ended in April 11, 1814 after Napoleon's first abdication.

The United Kingdom was an important force in encouraging and financing alliances against Napoleonic France.

a. Digital Transition Content Security Act
b. Federal Funding Accountability and Transparency Act of 2006
c. Jessica's Law
d. Continental System

5.

_________ was the name of an administrative district of the Viceroyalty of New Spain from 1764 to 1803 that represented territory west of the Mississippi River basin, plus New Orleans. Spain acquired the territory from France: see _________.

History

The area, comprising what is now known as the _________ Purchase, was turned over to the French for a few days in 1803 before it, in turn, was turned over to the United States.

a. Louisiana
b. Chiaha
c. Digital Transition Content Security Act
d. Federal Funding Accountability and Transparency Act of 2006

1. b
2. a
3. a
4. d
5. a

CHAPTER OUTLINE: KEY TERMS, PEOPLE, PLACES, CONCEPTS

Chapter 8

Toward a National Economy

- York
- Market Revolution
- Factory
- Boston
- Boston Manufacturing Company
- Erie Canal
- Union
- Constitutional Convention
- Sam Bass
- Irish American
- German American
- John Fitch
- Black Codes
- Columbian Exchange
- George Corbin Washington
- Report on Manufactures
- South Carolina
- Washington
- Alabama

______________ Black Belt

______________ Missouri Compromise

______________ Tennessee

______________ Richard Allen

______________ American Colonization Society

______________ Black nationalism

______________ Burr conspiracy

______________ Colonization Societies

______________ Democratic Party

______________ Flatboat

______________ National Road

______________ Wilderness Road

______________ American Revolution

______________ DeWitt Clinton

______________ Wabash and Erie Canal

______________ George Mason III

______________ Gibbons v. Ogden

______________ Louisiana

______________ Louisiana Purchase

Chapter 8. Toward a National Economy

McCulloch v. Maryland

Monticello

Commerce

York	York was an African American slave best known for his participation with the Lewis and Clark Expedition. As William Clark's slave, he had to do diffficult manual labour without pay. After the expedition's return he pressed for his freedom, which Clark opposed, he possibly agreed ten years later, though some historians dispute this and say he was never freed.
Market Revolution	The Market Revolution in the United States was a drastic change in the manual labor system originating in the South (and soon moving to the North) and later spreading to the entire world. Traditional commerce was made obsolete by improvements in transportation and communication. This change prompted the reincarnation of the mercantilist ideas that were thought to have died out.
Factory	Factory was the English term for the trading posts system originally established by Europeans in foreign territories, first within different states of medieval Europe, and later in their colonial possessions. Factories served simultaneously as market, warehouse, customs, defense and support to the navigation or exploration, headquarters or de facto government of local communities, with the head of the factory being called a factor. This system was adopted by Americans to exchange goods with local non western societies.
Boston	Boston is the capital of and largest city in Massachusetts, and is one of the oldest cities in the United States. The largest city in New England, Boston is regarded as the unofficial 'Capital of New England' for its economic and cultural impact on the entire New England region. The city proper had a 2009 estimated population of 645,169, making it the twentieth largest in the country.
Boston Manufacturing Company	The Boston Manufacturing Company was organized in 1813 by Francis Cabot Lowell, a wealthy Boston merchant, in partnership a group of investors known as The Boston Associates, for the manufacture of cotton textiles. Boston Manufacturing Company gathered many of their trade secrets from the earlier horse-drawn Beverly Cotton Manufactory, of Beverly, Massachusetts, of 1788. While the Rhode Island System that followed was famously employed by Samuel Slater, the Boston Associates would improve upon it in what would become known as the 'Waltham System', an idea that would later be successfully copied at Lowell, Massachusetts and several other industrial cities established in the 19th century. It would soon change the face of New England and its economy from one based largely on agriculture to one dominated by industry.
Erie Canal	The Erie Canal is a waterway in New York that runs about 363 miles (584 km) from Albany, New York, on the Hudson River to Buffalo, New York, at Lake Erie, completing a navigable water route from the Atlantic Ocean to the Great Lakes. The canal contains 36 locks and encompasses a total elevation differential of around 565 ft. (169 m).

Chapter 8. Toward a National Economy

Union	During the American Civil War, the Union was a name used to refer to the federal government of the United States, which was supported by the twenty free states and five border slave states. It was opposed by 11 Southern slave states that had declared a secession to join together to form the Confederacy. Although the Union states included the Western states of California, Oregon, and (after 1864) Nevada, as well as states generally considered to be part of the Midwest, the Union has been also often loosely referred to as 'the North', both then and now.
Constitutional Convention	The United States Constitutional Convention took place from May 25 to September 17, 1787, in Philadelphia, Pennsylvania, to address problems in governing the United States of America, which had been operating under the Articles of Confederation following independence from Great Britain. Although the Convention was purportedly intended only to revise the Articles of Confederation, the intention from the outset of many of its proponents, chief among them James Madison and Alexander Hamilton, was to create a new government rather than fix the existing one. The delegates elected George Washington to preside over the convention.
Sam Bass	Sam Bass was a nineteenth-century American train robber and outlaw. Early life Bass was orphaned at the age of 10. For the next five years, he and his siblings lived with an abusive uncle. In 1869, he set out on his own and spent the next year in Mississippi.
Irish American	Irish Americans (Irish: Gael-Mheiriceánaigh) are citizens of the United States who can trace their ancestry to Ireland. A total of 36,278,332 Americans--estimated at 11.9% of the total population--reported Irish ancestry in the 2008 American Community Survey conducted by the U.S. Census Bureau. The only self-reported ancestral group larger than Irish Americans is German Americans.
German American	German Americans comprise about 51 million people, or 17% of the U.S. population, the country's largest self-reported ancestral group. California, Texas and Pennsylvania have the largest numbers of German origin, although upper Midwestern states, including Iowa, Minnesota, Wisconsin, Nebraska, and The Dakotas, have the highest proportion of German Americans at over one-third.

None of the historical German states had overseas colonies, so not until the 1680s did the first significant groups of German immigrants arrive in the British colonies, settling primarily in New York and Pennsylvania.

John Fitch

John Fitch was an American inventor, clockmaker, and silversmith who, in 1787, built the first recorded steam-powered boat in the United States. Two decades later, Robert Fulton was able to make steamboats profitable.

Early life

Fitch was born in Jewell, Iowa on January 21,1998, on a farm that is part of present-day Iowa He received little formal schooling and eventually Though of killing himself to a clockmaker, during which time Fitch was not allowed to learn or even observe watchmaking (he later taught himself how to repair clocks and watches).

Black Codes

The Black Codes were unofficial laws put in place in the United States to limit the basic human rights and civil liberties of blacks. Even though the U.S. constitution originally discriminated against blacks (as 'other persons') and both Northern and Southern states had passed discriminatory legislation from the early 19th century, the term Black Codes is used most often to refer to legislation passed by Southern states at the end of the Civil War to control the labor, migration and other activities of newly-freed slaves.

In Texas, the Eleventh Legislature produced these codes in 1866, right after the United States Civil War.

Columbian Exchange

The Columbian Exchange was a dramatically widespread exchange of animals, plants, culture, human populations (including slaves), communicable diseases, and ideas between the Eastern and Western hemispheres (Old World and New World). It was one of the most significant events concerning ecology, agriculture, and culture in all of human history. Christopher Columbus' first voyage to the Americas in 1492 launched the era of large-scale contact between the Old and the New Worlds that resulted in this ecological revolution, hence the name 'Columbian' Exchange.

Chapter 8. Toward a National Economy

George Corbin Washington	George Corbin Washington was a United States Congressman from the third and fifth districts of Maryland, serving four terms from 1827 to 1833, and 1835 to 1837. He was also a grandnephew of U.S. President George Washington. Washington was born at Haywood Farms near Oak Grove of Westmoreland County, Virginia. He attended Phillips Academy and Harvard University, studied law, but devoted himself to agricultural pursuits on his plantation in Maryland.
Report on Manufactures	The Report on Manufactures is the third report, and magnum opus, of American Founding Father and 1st U.S. Treasury Secretary Alexander Hamilton. It was presented to Congress on December 5, 1791 and recommended economic policies to stimulate the new republic's economy and ensure the independence won with the conclusion of the Revolutionary War in 1783. Hamilton's 'Report on Manufactures' laid forth economic principles rooted in both the Mercantilist System of Elizabeth I's England and the practices of Jean-Baptiste Colbert of France.
South Carolina	South Carolina is a state in the Deep South that borders Georgia to the south and North Carolina to the north. Originally part of the Province of Carolina, the Province of South Carolina was one of the 13 colonies that declared independence from the British Crown during the American Revolution. The colony was originally named by King Charles II of England in honor of his father Charles I, as Carolus is Latin for Charles.
Washington	Washington was one of the first steamboats to operate in the states of California and Oregon. Operations in California Washington operated in California on the Sacramento River. The vessel was purchased in California in 1851 by pioneer steamboat captain Alexander Sinclair Murray (b.1828).

Alabama	Alabama is a state located in the southeastern region of the United States of America. It is bordered by Tennessee to the north, Georgia to the east, Florida and the Gulf of Mexico to the south, and Mississippi to the west. Alabama ranks 30th in total land area and ranks second in the size of its inland waterways. The state ranks 23rd in population with 4.7 million residents in 2009.
Black Belt	The Black Belt is a region of the Southern United States. Although the term originally describes the prairies and dark soil of central Alabama and northeast Mississippi, it has long been used to describe a broad region in the American South characterized by a high percentage of black people. They were originally enslaved laborers on the region's cotton plantations and many stayed as rural workers, tenant farmers and sharecroppers after the American Civil War.
Missouri Compromise	The Missouri Compromise was an agreement passed in 1820 between the pro-slavery and anti-slavery factions in the United States Congress, involving primarily the regulation of slavery in the western territories. It prohibited slavery in the former Louisiana Territory north of the parallel 36° 30′ north except within the boundaries of the proposed state of Missouri. Prior to the agreement, the House of Representatives had refused to accept this compromise, and a conference committee was appointed.
Tennessee	Tennessee is a U.S. state located in the Southeastern United States. It has a population of 6,214,888, making it the nation's 17th-largest state by population, and covers 42,169 square miles (109,220 km^2), making it the 36th-largest by total land area. Tennessee is bordered by Kentucky and Virginia to the north, North Carolina to the east, Georgia, Alabama, and Mississippi to the south, and Arkansas and Missouri to the west.
Richard Allen	Richard Allen was a minister, educator, writer, and the founder in 1816 of the African Methodist Episcopal (AME), the first independent black denomination in the United States. He opened his first church in 1794 in Philadelphia, Pennsylvania. He was elected the first bishop of the AME Church.
American Colonization Society	The American Colonization Society founded in 1816, was the primary vehicle to support the 'return' of free African Americans to what was considered greater freedom in Africa. It helped to found the colony of Liberia in 1821-22 as a place for freedmen. Among its founders were Charles Fenton Mercer, Henry Clay, John Randolph, and Richard Bland Lee.

	Paul Cuffee, a wealthy mixed-race New England shipowner and activist, was an early advocate of settling freed blacks in Africa. He gained support from black leaders and members of the US Congress for an emigration plan.
Black nationalism	Black nationalism advocates a racial definition (or redefinition) of indigenous national identity, as opposed to multiculturalism. There are different indigenous nationalist philosophies but the principles of all African nationalist ideologies are unity, and self-determination or independence from European society. Martin Delany is considered to be the grandfather of African nationalism.
Burr conspiracy	The Burr conspiracy in the beginning of the 19th century was a suspected treasonous cabal of planters, politicians, and army officers led by former U.S. Vice President Aaron Burr. According to the accusations against him, Burr's goal was to create an independent nation in the center of North America and/or the Southwest and parts of Mexico. Burr's explanation: To take possession of, and farm, 40,000 acres (160 km²) in the Texas Territory leased to him by the Spanish.
Colonization Societies	A number of Colonization Societies which promoted the return of Negroes to Africa have existed in the history of the United States. Thomas Jefferson was a Founding Father who promoted the racial separation of American Indians and the colonization of Negroes to places far away from Virginia. Jefferson was the most important early advocate of colonization.
Democratic Party	The Democratic Party is one of two major contemporary political parties in the United States, along with the Republican Party. The party's social liberal and progressive platform is largely considered center-left in the U.S. political spectrum. The party has the lengthiest record of continuous operation in the United States.
Flatboat	A flatboat is a rectangular flat-bottomed boat with (mostly) square ends used to transport freight and passengers on inland waterways. The flatboat could be any size, but essentially it is large, sturdy tub with a hull that displaces water and so floats in the water. This differentiates the flatboat from the raft, which floats on the water.
National Road	The National Road or Cumberland Road was one of the first major improved highways in the United States to be built by the federal government. Construction began in 1811 at Cumberland, Maryland, on the Potomac River. It crossed the Allegheny Mountains and southwestern Pennsylvania, reaching Wheeling, Virginia (now West Virginia), on the Ohio River in 1818. Plans were made to continue through St. Louis, Missouri, on the Mississippi River to Jefferson City, Missouri, but funding ran out and construction stopped at Vandalia, Illinois, in 1838.

Wilderness Road

The Wilderness Road was the principal route used by settlers for more than fifty years to reach Kentucky from the East. In 1775, Daniel Boone blazed a trail for the Transylvania Company from Fort Chiswell in Virginia through the Cumberland Gap into central Kentucky. It was later lengthened, following Native American trails, to reach the Falls of the Ohio at Louisville.

American Revolution

The American Revolution was the political upheaval during the last half of the 18th century in which thirteen colonies in North America joined together to break free from the British Empire, combining to become the United States of America. They first rejected the authority of the Parliament of Great Britain to govern them from overseas without representation, and then expelled all royal officials. By 1774, each colony had established a Provincial Congress, or an equivalent governmental institution, to govern itself, but still within the empire. The British responded by sending combat troops to re-impose direct rule.

DeWitt Clinton

DeWitt Clinton was an early American politician who served as United States Senator and the sixth Governor of New York. In this last capacity he was largely responsible for the construction of the Erie Canal. Unlike his adversary Martin Van Buren, who invented machine politics, Clinton became the leader of New York's People's Party.

Wabash and Erie Canal

The Wabash and Erie Canal was a shipping canal that linked the Great Lakes to the Ohio River via an artificial waterway. The canal provided traders with access from the Great Lakes all the way to the Gulf of Mexico. Over 460 miles long, it was the longest canal ever built in North America.

The canal known as the Wabash ' Erie in the 1850s and thereafter, was actually a combination of four canals: the Miami and Erie Canal from the Maumee River near Toledo, Ohio to Junction, Ohio, the original Wabash and Erie Canal from Junction, Ohio to Terre Haute, Indiana, the Cross Cut Canal from Terre Haute, Indiana to Worthington, Indiana (Point Commerce), and the Central Canal from Worthington to Evansville, Indiana.

George Mason III

George Mason III was an early American planter, businessman, and statesman. Mason was the father of George Mason IV, a Founding Father of the United States.

Early life

Mason was born in 1690 at Chopawamsic plantation in Stafford County, Virginia.

Gibbons v. Ogden

Gibbons v. Ogden, 22 U.S. 1 (1824), was a landmark decision in which the Supreme Court of the United States held that the power to regulate interstate commerce was granted to Congress by the Commerce Clause of the United States Constitution. The case was argued by some of America's most admired and capable attorneys at the time. Exiled Irish patriot Thomas Addis Emmet and Thomas J. Oakley argued for Ogden, while William Wirt and Daniel Webster argued for Gibbons.

Background
The acts of the Legislature of the State of New York granted to Robert R. Livingston and Robert Fulton exclusive navigation privileges of all the waters within the jurisdiction of that State, with boats moved by fire or steam, for a term of years. Livingston and Fulton granted a license to Aaron Ogden. Thomas Gibbons operated a competing steamboat service between Elizabethtown, New Jersey and New York City that had been licensed by the United States Congress in regulating the coasting trade; he also took on Cornelius Vanderbilt as his business manager.

Case
Aaron Ogden filed a complaint in the Court of Chancery of New York asking the court to restrain Thomas Gibbons from operating on these waters. Ogden's lawyer contended that states often passed laws on issues regarding interstate matters and that states should have fully concurrent power with Congress on matters concerning interstate commerce

The Court of Chancery of New York and the Court of Errors of New York found in favor of Ogden and issued an injunction to restrict Gibbons from operating his boats. Gibbons appealed the case to the Supreme Court, which reversed the decision.

Decision of the Court
The Supreme Court ruled in favor of Gibbons. The sole argued source of Congress's power to promulgate the law at issue was the Commerce Clause. Accordingly, the Court had to answer whether the law regulated 'commerce' that was 'among the several states.' With respect to 'commerce,' the Court held that commerce is more than mere traffic--that it is the trade of commodities--it is also intercourse. This broader definition includes navigation. The Court interpreted 'among' as 'intermingled with.'

Marshall's ruling determined that 'a Congressional power to regulate navigation is as expressly granted as if that term had been added to the word 'commerce'.'

The court went on to conclude that Congressional power over commerce should extend to the regulation of all aspects of it, overriding state law to the contrary:

> 'If, as has always been understood, the sovereignty of Congress, though limited to specified objects, is plenary as to those objects, the power over commerce with foreign nations and among the several states is vested in Congress as absolutely as it would be in a single government, having in its constitution the same restrictions on the exercise of the power as are found in the Constitution of the United States.'

Importance of the case
Steven Redd argues that the decision in Gibbons v. Ogden survived until 1895, when the court began to limit the congressional power with the case of United States v. E. C. Knight Co., 156 U.S. 1 (1895). This marked the start of a 40-year period of history during which the Supreme Court limited the federal government's ability to regulate under the Interstate Commerce Clause. During the 1930s the Supreme Court changed course again and began to grant more federal authority under Commerce Clause, going beyond even the authority recognized in Gibbons v. Odgen. The Court went so far as to say that even activity entirely within one state could be regulated by the federal government if the activity had an effect on interstate commerce. Jones ' Laughlin Steel Corporation, 301 US 1 (1937).

However, Strict Constructionists (those who believe that the Constitution must be given the narrowest possible construction) hold a different view of the meaning of Commerce Clause as established in Gibbons that it was limited in scope because the decision could be interpreted to say that navigation only pertained to the federal Commerce Clause because it was necessary to business as it allowed for the interstate transportation of goods. Therefore, under this theory the E.C Knight decision may be viewed not as a radical departure, but as a continuation of the original jurisprudence.

Note that in Gibbons v. Ogden the court specifically stated there are limits upon the federal commerce power, but chose not to put into detail what those limits were aside from goods specifically made, moved, and sold within one state were exclusively beyond the reach of the federal commerce power. This part of the Gibbons ruling stands in direct contrast to the post-New Deal decision in Wickard v. Filburn, 317 U.S. 111 (1942).

Opinion excerpts

- The power to 'regulate Commerce' is:
- In interpreting the power of Congress as to commerce 'among the several states':
- Defining how far the power of Congress extends:

.

Louisiana

Louisiana was the name of an administrative district of the Viceroyalty of New Spain from 1764 to 1803 that represented territory west of the Mississippi River basin, plus New Orleans. Spain acquired the territory from France: see Louisiana.

History

The area, comprising what is now known as the Louisiana Purchase, was turned over to the French for a few days in 1803 before it, in turn, was turned over to the United States.

Louisiana Purchase

The Louisiana Purchase was the acquisition by the United States of America of 828,800 square miles (2,147,000 km^2) of France's claim to the territory of Louisiana in 1803. The U.S. paid 60 million francs ($11,250,000) plus cancellation of debts worth 18 million francs ($3,750,000), for a total sum of 15 million dollars for the Louisiana territory ($219 million in 2010 dollars). What was purchased was France's claim only, not the actual territory, which belonged to the tribes which inhabited the area. The territory itself was acquired slowly throughout the nineteenth century by purchases to Native American tribes and wars.

McCulloch v. Maryland	McCulloch v. Maryland, 17 U.S. 316 (1819), was a landmark decision by the Supreme Court of the United States. The state of Maryland had attempted to impede operation of a branch of the Second Bank of the United States by imposing a tax on all notes of banks not chartered in Maryland. Though the law, by its language, was generally applicable to all banks not chartered in Maryland, the Second Bank of the United States was the only out-of-state bank then existing in Maryland, and the law was recognized in the court's opinion as having specifically targeted the U.S. Bank.
Monticello	The Monticello was a Confederate blockade runner during the American Civil War. She was a two-masted schooner out of Havana, Cuba and of unknown nationality. She ran ashore about 6 to 8 miles east of Fort Morgan and the main inlet to Mobile Bay in Alabama on June 26, 1862, after sailing from Havana, and was then set on fire by the crew to prevent her capture.
Commerce	While business refers to the value-creating activities of an organization for profit, commerce means the whole system of an economy that constitutes an environment for business. The system includes legal, economic, political, social, cultural, and technological systems that are in operation in any country. Thus, commerce is a system or an environment that affects the business prospects of an economy or a nation-state.

PRACTICE QUIZ
Chapter 8. Toward a National Economy

---

1. _________, 22 U.S. 1 (1824), was a landmark decision in which the Supreme Court of the United States held that the power to regulate interstate commerce was granted to Congress by the Commerce Clause of the United States Constitution. The case was argued by some of America's most admired and capable attorneys at the time. Exiled Irish patriot Thomas Addis Emmet and Thomas J. Oakley argued for Ogden, while William Wirt and Daniel Webster argued for Gibbons.

Background

The acts of the Legislature of the State of New York granted to Robert R. Livingston and Robert Fulton exclusive navigation privileges of all the waters within the jurisdiction of that State, with boats moved by fire or steam, for a term of years. Livingston and Fulton granted a license to Aaron Ogden. Thomas Gibbons operated a competing steamboat service between Elizabethtown, New Jersey and New York City that had been licensed by the United States Congress in regulating the coasting trade; he also took on Cornelius Vanderbilt as his business manager.

Case

Aaron Ogden filed a complaint in the Court of Chancery of New York asking the court to restrain Thomas Gibbons from operating on these waters. Ogden's lawyer contended that states often passed laws on issues regarding interstate matters and that states should have fully concurrent power with Congress on matters concerning interstate commerce

The Court of Chancery of New York and the Court of Errors of New York found in favor of Ogden and issued an injunction to restrict Gibbons from operating his boats. Gibbons appealed the case to the Supreme Court, which reversed the decision.

Decision of the Court

The Supreme Court ruled in favor of Gibbons. The sole argued source of Congress's power to promulgate the law at issue was the Commerce Clause. Accordingly, the Court had to answer whether the law regulated 'commerce' that was 'among the several states.' With respect to 'commerce,' the Court held that commerce is more than mere traffic--that it is the trade of commodities--it is also intercourse. This broader definition includes navigation. The Court interpreted 'among' as 'intermingled with.'

Marshall's ruling determined that 'a Congressional power to regulate navigation is as expressly granted as if that term had been added to the word 'commerce'.'

The court went on to conclude that Congressional power over commerce should extend to the regulation of all aspects of it, overriding state law to the contrary:

> 'If, as has always been understood, the sovereignty of Congress, though limited to specified objects, is plenary as to those objects, the power over commerce with foreign nations and among the several states is vested in Congress as absolutely as it would be in a single government, having in its constitution the same restrictions on the exercise of the power as are found in the Constitution of the United States.'

Importance of the case

Steven Redd argues that the decision in _________ survived until 1895, when the court began to limit the congressional power with the case of United States v. E. C. Knight Co., 156 U.S. 1 (1895). This marked the start of a 40-year period of history during which the Supreme Court limited the federal government's ability to regulate under the Interstate Commerce Clause. During the 1930s the Supreme Court changed course again and began to grant more federal authority under Commerce Clause, going beyond even the authority recognized in Gibbons v. Odgen. The Court went so far as to say that even activity entirely within one state could be regulated by the federal government if the activity had an effect on interstate commerce. Jones ' Laughlin Steel Corporation, 301 US 1 (1937).

However, Strict Constructionists (those who believe that the Constitution must be given the narrowest possible construction) hold a different view of the meaning of Commerce Clause as established in Gibbons that it was limited in scope because the decision could be interpreted to say that navigation only pertained to the federal Commerce Clause because it was necessary to business as it allowed for the interstate transportation of goods. Therefore, under this theory the E.C Knight decision may be viewed not as a radical departure, but as a continuation of the original jurisprudence.

Note that in _________ the court specifically stated there are limits upon the federal commerce power, but chose not to put into detail what those limits were aside from goods specifically made, moved, and sold within one state were exclusively beyond the reach of the federal commerce power. This part of the Gibbons ruling stands in direct contrast to the post-New Deal decision in Wickard v. Filburn, 317 U.S. 111 (1942).

Opinion excerpts

- The power to 'regulate Commerce' is:

- In interpreting the power of Congress as to commerce 'among the several states':

- Defining how far the power of Congress extends:

.

a. Gibbons v. Ogden
b. Thomas Sumter
c. Martin Van Buren
d. John Tyler

2. The _________ is one of two major contemporary political parties in the United States, along with the Republican Party. The party's social liberal and progressive platform is largely considered center-left in the U.S. political spectrum. The party has the lengthiest record of continuous operation in the United States.

a. Digital Transition Content Security Act
b. Chinh-Hunnicutt affair
c. Conway Cabal
d. Democratic Party

3. _________ was an African American slave best known for his participation with the Lewis and Clark Expedition. As William Clark's slave, he had to do diffficult manual labour without pay. After the expedition's return he pressed for his freedom, which Clark opposed, he possibly agreed ten years later, though some historians dispute this and say he was never freed.

a. Thomas Gage
b. Francisco de Montejo
c. Juan de Grijalva
d. York

4. _________ advocates a racial definition (or redefinition) of indigenous national identity, as opposed to multiculturalism. There are different indigenous nationalist philosophies but the principles of all African nationalist ideologies are unity, and self-determination or independence from European society. Martin Delany is considered to be the grandfather of African nationalism.

   a. Back-to-Africa movement
   b. Black Consciousness Movement
   c. Black Liberation Army
   d. Black nationalism

5. _________s comprise about 51 million people, or 17% of the U.S. population, the country's largest self-reported ancestral group. California, Texas and Pennsylvania have the largest numbers of German origin, although upper Midwestern states, including Iowa, Minnesota, Wisconsin, Nebraska, and The Dakotas, have the highest proportion of _________s at over one-third.

   None of the historical German states had overseas colonies, so not until the 1680s did the first significant groups of German immigrants arrive in the British colonies, settling primarily in New York and Pennsylvania.

   a. Mexican American
   b. German American
   c. Nisei
   d. Macedonian American

ANSWER KEY
Chapter 8. Toward a National Economy

1. a
2. d
3. d
4. d
5. b

CHAPTER OUTLINE: KEY TERMS, PEOPLE, PLACES, CONCEPTS

Chapter 9

Jacksonian Democracy

______________ Democratic Party

______________ Indian removal

______________ American Party

______________ Party system

______________ John Quincy

______________ Northwest Ordinance

______________ Politics

______________ Kitchen Cabinet

______________ Republican Party

______________ State bank

______________ Thomas Hart Benton

______________ McCulloch v. Maryland

______________ Union

______________ Cherokee

______________ Choctaw

______________ Nullification

______________ Spanish Florida

______________ Black Hawk

______________ Cherokee Nation v. Georgia

_____ Nation

_____ Osceola

_____ Worcester v. Georgia

_____ Alabama

_____ George Corbin Washington

_____ Missouri Compromise

_____ South Carolina

_____ Trail of Tears

_____ Turners

_____ Denmark Vesey

_____ Washington

_____ William Wirt

_____ Nullification Crisis

_____ Force Bill

_____ Proclamation to the People of South Carolina

_____ The Sky People

_____ Specie Circular

_____ York

_____ Ralph Waldo Emerson

Chapter 9. Jacksonian Democracy

______ Horace Greeley

______ Independents

______ Tecumseh

______ John Tyler

Democratic Party

The Democratic Party is one of two major contemporary political parties in the United States, along with the Republican Party. The party's social liberal and progressive platform is largely considered center-left in the U.S. political spectrum. The party has the lengthiest record of continuous operation in the United States.

Indian removal

Indian removal was a nineteenth century policy of the government of the United States to relocate Native American tribes living east of the Mississippi River to lands west of the river. The Indian Removal Act was signed into law by President Andrew Jackson on May 26, 1830.

Overview
Since the presidency of Thomas Jefferson, America's policy had been to allow Native Americans to remain east of the Mississippi as long as they became assimilated or 'civilized'.

American Party

A political party by the name of the American Party has existed several times in the United States:

- The Toleration Party, also known as the American Party, was established in Connecticut to oppose the Federalist Party
- The antebellum American Party grew out of the Know Nothing movement and was based on nativism
- There were also several other late 19th-century political parties with the same name, notably one founded in 1887, and another that participated in the elections of 1876, 1880 and 1884. wikimedia.org/wikipedia/commons/thumb/4/4c/Wikisource-logo.svg/12px-Wikisource-logo.svg.png' width='12' height='13' /> 'American Party, The'. Collier's New Encyclopedia. 1921.<span style=' none;? display:> </SPAN></SPAN></LI><LI>American Party organized by Ex-Governor of New York William Sulzer</LI><LI>American Party an anti-Mormon party that existed in Utah from 1905 to 1911</LI><LI>Ku Klux Party, also known as the American Party, which ran Gilbert Nations for President of the United States and former congressman Charles H. Randall for vice-president in 1924. The ticket received 23867 votes.</LI><LI>American Party of Nebraska which ran Mary Kennery (or Kennedy) as a favorite daughter for President of the United States in 1952.</LI><LI>American Party which ran Herman W. Kolpack for President of the United States in 1952.</LI><LI>American Party was a successor of the 1968 American Independent Party. The current American Independent Party split from it in 1976.</LI><LI>American Party http://www.americanparty.mobi now holds the U.S. trademark for this name</LI></UL>. </div></td></tr></table><p></p></div>

Chapter 9. Jacksonian Democracy

Party system	A party system is a concept in comparative political science concerning the system of government by political parties in a democratic country. The idea is that political parties have basic similarities: they control the government, have a stable base of mass popular support, and create internal mechanisms for controlling funding, information and nominations. The concept was originated by European scholars studying the United States, especially James Bryce and Moisey Ostrogorsky, and has been expanded to cover other democracies.
John Quincy	Colonel John Quincy was an American soldier, politician and member of the Quincy political family. His granddaughter Abigail Adams named her son, John Quincy Adams, in his honor. The city of Quincy, Massachusetts is named in his honor, as well.
Northwest Ordinance	The Northwest Ordinance was an act of the Congress of the Confederation of the United States. The primary effect of the ordinance was the creation of the Northwest Territory as the first organized territory of the United States out of the region south of the Great Lakes, north and west of the Ohio River, and east of the Mississippi River. On August 7, 1789, the U.S. Congress affirmed the Ordinance with slight modifications under the Constitution.
Politics	Politics is an essay written by Ralph Waldo Emerson. It is part of his Essays: Second Series, published in 1844. A premier philosopher, poet and leader of American transcendentalism, he used this essay to belie his feelings on government, specifically American government. His impact on New England thought and his views on pragmatism influenced the likes of Henry David Thoreau, Orestes Brownson, and Frederich Nietzsche, among others.
Kitchen Cabinet	The Kitchen Cabinet was a term used by political opponents of President of the United States Andrew Jackson to describe the collection of unofficial advisers he consulted in parallel to the United States Cabinet (the 'parlor cabinet') following his purge of the cabinet at the end of the Eaton affair and his break with Vice President John C. Calhoun in 1831. In an unprecedented dismissal of five of the eight Cabinet officials in the middle of his first term, Jackson dismissed Calhoun's allies Samuel D. Ingham, John Branch, and John M. Berrien as well as his own supporters, Secretary of State Martin Van Buren and Secretary of War John Eaton. However, Jackson retained Van Buren in Washington as the minister to Great Britain.

Republican Party	The Republican Party is one of the two major contemporary political parties in the United States, along with the Democratic Party. Founded by anti-slavery expansion activists in 1854, it is often called the Grand Old Party (GOP). The party's platform generally reflects American conservatism in the U.S. political spectrum and is considered center-right, in contrast to the more liberal-leaning Democrats.
State bank	A state bank is generally a financial institution that is chartered by a state. It differs from a reserve bank in that it does not necessarily control monetary policy (indeed, the state in question may have no legal capacity to create monetary policy), but instead usually offers only retail and commercial services.
Thomas Hart Benton	Thomas Hart Benton was an American painter and muralist. Along with Grant Wood and John Steuart Curry, he was at the forefront of the Regionalist art movement. His fluid, almost sculpted paintings showed everyday scenes of life in the United States.
McCulloch v. Maryland	McCulloch v. Maryland, 17 U.S. 316 (1819), was a landmark decision by the Supreme Court of the United States. The state of Maryland had attempted to impede operation of a branch of the Second Bank of the United States by imposing a tax on all notes of banks not chartered in Maryland. Though the law, by its language, was generally applicable to all banks not chartered in Maryland, the Second Bank of the United States was the only out-of-state bank then existing in Maryland, and the law was recognized in the court's opinion as having specifically targeted the U.S. Bank.
Union	During the American Civil War, the Union was a name used to refer to the federal government of the United States, which was supported by the twenty free states and five border slave states. It was opposed by 11 Southern slave states that had declared a secession to join together to form the Confederacy. Although the Union states included the Western states of California, Oregon, and (after 1864) Nevada, as well as states generally considered to be part of the Midwest, the Union has been also often loosely referred to as 'the North', both then and now.
Cherokee	The Cherokee are a Native American people historically settled in the Southeastern United States . Linguistically, they are part of the Iroquoian language family. In the 19th century, historians and ethnographers recorded their oral tradition that told of the tribe having migrated south in ancient times from the Great Lakes region, where other Iroquoian-speaking peoples were located.
Choctaw	The Choctaw are a Native American people originally from the Southeastern United States (Mississippi, Florida, Alabama, and Louisiana). The Choctaw language belongs to the Muskogean linguistic group. Noted 20th century anthropologist John Swanton suggested that the name was derived from a Choctaw leader.

Chapter 9. Jacksonian Democracy

Nullification	Nullification is a legal theory that a U.S. State has the right to nullify, or invalidate, any federal law which that state has deemed unconstitutional. The theory is based on a view that the sovereign States formed the Union, and as creators of the compact hold final authority regarding the limits of the power of the central government. Under this, the compact theory, the States and not the Federal Bench are the ultimate interpreters of the extent of the federal government's power.
Spanish Florida	Spanish Florida refers to the Spanish territory of Florida, which formed part of the Captaincy General of Cuba, the Viceroyalty of New Spain, and the Spanish Empire. Originally extending over what is now the southeastern United States, but with no defined boundaries, la Florida was a component of the Spanish colonization of the Americas and the expansion of the Spanish Empire. Wide-ranging expeditions were mounted into the hinterland during the 16th century, but Spain never exercised complete control over la Florida outside an area of what is now the state of Florida, southern Georgia, southern Alabama, southeastern Louisiana, and other areas along the northern coast of the Gulf of Mexico.
Black Hawk	Black Hawk was a leader and warrior of the Sauk American Indian tribe in what is now the United States. Although he had inherited an important historic medicine bundle, he was not one of the Sauk's hereditary civil chiefs. His status came from leading war parties as a young man, and from his leadership of a band of Sauks during the Black Hawk War of 1832.
Cherokee Nation v. Georgia	Cherokee Nation v. Georgia, 30 U.S. 1 (1831), was a United States Supreme Court case. The Cherokee Nation sought a federal injunction against laws passed by the state of Georgia depriving them of rights within its boundaries, but the Supreme Court did not hear the case on its merits. It ruled that it had no original jurisdiction in the matter, as the Cherokee were a dependent nation, with a relationship to the United States like that of a ward to its guardian.
Nation	Nation has different meanings in different contexts. In worldwide diplomacy, nation can mean country or sovereign state. The United Nations, for instance, speaks of how it was founded after the Second World War with '51 countries' and currently has '192 member states'.
Osceola	Osceola was an influential leader with the Seminole in Florida. Osceola led a small band of warriors in the Seminole resistance during the Second Seminole War when the United States tried to remove the Seminoles from their lands. He exercised a great deal of influence on Micanopy, the highest-ranking chief of the Seminoles.

Worcester v. Georgia	Worcester v. Georgia, 31 U.S. (6 Pet). 515 (1832), was a case in which the United States Supreme Court vacated the conviction of Samuel Worcester, holding that the Georgia criminal statute, prohibiting non-Indians from being present on Indian lands without a license from the state, was unconstitutional. The opinion is most famous for its dicta, which lays out the relationship between tribes and the state and federal governments, building the foundations of the doctrine of tribal sovereignty in the United States.
Alabama	Alabama is a state located in the southeastern region of the United States of America. It is bordered by Tennessee to the north, Georgia to the east, Florida and the Gulf of Mexico to the south, and Mississippi to the west. Alabama ranks 30th in total land area and ranks second in the size of its inland waterways. The state ranks 23rd in population with 4.7 million residents in 2009.
George Corbin Washington	George Corbin Washington was a United States Congressman from the third and fifth districts of Maryland, serving four terms from 1827 to 1833, and 1835 to 1837. He was also a grandnephew of U.S. President George Washington. Washington was born at Haywood Farms near Oak Grove of Westmoreland County, Virginia. He attended Phillips Academy and Harvard University, studied law, but devoted himself to agricultural pursuits on his plantation in Maryland.
Missouri Compromise	The Missouri Compromise was an agreement passed in 1820 between the pro-slavery and anti-slavery factions in the United States Congress, involving primarily the regulation of slavery in the western territories. It prohibited slavery in the former Louisiana Territory north of the parallel 36° 30′ north except within the boundaries of the proposed state of Missouri. Prior to the agreement, the House of Representatives had refused to accept this compromise, and a conference committee was appointed.

Chapter 9. Jacksonian Democracy

South Carolina	South Carolina is a state in the Deep South that borders Georgia to the south and North Carolina to the north. Originally part of the Province of Carolina, the Province of South Carolina was one of the 13 colonies that declared independence from the British Crown during the American Revolution. The colony was originally named by King Charles II of England in honor of his father Charles I, as Carolus is Latin for Charles.
Trail of Tears	The Trail of Tears is a name given to the forced relocation and movement of Native American nations from southeastern parts of the United States following the Indian Removal Act of 1830. The removal included many members of the Cherokee, Muscogee (Creek), Seminole, Chickasaw, and Choctaw nations, among others in the United States, from their homelands to Indian Territory (eastern sections of the present-day state of Oklahoma). The phrase originated from a description of the removal of the Choctaw Nation in 1831. Many Native Americans suffered from exposure, disease and starvation en route to their destinations. Many died, including 4,000 of the 15,000 relocated Cherokee.
Turners	Turners are members of German-American gymnastic clubs. A German gymnastic movement was started by Turnvater (turners' father) Friedrich Ludwig Jahn in the early 19th century when Germany was occupied by Napoleon. The Turnvereine ('gymnastic unions') were not only athletic, but also political, reflecting their origin in similar 'nationalistic gymnastic' organizations in Europe.
Denmark Vesey	Denmark Vesey, (1767? - July 2, 1822) was an African American slave brought to the United States from the Caribbean of Coromantee background. After purchasing his freedom, he planned what would have been one of the largest slave rebellions in the United States. Word of the plans was leaked, and at Charleston, South Carolina, authorities arrested the plot's leaders before the uprising could begin.
Washington	Washington was one of the first steamboats to operate in the states of California and Oregon. Operations in California Washington operated in California on the Sacramento River. The vessel was purchased in California in 1851 by pioneer steamboat captain Alexander Sinclair Murray (b.1828).

William Wirt

William Wirt was an American author and statesman who is credited with turning the position of United States Attorney General into one of influence.

History

He was born in Bladensburg, Maryland, to a Swiss father and a German mother. Both parents having died before he was eight years old, Jasper Wirt, his uncle, became his guardian.

Nullification Crisis

The Nullification Crisis was a sectional crisis during the presidency of Andrew Jackson created by South Carolina's 1832 Ordinance of Nullification. This ordinance declared by the power of the State that the federal Tariffs of 1828 and 1832 were unconstitutional and therefore null and void within the sovereign boundaries of South Carolina. The controversial and highly protective Tariff of 1828 (known to its detractors as the 'Tariff of Abominations') was enacted into law during the presidency of John Quincy Adams.

Force Bill

The United States Force Bill, formally titled 'An Act further to provide for the collection of duties on imports', 4 Stat. 632 (1833), enacted by the 22nd U.S. Congress, consists of eight sections expanding Presidential power. The relevant sections are:

- Section 1 deals with unlawful obstructions to the collections of import duties; by securing ports and harbors for the protection of duty collectors, allowing for the detention of vessels and cargoes to enforce revenue laws, and authorizes the President to use armed expands the jurisdiction of federal courts to cases arising from revenue collections by the U.S. government and allows injured parties in revenue cases to sue in court. It deems property detained by customs officers to be in the custody of the law, subject to disposition by court order only, and criminalizes anyone who circumvents the legal process in regaining detained property as guilty of a misdemeanor.
- Section 5 deals with States, or portions within a state, who employ force, or any other unlawful means, to obstruct the execution of U.S. federal law, or interfere with the process of any Federal court.

Proclamation to the People of South Carolina	In United States history the Proclamation to the People of South Carolina was a proclamation written by Edward Livingston and issued by Andrew Jackson in 1832. Issued at the height of the Nullification Crisis, the proclamation denounces the doctrine of Nullification as 'incompatible with the existence of the Union, contradicted expressly by the letter of the Constitution, unauthorized by its spirit, inconsistent with every principle on which It was founded, and destructive of the great object for which it was formed. proclamation, including Abel P. Upshur and Littleton Waller Tazewell. Upshur wrote a series of letters entitled 'An Exposition of the Virginia Resolutions of 1798' (1833) in which he defends nullification.
The Sky People	The Sky People is a 2006 science fiction novel by American writer S. M. Stirling. Plot introduction It takes place on the planet Venus in an alternate solar system where probes from the United States of America and the Soviet Union, find intelligent life and civilizations on both Venus and Mars. The book is heavily influenced by the works of writers such as Ray Bradbury, Edgar Rice Burroughs, Arthur C. Clarke, and Larry Niven, among others.
Specie Circular	The Specie Circular was an executive order issued by U.S. President Andrew Jackson in 1836 and carried out by President Martin Van Buren. It required payment for government land to be in gold and silver. History The Act was a reaction to the growing concerns about excessive speculations of land after the Indian removal, which was mostly done with soft currency.
York	York was an African American slave best known for his participation with the Lewis and Clark Expedition. As William Clark's slave, he had to do diffficult manual labour without pay. After the expedition's return he pressed for his freedom, which Clark opposed, he possibly agreed ten years later, though some historians dispute this and say he was never freed.

Ralph Waldo Emerson	Ralph Waldo Emerson was an American lecturer, philosopher, essayist, and poet, best remembered for leading the Transcendentalist movement of the mid-19th century. He was seen as a champion of individualism and a prescient critic of the countervailing pressures of society, and he disseminated his thoughts through dozens of published essays and more than 1,500 public lectures across the United States. Emerson gradually moved away from the religious and social beliefs of his contemporaries, formulating and expressing the philosophy of Transcendentalism in his 1836 essay, Nature.
Horace Greeley	Horace Greeley was an American newspaper editor, a founder of the Liberal Republican Party, a reformer, and a politician. His New York Tribune was America's most influential newspaper from the 1840s to the 1870s and 'established Greeley's reputation as the greatest editor of his day.' Greeley used it to promote the Whig and Republican parties, as well as opposition to slavery and a host of reforms ranging from vegetarianism to socialism. Crusading against the corruption of Ulysses S. Grant's Republican administration, he was the new Liberal Republican Party's candidate in the 1872 U.S. presidential election.
Independents	The Independents were a group of modernist painters based in the New Hope, Pennsylvania, area of the United States during the early 1930s. They evolved out of The New Group (founded in 1930), a collection of artists dissatisfied with the hold that 'conservative' Pennsylvania Impressionists had on local exhibitions. Members of the Independents included Peter Keenan, Robert Hogue, R.A.D. Miller, Charles Evans, Henry Baker, Ralston Crawford, Charles Frederic Ramsey and Faye Swengel Badura.
Tecumseh	Tecumseh also known as Tecumtha or Tekamthi, was a Native American leader of the Shawnee and a large tribal confederacy that opposed the United States during Tecumseh's War and the War of 1812. He grew up in the Ohio country during the American Revolutionary War and the Northwest Indian War, where he was constantly exposed to warfare.

	His brother Tenskwatawa was a religious leader who advocated a return to the ancestral lifestyle of the tribes. A large following and a confederacy grew around his prophetic teachings.
John Tyler	John Tyler, Jr. (March 29, 1790 - January 18, 1862) was the tenth President of the United States (1841-1845) and the first to succeed to the office following the death of a predecessor. A longtime Democratic-Republican, Tyler was nonetheless elected Vice President on the Whig ticket.

1. _________ are members of German-American gymnastic clubs. A German gymnastic movement was started by Turnvater (_________' father) Friedrich Ludwig Jahn in the early 19th century when Germany was occupied by Napoleon. The Turnvereine ('gymnastic unions') were not only athletic, but also political, reflecting their origin in similar 'nationalistic gymnastic' organizations in Europe.

   a. Turners
   b. Digital Transition Content Security Act
   c. Jessica's Law
   d. Battle of Mount Gray

2. _________ was an American lecturer, philosopher, essayist, and poet, best remembered for leading the Transcendentalist movement of the mid-19th century. He was seen as a champion of individualism and a prescient critic of the countervailing pressures of society, and he disseminated his thoughts through dozens of published essays and more than 1,500 public lectures across the United States.

   Emerson gradually moved away from the religious and social beliefs of his contemporaries, formulating and expressing the philosophy of Transcendentalism in his 1836 essay, Nature.

   a. Margaret Mead
   b. Ralph Waldo Emerson
   c. Ruth Benedict
   d. Thomas Gage

3. The _________ was an act of the Congress of the Confederation of the United States. The primary effect of the ordinance was the creation of the Northwest Territory as the first organized territory of the United States out of the region south of the Great Lakes, north and west of the Ohio River, and east of the Mississippi River. On August 7, 1789, the U.S. Congress affirmed the Ordinance with slight modifications under the Constitution.

   a. Digital Transition Content Security Act
   b. Northwest Ordinance
   c. Federal Funding Accountability and Transparency Act of 2006
   d. Reagan coalition

---

4. A political party by the name of the _________ has existed several times in the United States:

- The Toleration Party, also known as the _________, was established in Connecticut to oppose the Federalist Party
- The antebellum _________ grew out of the Know Nothing movement and was based on nativism
- There were also several other late 19th-century political parties with the same name, notably one founded in 1887, and another that participated in the elections of 1876, 1880 and 1884. wikimedia.org/wikipedia/commons/thumb/4/4c/Wikisource-logo.svg/12px-Wikisource-logo.svg.png' width='12' height='13' /> '_________, The'. Collier's New Encyclopedia. 1921.<span style=' none;? display:> </SPAN></SPAN></LI><LI>_________ organized by Ex-Governor of New York William Sulzer</LI><LI>_________ an anti-Mormon party that existed in Utah from 1905 to 1911</LI><LI>Ku Klux Party, also known as the _________, which ran Gilbert Nations for President of the United States and former congressman Charles H. Randall for vice-president in 1924. The ticket received 23867 votes.</LI><LI>_________ of Nebraska which ran Mary Kennery (or Kennedy) as a favorite daughter for President of the United States in 1952.</LI><LI>_________ which ran Herman W. Kolpack for President of the United States in 1952.</LI><LI>_________ was a successor of the 1968 American Independent Party. The current American Independent Party split from it in 1976.</LI><LI>_________ http://www.americanparty.mobi now holds the U.S. trademark for this name</LI></UL>. </div></td></tr></table><p></p>

a. America's Independent Party
b. American Party
c. International Working People's Association
d. Executive Branch Reform Act

5. _________ refers to the Spanish territory of Florida, which formed part of the Captaincy General of Cuba, the Viceroyalty of New Spain, and the Spanish Empire. Originally extending over what is now the southeastern United States, but with no defined boundaries, la Florida was a component of the Spanish colonization of the Americas and the expansion of the Spanish Empire. Wide-ranging expeditions were mounted into the hinterland during the 16th century, but Spain never exercised complete control over la Florida outside an area of what is now the state of Florida, southern Georgia, southern Alabama, southeastern Louisiana, and other areas along the northern coast of the Gulf of Mexico.

a. Spanish Florida
b. Spanish missions in Georgia
c. Spanish missions in Louisiana
d. Spanish missions in New Mexico

ANSWER KEY
Chapter 9. Jacksonian Democracy

---

1. a
2. b
3. b
4. b
5. a

_______ Puritan

_______ Union

_______ Frontier

_______ Louisa May Alcott

_______ Lydia Maria Child

_______ Great Awakening

_______ Second Great Awakening

_______ Erie Canal

_______ Missionary

_______ Shakers

_______ Nauvoo Legion

_______ Oneida Community

_______ John Smith

_______ England

_______ Horace Greeley

_______ Samuel Gridley Howe

_______ Robert Dale Owen

_______ Constitutional Convention

_______ Temperance movement

Chapter 10. The Making of Middle-Class America

____________ Tennessee

____________ Race riot

____________ Neal S. Dow

____________ John Bartholomew Gough

____________ African American

____________ Alabama

____________ Frederick Douglass

____________ John Quincy

____________ Liberty Party

____________ Elijah Parish Lovejoy

____________ Massachusetts

____________ New England Anti-Slavery Society

____________ York

____________ The World

____________ Declaration of Sentiments

____________ Abby Kelley

____________ Seneca Falls Convention

____________ Elizabeth Cady Stanton

____________ Literature

_______________ Ralph Waldo Emerson

_______________ Transcendentalism

_______________ Edgar Allan Poe

_______________ Moby-Dick

_______________ Frederick Law Olmsted

_______________ Boston

_______________ Horace Mann

_______________ Brown University

_______________ Oberlin College

CHAPTER HIGHLIGHTS: KEY TERMS, PEOPLE, PLACES, CONCEPTS
Chapter 10. The Making of Middle-Class America

Puritan	The Puritans were a significant grouping of English Protestants in the 16th and 17th centuries, including, but not limited to, English Calvinists. Puritanism in this sense was founded by some Marian exiles from the clergy shortly after the accession of Elizabeth I of England in 1558, as an activist movement within the Church of England. The designation 'Puritan' is often incorrectly used, notably based on the assumption that hedonism and puritanism are antonyms: Historically, the word was used pejoratively to characterize the Protestant group as extremists similar to the Cathari of France, and according to Thomas Fuller in his Church History dated back to 1564, Archbishop Matthew Parker of that time used it and 'precisian' with the sense of modern 'stickler'.
Union	During the American Civil War, the Union was a name used to refer to the federal government of the United States, which was supported by the twenty free states and five border slave states. It was opposed by 11 Southern slave states that had declared a secession to join together to form the Confederacy. Although the Union states included the Western states of California, Oregon, and (after 1864) Nevada, as well as states generally considered to be part of the Midwest, the Union has been also often loosely referred to as 'the North', both then and now.
Frontier	A frontier is a political and geographical term referring to areas near or beyond a boundary. 'Frontier' was absorbed into English from French in the 15th century, with the meaning 'borderland'--the region of a country that fronts on another country . 'Frontier' means 'a region at the edge of a settled area'.
Louisa May Alcott	Louisa May Alcott was an American novelist. She is best known for the novel Little Women and its sequels Little Men and Jo's Boys. Little Women was set in the Alcott family home, Orchard House in Concord, Massachusetts, and published in 1868. This novel is loosely based on her childhood experiences with her three sisters.
Lydia Maria Child	Lydia Maria Child was an American abolitionist, women's rights activist, opponent of American expansionism, Indian rights activist, novelist, and journalist and Unitarian. Her journals, fiction and domestic manuals reached wide audiences from the 1820s through the 1850s. She at times shocked her audience, as she tried to take on issues of both male dominance and white supremacy in some of her stories.

Great Awakening	The Great Awakening was a religious revival in American religious history. Historians and theologians identify three or four waves of Great Awakening occurring from the early 18th century to the late 20th century, each characterized by widespread revivals led by evangelical Protestant ministers, a sharp increase of interest in religion, a profound sense of conviction and redemption on the part of those affected, a jump in evangelical church membership, and the formation of new religious movements and denominations. First Great Awakening The First Great Awakening began in 1725 and lasted to about 1750. Ministers from various evangelical Protestant denominations supported the Great Awakening,.
Second Great Awakening	The Second Great Awakening was a Christian religious revival movement during the early 19th century in the United States, which expressed Arminian theology by which every person could be saved through revivals. It enrolled millions of new members, and led to the formation of new denominations. Many converts believed that the Awakening heralded a new millennial age.
Erie Canal	The Erie Canal is a waterway in New York that runs about 363 miles (584 km) from Albany, New York, on the Hudson River to Buffalo, New York, at Lake Erie, completing a navigable water route from the Atlantic Ocean to the Great Lakes. The canal contains 36 locks and encompasses a total elevation differential of around 565 ft. (169 m).
Missionary	The Church of Jesus Christ of Latter-day Saints (LDS Church) is one of the most active modern practitioners of missionary work, with over fifty thousand full-time missionaries worldwide, as of the end of 2009. Commonly referred to as Mormon missionaries, most LDS Church missionaries are single young men and women in their late teens and early twenties and are assigned to a mission of the church which is usually far from the missionary's home. Missionaries do not receive a salary for the work they undertake, and most are financially supported by themselves or their families. Throughout the history of the church, over one million missionaries have been sent on missions.
Shakers	The United Society of Believers in Christ's Second Appearing, known as the Shakers, is a religious sect originally thought to be a development of the Religious Society of Friends. Founded upon the teachings of Ann Lee, Shakers today are mostly known for their cultural contributions (especially style of music and furniture).

However, the Shakers' enduring legacy includes their model of equality of the sexes (or gender equality), which they institutionalized in their society in the 1780s.

Nauvoo Legion

The Nauvoo Legion was a militia originally organized by the Latter Day Saints (Mormons) to defend the city of Nauvoo, Illinois, . To curry political favor with the ambiguously-political Saints, the Illinois state legislature granted Nauvoo a liberal city charter that gave the Nauvoo Legion extraordinary independence. Led by Joseph Smith, Jr., founder of the Latter Day Saint movement and mayor of Nauvoo, the Legion quickly became a formidable concentration of military power in the American West.

Oneida Community

The Oneida Community was a religious commune founded by John Humphrey Noyes in 1848 in Oneida, New York. The community believed that Jesus Christ had already returned in the year 70, making it possible for them to bring about Christ's millennial kingdom themselves, and be free of sin and perfect in this world, not just Heaven (a belief called Perfectionism).

The Oneida Community practiced Communalism (in the sense of communal property and possessions), Complex Marriage, Male Continence, Mutual Criticism and Ascending Fellowship.

John Smith

John Smith also known by the alias John Wilson, was a London housebreaker, most notable for his three evasions of execution. His first evasion granted him the nickname of Half-hanged Smith.

Biography

Early life and career

John Smith was the son of a Malton farmer.

England	England is a country that is part of the United Kingdom. It shares land borders with Scotland to the north and Wales to the west; the Irish Sea is to the north west, the Celtic Sea to the south west and the North Sea to the east, with the English Channel to the south separating it from continental Europe. Most of England comprises the central and southern part of the island of Great Britain in the North Atlantic.
Horace Greeley	Horace Greeley was an American newspaper editor, a founder of the Liberal Republican Party, a reformer, and a politician. His New York Tribune was America's most influential newspaper from the 1840s to the 1870s and 'established Greeley's reputation as the greatest editor of his day.' Greeley used it to promote the Whig and Republican parties, as well as opposition to slavery and a host of reforms ranging from vegetarianism to socialism. Crusading against the corruption of Ulysses S. Grant's Republican administration, he was the new Liberal Republican Party's candidate in the 1872 U.S. presidential election.
Samuel Gridley Howe	Samuel Gridley Howe was a prominent 19th century United States physician, abolitionist, and an advocate of education for the blind. Early life and education Howe was born on Pearl Street in Boston, Massachusetts on November 10, 1801. His father, Joseph Neals Howe, was a ship-owner and cordage manufacturer. His mother, Patty Gridley, was considered to be one of the most beautiful women of her day.
Robert Dale Owen	Robert Dale Owen was a longtime exponent in his adopted United States of the socialist doctrines of his father, Robert Owen, as well as a politician in the Democratic Party. Biography

Born in Glasgow, Scotland, Owen emigrated to the United States in 1825, and helped his father create the Utopian community of New Harmony, Indiana. After the community failed, Owen returned briefly to Europe, then moved to New York City and became the editor of the Free Enquirer, which he ran from 1828 to 1832. Owen's Moral Physiology, published in 1830 or 1831, was the first book to advocate birth control in the United States (specifically, coitus interruptus).

Constitutional Convention

The United States Constitutional Convention took place from May 25 to September 17, 1787, in Philadelphia, Pennsylvania, to address problems in governing the United States of America, which had been operating under the Articles of Confederation following independence from Great Britain. Although the Convention was purportedly intended only to revise the Articles of Confederation, the intention from the outset of many of its proponents, chief among them James Madison and Alexander Hamilton, was to create a new government rather than fix the existing one. The delegates elected George Washington to preside over the convention.

Temperance movement

A temperance movement is a social movement urging reduced use of alcoholic beverages. Temperance movements may criticize excessive alcohol use, promote complete abstinence, or pressure the government to enact anti-alcohol legislation.

Tennessee

Tennessee is a U.S. state located in the Southeastern United States. It has a population of 6,214,888, making it the nation's 17th-largest state by population, and covers 42,169 square miles (109,220 km^2), making it the 36th-largest by total land area. Tennessee is bordered by Kentucky and Virginia to the north, North Carolina to the east, Georgia, Alabama, and Mississippi to the south, and Arkansas and Missouri to the west.

Race riot

A race riot is an outbreak of violent civil disorder in which race is a key factor. A phenomenon frequently confused with the concept of 'race riot' is sectarian violence, which involves public mass violence or conflict over non-racial factors.

Neal S. Dow

Neal S. Dow nicknamed the 'Napoleon of Temperance' and the 'Father of Prohibition', was mayor of Portland, Maine. He sponsored the 'Maine law of 1851', which prohibited the manufacture and sale of liquor. Dow was widely criticized for his heavy handed tactics during the Portland Rum Riot of 1855.

John Bartholomew Gough

John Bartholomew Gough was a United States temperance orator.

Biography

He was born at Sandgate, Kent, England, and was educated by his mother, a schoolmistress. At the age of twelve, after his father died, he was sent to the United States to seek his fortune.

African American

African Americans (also referred to as Black Americans or Afro-Americans, and formerly as American Negroes) are citizens or residents of the United States who have origins in any of the black populations of Africa. In the United States, the terms are generally used for Americans with at least partial Sub-Saharan African ancestry. Most African Americans are the direct descendants of captive Africans who survived the slavery era within the boundaries of the present United States, although some are--or are descended from--immigrants from African, Caribbean, Central American or South American nations. As an adjective, the term is usually written as African-American.

Alabama

Alabama is a state located in the southeastern region of the United States of America. It is bordered by Tennessee to the north, Georgia to the east, Florida and the Gulf of Mexico to the south, and Mississippi to the west. Alabama ranks 30th in total land area and ranks second in the size of its inland waterways. The state ranks 23rd in population with 4.7 million residents in 2009.

Frederick Douglass

Frederick Douglass was an American social reformer, orator, writer and statesman. After escaping from slavery, he became a leader of the abolitionist movement, known for his dazzling oratory and incisive antislavery writing. He stood as a living counter-example to slaveholders' arguments that slaves did not have the intellectual capacity to function as independent American citizens.

John Quincy

Colonel John Quincy was an American soldier, politician and member of the Quincy political family. His granddaughter Abigail Adams named her son, John Quincy Adams, in his honor. The city of Quincy, Massachusetts is named in his honor, as well.

Liberty Party

The Liberty Party was a minor political party in the United States in the 1840s, 1850s, and 1860s. The party was an early advocate of the abolitionist cause. It broke away from the American Anti-Slavery Society (AASS) to advocate the view that the Constitution was an anti-slavery document; the libertarian William Lloyd Garrison, leader of the AASS, held the contrary view that the Constitution should be condemned as an evil pro-slavery document.

Elijah Parish Lovejoy

Elijah Parish Lovejoy was an American Presbyterian minister, journalist, newspaper editor and abolitionist. He was murdered by an opposition mob in Alton, Illinois for his publication of abolitionist materials, as they attacked the warehouse where his press was operated.

	Lovejoy had a deeply religious upbringing, as his father was a Congregational minister and his mother a devout Christian.
Massachusetts	'Massachusetts', words and music by Arlo Guthrie, was made the official folk song of Massachusetts in July, 1981.
New England Anti-Slavery Society	The New England Anti-Slavery Society was formed by William Lloyd Garrison, editor of The Liberator, in 1831. The Liberator was also its official publication. Separate black anti-slavery societies had already existed in Massachusetts, New York, Ohio, Connecticut, and New Jersey, however, a strong feeling against the organization of separate anti-slavery societies was emerging. In January 1833, Thomas Dalton, president of the Massachusetts General Colored Association, led a successful petition to merge with the New England Anti-Slavery Society.
York	York was an African American slave best known for his participation with the Lewis and Clark Expedition. As William Clark's slave, he had to do diffficult manual labour without pay. After the expedition's return he pressed for his freedom, which Clark opposed, he possibly agreed ten years later, though some historians dispute this and say he was never freed.
The World	The World was a large nightclub in New York City, which operated from the mid-1980s until 1991 at 254 East 2nd Street, in Manhattan's East Village neighborhood. The venue, which included a secondary establishment called 'The It Club,' was housed in a former catering hall and theater. The World attracted a clientele that was economically, racially, and sexually diverse, and included artists, celebrities, and fashion designers, such as Keith Haring, Madonna, Brooke Shields, Prince, Stephen Sprouse, and Carolina Herrera.

Declaration of Sentiments

The Declaration of Sentiments, is a document signed in 1848 by 68 women and 32 men, 100 out of some 300 attendees at the first women's rights convention, in Seneca Falls, New York, now known as the Seneca Falls Convention. The principal author of the Declaration of Rights and Sentiments was Elizabeth Cady Stanton, who based it on the form of the United States Declaration of Independence. According to the North Star, published by Frederick Douglass, whose attendance at the convention and support of the Declaration helped pass the resolutions put forward, the document was the 'grand basis for attaining the civil, social, political, and religious rights of women.'

At a time when traditional roles were still very much in place, the Declaration caused much controversy.

Abby Kelley

Abby Kelley Foster (January 15, 1811 - January 14, 1887) was an American abolitionist and radical social reformer active from the 1830s to 1870s. She became a fundraiser, lecturer and committee organizer for the influential American Anti-Slavery Society, where she worked closely with William Lloyd Garrison and other radicals. She married fellow abolitionist and lecturer Stephen Symonds Foster, and they both worked for equal rights for women.

Seneca Falls Convention

The Seneca Falls Convention was an early and influential women's rights convention held in Seneca Falls, New York, July 19-20, 1848. It was organized by local New York women upon the occasion of a visit by Boston-based Lucretia Mott, a Quaker famous for her speaking ability, a skill rarely cultivated by American women at the time. The local women, primarily members of a radical Quaker group, organized the meeting along with Elizabeth Cady Stanton, a skeptical non-Quaker who followed logic more than religion.

The meeting spanned two days and six sessions, and included a lecture on law, a humorous presentation, and multiple discussions about the role of women in society.

Elizabeth Cady Stanton

Elizabeth Cady Stanton was an American social activist, abolitionist, and leading figure of the early woman's movement. Her Declaration of Sentiments, presented at the first women's rights convention held in 1848 in Seneca Falls, New York, is often credited with initiating the first organized woman's rights and woman's suffrage movements in the United States.

	Before Stanton narrowed her political focus almost exclusively to women's rights, she had been an active abolitionist together with her husband, Henry Brewster Stanton and cousin, Gerrit Smith.
Literature	Literature is the art of written works, and is not bound to published sources (although, under circumstances unpublished sources can be exempt). Literally translated, the word literature means 'acquaintance with letters' (as in the 'arts and letters'). The two major classification of literature are poetry and prose.
Ralph Waldo Emerson	Ralph Waldo Emerson was an American lecturer, philosopher, essayist, and poet, best remembered for leading the Transcendentalist movement of the mid-19th century. He was seen as a champion of individualism and a prescient critic of the countervailing pressures of society, and he disseminated his thoughts through dozens of published essays and more than 1,500 public lectures across the United States. Emerson gradually moved away from the religious and social beliefs of his contemporaries, formulating and expressing the philosophy of Transcendentalism in his 1836 essay, Nature.
Transcendentalism	Transcendentalism is a group of new ideas in literature and philosophy that emerged in New England in the early-to-middle 19th century. It is sometimes called American Transcendentalism to distinguish it from other uses of the word transcendental. The movement developed in the 1830s and 40s as a protest against the general state of culture and society, and in particular, the state of intellectualism at Harvard University and the doctrine of the Unitarian church taught at Harvard Divinity School.
Edgar Allan Poe	Edgar Allan Poe was an American author, poet, editor and literary critic, considered part of the American Romantic Movement. Best known for his tales of mystery and the macabre, Poe was one of the earliest American practitioners of the short story and is considered the inventor of the detective fiction genre. He is further credited with contributing to the emerging genre of science fiction.
Moby-Dick	Moby-Dick, is a novel first published in 1851 by American author Herman Melville. Moby-Dick is widely considered to be a Great American Novel and a treasure of world literature. The story tells the adventures of the wandering sailor Ishmael, and his voyage on the whaleship Pequod, commanded by Captain Ahab.

Frederick Law Olmsted	Frederick Law Olmsted was an American journalist, landscape designer and is popularly considered to be the father of American landscape architecture, although many scholars have bestowed that title upon Andrew Jackson Downing. Olmsted was famous for co-designing many well-known urban parks with his senior partner, Calvert Vaux, including Central Park and Prospect Park in New York City. Other projects that Olmsted has been involved in include the country's oldest coordinated system of public parks and parkways in Buffalo, New York; the country's oldest state park, the Niagara Reservation in Niagara Falls, New York; one of the first planned communities in the United States, Riverside, Illinois; Mount Royal Park in Montreal, Quebec; the Emerald Necklace in Boston, Massachusetts; also the Emerald Necklace of parks in Rochester, New York; Deering Oaks Park in Portland, Maine; the Belle Isle Park, in the Detroit River for Detroit, Michigan; the Presque Isle Park in Marquette, Michigan; the Grand Necklace of Parks in Milwaukee, Wisconsin; the Cherokee Park and entire parks and parkway system in Louisville, Kentucky; the George Washington Vanderbilt II Biltmore Estate in Asheville, North Carolina; the master plans for the University of California, Berkeley and Stanford University near Palo Alto, California; and the Montebello Park in St. Catharines, Ontario.
Boston	Boston is the capital of and largest city in Massachusetts, and is one of the oldest cities in the United States. The largest city in New England, Boston is regarded as the unofficial 'Capital of New England' for its economic and cultural impact on the entire New England region. The city proper had a 2009 estimated population of 645,169, making it the twentieth largest in the country.
Horace Mann	Horace Mann was an American education reformer, and a member of the Massachusetts House of Representatives from 1827 to 1833. He served in the Massachusetts Senate from 1834 to 1837. In 1848, after serving as Secretary of the Massachusetts State Board of Education since its creation, he was elected to the US House of Representatives. Mann was a brother-in-law to author Nathaniel Hawthorne. Arguing that universal public education was the best way to turn the nation's unruly children into disciplined, judicious republican citizens, Mann won widespread approval from modernizers, especially in his Whig Party, for building public schools.

Brown University	Brown University is a private, Ivy League university located in Providence, Rhode Island, United States. Founded in 1764 prior to American independence from the British Empire as the College in the English Colony of Rhode Island and Providence Plantations early in the reign of King George III (1760-1820), Brown is the third oldest institution of higher education in New England and seventh oldest in the United States. Several of the buildings on the Brown campus from its founding 18th century period through the 20th century offer fine representation of the Georgian style of American colonial era architecture.
Oberlin College	Oberlin College is a private liberal arts college in Oberlin, Ohio, noteworthy for having been the first American institution of higher learning to regularly admit female and black students. Connected to the college is the Oberlin Conservatory of Music, the oldest continuously operating conservatory in the country. The college's motto is 'Learning and Labor.' Oberlin is known for having more alumni who earn PhDs than any other liberal arts college in the nation.

1. _________ is a country that is part of the United Kingdom. It shares land borders with Scotland to the north and Wales to the west; the Irish Sea is to the north west, the Celtic Sea to the south west and the North Sea to the east, with the English Channel to the south separating it from continental Europe. Most of _________ comprises the central and southern part of the island of Great Britain in the North Atlantic.

   a. Thomas Gage
   b. England
   c. Nathaniel Bacon
   d. John Hopwood

2. _________ nicknamed the 'Napoleon of Temperance' and the 'Father of Prohibition', was mayor of Portland, Maine. He sponsored the 'Maine law of 1851', which prohibited the manufacture and sale of liquor. Dow was widely criticized for his heavy handed tactics during the Portland Rum Riot of 1855.

   a. Charles A. Boutelle
   b. Thomas Gage
   c. Neal S. Dow
   d. Juan de Grijalva

3. _________ was a United States temperance orator.

   Biography

   He was born at Sandgate, Kent, England, and was educated by his mother, a schoolmistress. At the age of twelve, after his father died, he was sent to the United States to seek his fortune.

   a. William J. Bailey
   b. Henry Winthrop
   c. Thomas Gage
   d. John Bartholomew Gough

4. _________ was an American social activist, abolitionist, and leading figure of the early woman's movement. Her Declaration of Sentiments, presented at the first women's rights convention held in 1848 in Seneca Falls, New York, is often credited with initiating the first organized woman's rights and woman's suffrage movements in the United States.

Before Stanton narrowed her political focus almost exclusively to women's rights, she had been an active abolitionist together with her husband, Henry Brewster Stanton and cousin, Gerrit Smith.

a. Mary Greenleaf Clement Leavitt
b. Thomas Gage
c. Francisco de Montejo
d. Elizabeth Cady Stanton

5. During the American Civil War, the _________ was a name used to refer to the federal government of the United States, which was supported by the twenty free states and five border slave states. It was opposed by 11 Southern slave states that had declared a secession to join together to form the Confederacy. Although the _________ states included the Western states of California, Oregon, and (after 1864) Nevada, as well as states generally considered to be part of the Midwest, the _________ has been also often loosely referred to as 'the North', both then and now.

a. Avery O. Craven Award
b. Union
c. Opposition to the American Civil War
d. Ordinance of Secession

ANSWER KEY
Chapter 10. The Making of Middle-Class America

1. b
2. c
3. d
4. d
5. b

CHAPTER OUTLINE: KEY TERMS, PEOPLE, PLACES, CONCEPTS

Chapter 11

Westward Expansion

_______________ Border

_______________ Southwest Territory

_______________ American Revolution

_______________ William Henry Harrison

_______________ John Tyler

_______________ Program Assessment Rating Tool

_______________ Aztec

_______________ Republic of Texas

_______________ Santa Anna

_______________ Louisiana

_______________ Louisiana Purchase

_______________ Manifest Destiny

_______________ USS Princeton

_______________ Frontier

_______________ John Jacob Astor

_______________ Robert Gray

_______________ Lewis and Clark Expedition

_______________ Oregon Trail

_______________ Pacific Fur Company

Chapter 11. Westward Expansion

Early American currency

Fort Bridger

Turners

President

Thomas Hart Benton

Winfield Scott

Missouri Compromise

Wilmot Proviso

Resolution

Free Soil Party

James Murray Mason

Millard Fillmore

William H. Seward

Columbia

Fugitive slave

Border

Border is a 1997 blockbuster Bollywood war film based on the Indo-Pakistani War of 1971. J. P. Dutta directed and produced this war epic which stars Sunny Deol, Jackie Shroff, Sunil Shetty, Akshay Khanna, Pooja Bhatt, Sharbani Mukherjee and Tabu.

Director J.P. Dutta won Best Director at the same award function, while his father O.P. Dutta won for Best Dialogues.

The movie is an adaptation from real life events that happened at the Battle of Longewala fought in Rajasthan (Western Theatre) during the Indo-Pakistani War of 1971 and Bangladesh Liberation War.

Southwest Territory

The Territory South of the River Ohio, more commonly known as the Southwest Territory, was an organized incorporated territory of the United States that existed from May 26, 1790, until June 1, 1796, when it was admitted to the United States as the State of Tennessee.

The Southwest Territory was created by the Southwest Ordinance enacted on May 26, 1790, out of land (the Washington District) that was ceded to the U.S. federal government by the State of North Carolina. The name 'Territory South of the River Ohio' suggests a much larger territory than modern-day Tennessee.

American Revolution

The American Revolution was the political upheaval during the last half of the 18th century in which thirteen colonies in North America joined together to break free from the British Empire, combining to become the United States of America. They first rejected the authority of the Parliament of Great Britain to govern them from overseas without representation, and then expelled all royal officials. By 1774, each colony had established a Provincial Congress, or an equivalent governmental institution, to govern itself, but still within the empire. The British responded by sending combat troops to re-impose direct rule.

Chapter 11. Westward Expansion

William Henry Harrison	William Henry Harrison was the ninth President of the United States, an American military officer and politician, and the first president to die in office. The oldest president elected until Ronald Reagan in 1980, and last President to be born before the United States Declaration of Independence, Harrison died on his 32nd day in office of complications from a cold - the shortest tenure in United States presidential history. His death sparked a brief constitutional crisis, but that crisis ultimately resolved many questions about presidential succession left unanswered by the Constitution until passage of the 25th Amendment.
John Tyler	John Tyler, Jr. (March 29, 1790 - January 18, 1862) was the tenth President of the United States (1841-1845) and the first to succeed to the office following the death of a predecessor. A longtime Democratic-Republican, Tyler was nonetheless elected Vice President on the Whig ticket.
Program Assessment Rating Tool	The Program Assessment Rating Tool, is a program run through the United States Office of Management and Budget instituted by President George W. Bush in 2002 to rate all federal programs on their effectiveness. As of July 2008, 98 percent of all federal programs have been reviewed. History The Program Assessment Rating Tool was introduced in the 2004 Fiscal Year Federal budget, and explained by the Bush Administration as a program that built upon previous efforts of American Presidents to make sure federal programs were accountable and achieved results.
Aztec	The Aztec people were certain ethnic groups of central Mexico, particularly those groups who spoke the Nahuatl language and who dominated large parts of Mesoamerica in the 14th, 15th and 16th centuries, a period referred to as the late post-classic period in Mesoamerican chronology.

Aztec (Aztecatl) is the Nahuatl word for 'people from Aztlan', a mythological place for the Nahuatl-speaking culture of the time, and later adopted as the word to define the Mexica people. Often the term 'Aztec' refers exclusively to the Mexica people of Tenochtitlan (now the location of Mexico City), situated on an island in Lake Texcoco, who referred to themselves as Mexica Tenochca or Colhua-Mexica. Sometimes the term also includes the inhabitants of Tenochtitlan's two principal allied city-states, the Acolhuas of Texcoco and the Tepanecs of Tlacopan, who together with the Mexica formed the Aztec Triple Alliance which has also become known as the 'Aztec Empire'.

Republic of Texas

The Republic of Texas was an independent nation in North America, bordering the United States and Mexico, that existed from 1836 to 1846.

Formed as a break-away republic from Mexico by the Texas Revolution, the state claimed borders that encompassed an area that included all of the present U.S. state of Texas, as well as parts of present-day New Mexico, Oklahoma, Kansas, Colorado, and Wyoming based upon the Treaties of Velasco between the newly created Texas Republic and Mexico. The eastern boundary with the United States was defined by the Adams-Onís Treaty between the United States and Spain, in 1819. Its southern and western-most boundary with Mexico was under dispute throughout the existence of the Republic, with Texas claiming that the boundary was the Rio Grande, and Mexico claiming the Nueces River as the boundary.

Santa Anna

Santa Anna was a Native American War Chief of the Penateka band of the Comanche Indians.

Early life

Santa Anna was a member of the same band of the Comanche as the more famous Buffalo Hump. He was an important chief, though probably less influential than Buffalo Hump during the 1830s and 1840s.

Louisiana

Louisiana was the name of an administrative district of the Viceroyalty of New Spain from 1764 to 1803 that represented territory west of the Mississippi River basin, plus New Orleans. Spain acquired the territory from France: see Louisiana.

History

The area, comprising what is now known as the Louisiana Purchase, was turned over to the French for a few days in 1803 before it, in turn, was turned over to the United States.

Louisiana Purchase

The Louisiana Purchase was the acquisition by the United States of America of 828,800 square miles (2,147,000 km^2) of France's claim to the territory of Louisiana in 1803. The U.S. paid 60 million francs ($11,250,000) plus cancellation of debts worth 18 million francs ($3,750,000), for a total sum of 15 million dollars for the Louisiana territory ($219 million in 2010 dollars). What was purchased was France's claim only, not the actual territory, which belonged to the tribes which inhabited the area. The territory itself was acquired slowly throughout the nineteenth century by purchases to Native American tribes and wars.

Manifest Destiny

Manifest Destiny was the 19th century American belief that the United States (often in the ethnically specific form of the 'Anglo-Saxon race') was destined to expand across the continent. It was used by Democrat-Republicans in the 1840s to justify the war with Mexico; the concept was denounced by Whigs, and fell into disuse after the mid-19th century.

Advocates of Manifest Destiny believed that expansion was not only wise but that it was readily apparent (manifest) and inexorable (destiny).

USS Princeton	Six United States Navy ships have borne the name Princeton, after the town of Princeton, New Jersey, site of an American victory in the Revolutionary War. • The first Princeton, a screw sloop, launched and commissioned in 1843, the first screw-driven vessel in the Navy o USS Princeton Disaster of 1844, a fatal gun explosion aboard the first USS Princeton • The second Princeton, a transport and training ship, launched in 1851 and commissioned in 1852 • The third Princeton (PG-13), a gunboat launched in 1897 and commissioned in 1898 • The fourth Princeton (CVL-23), a light aircraft carrier, commissioned in 1943, sunk at Leyte Gulf in 1944. • The fifth Princeton (CV-37), an aircraft carrier commissioned in 1945, serving in the Korean War and Vietnam War, reclassified LPH-5 in 1959, decommissioned 1970 • The sixth Princeton (CG-59), a guided missile cruiser commissioned in 1989, currently in active service .
Frontier	A frontier is a political and geographical term referring to areas near or beyond a boundary. 'Frontier' was absorbed into English from French in the 15th century, with the meaning 'borderland'--the region of a country that fronts on another country . 'Frontier' means 'a region at the edge of a settled area'.
John Jacob Astor	John Jacob Astor born Johann Jacob Astor, was the first prominent member of the Astor family and the first multi-millionaire in the United States. He was the creator of the first trust in America, from which he made his fortune in fur trading, real estate and opium. Astor's career began with working in Germany as assistant in his father's business as travelling butcher.

Chapter 11. Westward Expansion

Robert Gray	Robert Gray was an American merchant sea-captain who is known for his achievements in connection with two trading voyages to the northern Pacific coast of North America, between 1790 and 1793, which pioneered the American maritime fur trade in that region. In the course of those voyages, Gray explored portions of that coast and, in 1790, completed the first American circumnavigation of the world.
Lewis and Clark Expedition	The Lewis and Clark Expedition, or 'Corps of Discovery Expedition' (1804-1806) was the first transcontinental expedition to the Pacific Coast by the United States. Commissioned by President Thomas Jefferson and led by two Virginia-born veterans of Indian wars in the Ohio Valley, Meriwether Lewis and William Clark, the expedition had several goals. Their objects were both scientific and commercial - to study the area's plants, animal life, and geography, and to discover how the region could be exploited economically.
Oregon Trail	The Oregon Trail is a 2,000 miles (3,200 km) historic east-west wagon route that connected various towns on the Missouri River to valleys in Oregon and locations in between. It was the oldest of the northern commercial and emigrant trails and was originally discovered and used by fur trappers and traders in the fur trade from about 1811 to 1840. In its earliest days much of the future Oregon trail was not passable to wagons but was passable everywhere only to men walking or riding horses and leading mule trains. Early parties of fur traders and settlers gradually made improvements over or through barriers on the trail that converted the original mule paths into a rough but contiguous wagon road.
Pacific Fur Company	The Pacific Fur Company was founded June 23, 1810, in New York City. Half of the stock of the company was held by the American Fur Company, owned exclusively by John Jacob Astor, and Astor provided all of the capital for the enterprise. The other half of the stock was ascribed to working partners or kept in reserve.
Early American currency	Early American currency went through several stages of development in the colonial and post-Revolutionary history of the United States. Because few coins were minted in the thirteen colonies that became the United States in 1776, foreign coins like the Spanish dollar were widely circulated. Colonial governments sometimes issued paper money to facilitate economic activity.
Fort Bridger	Fort Bridger was originally a 19th century fur trading outpost established in 1842 on Blacks Fork of the Green River and later a vital resupply point for wagon trains on the Oregon Trail, California Trail and Mormon Trail. The Army established a military post here in 1858 during the Utah War until it was finally closed in 1890. A small town, Fort Bridger, Wyoming, remains near the fort and takes its name from it. Bridger's Trading Post

	The post was established by the mountain man Jim Bridger, after whom it is named, and Louis Vasquez.
Turners	Turners are members of German-American gymnastic clubs. A German gymnastic movement was started by Turnvater (turners' father) Friedrich Ludwig Jahn in the early 19th century when Germany was occupied by Napoleon. The Turnvereine ('gymnastic unions') were not only athletic, but also political, reflecting their origin in similar 'nationalistic gymnastic' organizations in Europe.
President	President was a steamboat which currently lies dismantled in St. Elmo, Illinois. Originally named Cincinnati, it was built in 1924, and is the only remaining 'Western Rivers' style sidewheel river excursion steamboat in the United States. She was listed on the National Register of Historic Places and declared a National Historic Landmark in 1989. Her home ports have been Cincinnati, Ohio, New Orleans, Louisiana, Vicksburg, Mississippi, St. Louis, Missouri and Davenport, Iowa.
Thomas Hart Benton	Thomas Hart Benton was an American painter and muralist. Along with Grant Wood and John Steuart Curry, he was at the forefront of the Regionalist art movement. His fluid, almost sculpted paintings showed everyday scenes of life in the United States.
Winfield Scott	Winfield Scott was a United States Army general, and unsuccessful presidential candidate of the Whig Party in 1852. Known as 'Old Fuss and Feathers' and the 'Grand Old Man of the Army,' he served on active duty as a general longer than any other man in American history and many historians rate him the ablest American commander of his time. Over the course of his forty-seven-year career, he commanded forces in the War of 1812, the Mexican-American War, the Black Hawk War, the Second Seminole War, and, briefly, the American Civil War, conceiving the Union strategy known as the Anaconda Plan that would be used to defeat the Confederacy.

Chapter 11. Westward Expansion

Missouri Compromise

The Missouri Compromise was an agreement passed in 1820 between the pro-slavery and anti-slavery factions in the United States Congress, involving primarily the regulation of slavery in the western territories. It prohibited slavery in the former Louisiana Territory north of the parallel 36° 30′ north except within the boundaries of the proposed state of Missouri. Prior to the agreement, the House of Representatives had refused to accept this compromise, and a conference committee was appointed.

Wilmot Proviso

The Wilmot Proviso, one of the major events leading to the American Civil War, would have banned slavery in any territory to be acquired from Mexico in the Mexican War or in the future, including the area later known as the Mexican Cession, but which some proponents construed to also include the disputed lands in south Texas and New Mexico east of the Rio Grande.

Congressman David Wilmot first introduced the Proviso in the United States House of Representatives on August 8, 1846 as a rider on a $2,000,000 appropriations bill intended for the final negotiations to resolve the Mexican-American War. (In fact this was only three months into the two-year war).

Resolution

The Resolution was an American trading vessel whose crew were massacred by Haida chief Cuomo and his followers in 1794, at Cuomo Inlet near Moresby Island in the Queen Charlotte Islands of the North Coast of British Columbia, Canada.

Free Soil Party

The Free Soil Party was a short-lived political party in the United States active in the 1848 and 1852 presidential elections, and in some state elections. It was a third party and a single-issue party that largely appealed to and drew its greatest strength from New York State. The party leadership consisted of former anti-slavery members of the Whig Party and the Democratic Party.

James Murray Mason

James Murray Mason was a United States Representative and United States Senator from Virginia. He was a grandson of George Mason and represented the Confederate States of America as appointed commissioner of the Confederacy to the United Kingdom and France between 1861 and 1865 during the American Civil War.

Early life and education

He was born on Analostan Island (now Theodore Roosevelt Island) in the District of Columbia, and was a graduate of the University of Pennsylvania (1818), receiving a law degree from the College of William and Mary in 1820.

Millard Fillmore

Millard Fillmore was the 13th President of the United States, serving from 1850 until 1853, and the last member of the Whig Party to hold the office of president. Being Zachary Taylor`s Vice President, he assumed the presidency after Taylor`s death.

He opposed the proposal to keep slavery out of the territories annexed during the Mexican-American War (to appease the South), and so supported the Compromise of 1850, which he signed, including the Fugitive Slave Act ('Bloodhound Law') which was part of the compromise.

William H. Seward

William Henry Seward (May 16, 1801 - October 10, 1872) was the 12th Governor of New York, United States Senator and the United States Secretary of State under Abraham Lincoln and Andrew Johnson. A determined opponent of the spread of slavery in the years leading up to the American Civil War, he was a dominant figure in the Republican Party in its formative years, and was widely regarded as the leading contender for the party's presidential nomination in 1860 - yet his very outspokenness may have cost him the nomination. Despite his loss, he became a loyal member of Lincoln's wartime cabinet, and played a role in preventing foreign intervention early in the war. On the night of Lincoln's assassination, he survived an attempt on his life in the conspirators' effort to decapitate the Union government. As Johnson's Secretary of State, he engineered the purchase of Alaska from Russia in an act that was ridiculed at the time as 'Seward's Folly', but which somehow exemplified his character. His contemporary Carl Schurz described Seward as 'one of those spirits who sometimes will go ahead of public opinion instead of tamely following its footprints.'

Early life and career
Seward was born in Florida, New York, on May 16, 1801, one of five children of Samuel Sweezy Seward and his wife Mary Jennings Seward. Samuel Seward, described as 'a prosperous, domineering doctor and businessman,' was the founder of the S. S. Seward Institute, today a secondary school in the Florida Union Free School District.

Seward served as president of the S.S. Seward Institute after the death of his father, even while serving as Secretary of State during the Lincoln and Johnson administrations.

Seward studied law at Union College, graduating in 1820 with highest honors, and as a member of Phi Beta Kappa. He was admitted to the New York State Bar in 1821. In that same year, he met Frances Adeline Miller, a classmate of his sister Cornelia at Emma Willard's Troy Female Seminary and the daughter of Judge Elijah Miller of Auburn, New York. In 1823, he moved to Auburn where he entered into law partnership with Judge Miller, and married Frances Miller on October 20, 1824. They raised five children:

- Augustus Henry Seward (1826-1876)
- Frederick William Seward (1830-1915)
- Cornelia Seward (1836-1837)
- William Henry Seward, Jr. (1839-1920)
- Frances Adeline 'Fanny' Seward (1844-1866)
- Olive Risley Seward (1841-1908), adopted

Seward entered politics with the help of his friend Thurlow Weed, whom he had met by chance after a stagecoach accident. Seward was an as an Anti-Masonic member of the New York State Senate (7th D). from 1831 to 1834, sitting in the 54th, 55th, 56th and 57th New York State Legislatures. In 1834, the 33-year-old Seward was named the Whig party candidate for Governor of New York, but lost to incumbent Democrat William Marcy who won 52% of the vote to Seward's 48%.

From 1836 to 1838, Seward served as agent for a group of investors who had purchased the over 3-million-acre (12,000 km^2) western New York holdings of the Holland Land Company. He moved the land office from Mayville, NY to Westfield, New York, where he was successful in easing tensions between the investors and local landowners. On July 16, 1837, he delivered to the students and faculty of the newly formed Westfield Academy a Discourse on Education, in which he advocated for universal education.

In 1838, Seward again challenged Marcy, and was elected Governor of New York by a majority of 51.4% to Marcy's 48.6%. He was narrowly re-elected to a second two-year term in 1840. As a state senator and governor, Seward promoted progressive political policies including prison reform and increased spending on education. He supported state funding for schools for immigrants operated by their own clergy and taught in their native language. This support, which included Catholic parochial schools, came back to haunt him in the 1850s, when anti-Catholic feelings were high, especially among ex-Whigs in the Republican Party.

Seward developed his views about slavery while still a boy. His parents, like other Hudson Valley residents of the early 19th century, owned several slaves. (Slavery was slowly abolished in New York from 1797 to 1827 through a gradual mandated process). Seward recalled his preference as a child for the company and conversation of the slaves in his father's kitchen to the 'severe decorum' in his family's front parlor. He discerned very quickly the inequality between races, writing in later years 'I early came to the conclusion that something was wrong...and [that] determined me...to be an abolitionist.' This belief would stay with Seward through his life and permeate his career.

Seward's wife Frances was deeply committed to the abolitionist movement. In the 1850s, the Seward family opened their Auburn home as a safehouse to fugitive slaves. Seward's frequent travel and political work suggest that it was Frances who played the more active role in Auburn abolitionist activities. In the excitement following the rescue and safe transport of fugitive slave William 'Jerry' Henry in Syracuse on October 1, 1851, Frances wrote to her husband, 'two fugitives have gone to Canada--one of them our acquaintance John.' Another time she wrote, 'A man by the name of William Johnson will apply to you for assistance to purchase the freedom of his daughter. You will see that I have given him something by his book. I told him I thought you would give him more.'

In 1846 Seward became the center of controversy in his hometown when he defended, in separate cases, two convicts accused of murder. Henry Wyatt, a white man, was charged in the stabbing death of a fellow prison inmate; William Freeman, of African American and Native American ancestry, was accused of breaking into a home and stabbing four people to death. In both cases the defendants were mentally ill and had been severely abused while in prison. Seward, having long been an advocate of prison reform and better treatment for the insane, sought to prevent both men from being executed by using a relatively new defense of insanity. In a case involving mental illness with heavy racial overtones Seward argued, 'The color of the prisoner's skin, and the form of his features, are not impressed upon the spiritual immortal mind which works beneath. In spite of human pride, he is still your brother, and mine, in form and color accepted and approved by his Father, and yours, and mine, and bears equally with us the proudest inheritance of our race--the image of our Maker. Hold him then to be a Man.'

Later, Seward quoted Freeman's brother-in-law, praising his eloquence: 'They have made William Freeman what he is, a brute beast; they don't make anything else of any of our people but brute beasts; but when we violate their laws, then they want to punish us as if we were men.' In the end both men were convicted. Although Wyatt was executed, Freeman, whose conviction was reversed on Seward's successful appeal to the New York Supreme Court, died in his cell of tuberculosis.

United States Senator and Presidential Candidate
Seward supported the Whig candidate, General Zachary Taylor, in the presidential election of 1848. He said of Taylor, 'He is the most gentle-looking and amiable of men.' Taylor was a slaveholding plantation owner, but was friendly to Seward anyway.

William Seward was elected as U.S. Senator from New York as a Whig in 1849, and emerged as the leader of the anti-slavery 'Conscience Whigs'. Seward opposed the Compromise of 1850, and was thought to have encouraged Taylor in his supposed opposition. More recent scholarship suggests that Taylor was not under Seward's influence and would have accepted the Compromise if he had not died. Seward believed that slavery was morally wrong, and said so many times, outraging Southerners. He acknowledged that slavery was legal under the Constitution, but denied that the Constitution recognized or protected slavery. He famously remarked in 1850 that 'there is a higher law than the Constitution'. He continued to argue this point of view over the next ten years. He presented himself as the leading enemy of the Slave Power - that is, the perceived conspiracy of southern slaveowners to seize the government and defeat the progress of liberty.

Seward was an opponent of the Fugitive Slave Act, and he defended runaway slaves in court. He supported personal liberty laws.

In February 1855, he was re-elected as a Whig to the U.S. Senate, and joined the Republican Party when the New York Whigs merged with the Anti-Nebraskans later the same year. Seward did not seriously compete for the presidential nomination (won by John C. Frémont) in 1856, but sought and was expected to receive the nomination in 1860. In October 1858, he delivered a famous speech in which he argued that the political and economic systems of North and South were incompatible, and that, due to this 'irrepressible conflict,' the inevitable 'collision' of the two systems would eventually result in the nation becoming 'either entirely a slaveholding nation, or entirely a free-labor nation.' Like Lincoln, he believed slavery could and should be extinguished by long-run historical forces rather than by coercion or war.

In 1859, confident of gaining the presidential nomination and advised by his political ally and friend Thurlow Weed that he would be better off avoiding political gatherings where his words might be misinterpreted by one faction or another, Seward left the country for an eight-month tour of Europe that included a visit to Syria, where Ayub Beg Tarabulsy gave him several Arabian horses. During that hiatus, his lesser-known rival Abraham Lincoln worked diligently to line up support in case Seward failed to win on the first ballot. After returning to the United States, Seward gave a conciliatory, pro-Union Senate speech that reassured moderates but alienated some radical Republicans. (Observing events from Europe, Karl Marx, who was ideologically sympathetic to Frémont, contemptuously regarded Seward as a 'Republican Richelieu' and the 'Demosthenes of the Republican Party' who had sabotaged Frémont's presidential ambitions). Around the same time, his friend Horace Greeley turned against him, opposing Seward on the grounds that his radical reputation made him unelectable. When Lincoln won the nomination, Seward loyally supported him and made a long speaking tour of the West in the autumn of 1860.

Secretary of State

'Our population is destined to roll its resistless waves to the icy barriers of the north, and to encounter oriental civilization on the shores of the Pacific.' --William H. Seward, 1846

Abraham Lincoln appointed Seward his Secretary of State in 1861. Seward played an integral role in resolving the Trent Affair and in negotiating the ensuing Lyons-Seward Treaty of 1862, which set forth strong measures by which the United States and Great Britain agreed to enforce an end to the Atlantic slave trade.

Seward pursued his vision of American expansion. 'Give me only this assurance, that there never be an unlawful resistance by an armed force to the ... United States, and give me fifty, forty, thirty more years of life, and I will engage to give you the possession of the American continent and the control of the world.' Having argued for taking American possession of vulnerable but useful places such as the Danish West Indies, Samaná, Panama, and Hawaii, Seward oversaw the annexation of only one, that of the Brook Islands in 1867. Despite minimal Congressional support, though, he developed American influence in the Hawaiian Islands, as well as in Japan and China to some extent.

Despite his endorsement of expansionist policies, Seward also strongly advocated non-interventionism. After Tsar Alexander II put down the 1863 January Uprising in Poland, French Emperor Napoleon III asked the United States to 'join in a protest to the Tsar.' Seward declined, 'defending 'our policy of non-intervention -- straight, absolute, and peculiar as it may seem to other nations," and insisted that '[t]he American people must be content to recommend the cause of human progress by the wisdom with which they should exercise the powers of self-government, forbearing at all times, and in every way, from foreign alliances, intervention, and interference.'

Assassination Attempt

On the night of April 14, 1865, Lewis Powell, an associate and co-conspirator of John Wilkes Booth, attempted to assassinate Seward at his Washington D.C. home. Powell's attack on Seward was meticulously coordinated with Booth's attack on President Abraham Lincoln and George Atzerodt's attack on Vice President Andrew Johnson in order to maximize the element of surprise and to sever the continuity of the United States government (it should be noted, however, that Atzerodt failed to follow through on his attack). Another member of the conspiracy, David Herold, led Powell to the Seward home on horseback and was responsible for holding Powell's horse while he committed the attack as well as guiding him out of the city during their escape. Powell was able to gain access to the Seward home by telling the butler, William H. Bell, that he was delivering medicine for Seward (who was bed-ridden from a carriage accident which had gravely injured him on April 5, 1865).

Upon entry to the home, Powell began up the stairs, but was stopped at the top of the stairs by Frederick, the Secretary's eldest son. Frederick told Powell that his father was asleep and that he (Frederick) would take the medicine to him. Unsure of what to do, Powell turned around and began descending the stairs, but then suddenly swung back around, drew a pistol, and pointed it at Frederick's head. The pistol misfired. Realizing he needed to act quickly, Powell ruthlessly began beating Frederick over the head with the barrel of his gun. The force of Powell's blows crippled Frederick Seward and left him sprawled on the floor, floating in and out of consciousness, in a pool of blood. Powell's gun was also rendered completely useless, as it had become jammed during the melee.

In Secretary Seward's bedroom was his daughter, Fanny Seward. Hearing the loud noises coming from the second floor hallway, Fanny opened the door to see her brother slumped on the floor and a wide-eyed Powell charging directly towards her, a dagger in his hand. Powell burst through the door, threw Fanny Seward to the side, and jumped on the Secretary's bed, repeatedly stabbing him in the face and neck area. Powell also attacked and injured another son (Augustus), and a soldier and nurse (Sgt. George Robinson) who had been assigned to stay with Seward. Outside the home, David Herold, who could clearly hear the screams coming from the house, fled with both horses, leaving Powell to fend for himself. Powell, convinced that he had mortally wounded the Secretary, fled down the stairs, and stabbed a messenger, Emerick Hansell, who had arrived just as Powell was escaping; Hansell was rendered permanently paralyzed from the stabbing. All five men that were injured that night survived, although Secretary Seward would carry the facial scars from the attack for the rest of his life. The events of that night took their toll on his wife, Frances, who died June 1865. His daughter Fanny died of tuberculosis in October 1866.

Powell was captured the next day (hiding in a tree in Washington D.C). and was executed on July 7, 1865, along with David Herold, George Atzerodt, and Mary Surratt, the three others convicted as conspirators in the Lincoln assassination.

Although it took Seward several months to recover from his wounds, he emerged as a major force in the administration of the new president, Andrew Johnson. He frequently defended his more moderate reconciliation policies towards the South, to the point of enraging Radical Republicans who had once regarded Seward as their ally.

In the fall of 1866, Seward joined Johnson, as well as Ulysses S. Grant and the young General George Armstrong Custer, along with several other administration figures, on the president's ill-fated 'Swing Around the Circle' campaign trip.

At one point Seward became so ill, probably from cholera, that he was sent back to Washington in a special car. Both Johnson and Grant, as well as several members of the Seward family, thought the Secretary was near death. But as with his April 1865 stabbing, Seward surprised many by making a good recovery.

The purchase of Alaska

Seward's most famous achievement as Secretary of State was his successful acquisition of Alaska from Russia. On March 30, 1867, he completed negotiations for the territory, which involved the purchase of 586,412 square miles (1,518,800 km²) of territory (more than twice the area of Texas) for $7,200,000, or approximately 2 cents per acre (equivalent to US$95 million in 2005). The purchase of this frontier land was variously mocked by the public as Seward's Folly, 'Seward's Icebox,' and Andrew Johnson's 'polar bear garden.' Alaska celebrates the purchase on Seward's Day, the last Monday of March. When asked what he considered to be his greatest achievement as Secretary of State, Seward replied 'The purchase of Alaska--but it will take the people a generation to find it out'.

Later life

Seward retired as Secretary of State after Ulysses S. Grant took office as president. During his last years, Seward traveled and wrote prolifically. Most notably, he traveled around the world in fourteen months and two days from August, 1870 to October, 1871. On October 10, 1872, Seward died in his office in his home in Auburn, New York, after having difficulty breathing. His last words were to his children saying, 'Love one another.' He was buried in Fort Hill Cemetery in Auburn, New York, with his wife and two children, Cornelia and Fanny. His headstone reads, 'He was faithful.'

His son, Frederick, edited and published his memoirs in three volumes.

In 1967, a century after the Alaska Purchase, the actor, Joseph Cotten, portrayed Seward in 'The Freeman Story', a part of his NBC anthology series, The Joseph Cotten Show. Virginia Gregg played Fanny Seward. Popular actor, Richard Mulligan, portrayed William Seward in the 1988 Lincoln mini-series, 'Random Letters'.

Seward's homes in Auburn and Florida, New York

Seward and his family owned a home in Auburn, New York which is now a museum; it was built in 1816 by Seward's father-in-law, Judge Elijah Miller. Seward married the Judge's daughter, Frances, in 1824 on the condition that they would live with Miller in his Auburn home. Seward made many changes to the home, adding an addition in the late 1840s and another one in 1866. When he died, Seward left the home to his son, William Seward, Jr.; it passed on to his grandson, William Henry Seward III, in 1920. At his death in 1951, it became a museum that opened to the public in 1955. Four generations of the family's artifacts are contained within the museum, located at 33 South Street in Auburn. The museum is open Tuesday through Saturday from 10am to 5pm.

Meanwhile, Seward's birthplace in Florida, New York was bought by the village in 2010, with the purpose of refurbishing it. (The property actually contains two houses: one in back--Seward's actual birthplace--which was converted into a barn; and one in front, built in the 1890s, used by the family that lived there for many years). The property (after spending an estimated $200,000, to be raised by private donations) is expected to be turned into a museum and opened to the public by 2013.

Legacy

- The purchase of Alaska.
- The Guano Islands Act of 1856
- The $50-dollar Treasury note, also called the Coin note, of the Series 1891, features a portrait of Seward on the obverse. Examples of this note are very rare and would likely se for about $50,000 at auction.
- His house in Auburn, New York is open as a public museum.
- The house in which he lived in Westfield, New York is now home to a bed and breakfast.
- He was a name partner of the law firm of Blatchford, Seward ' Griswold, today known as Cravath, Swaine ' Moore.
- Was famous in his lifetime for his red hair and energetic way of walking. Henry Adams described him as 'wonderfully resembling' a parrot in 'manner and profile'.

Memorials

- Seward Avenue in Auburn. Also in Auburn, Frances Street, Augustus Street, and Frederick Street are named for members of his family. The four streets form a block.
- Seward Elementary School in Auburn.
- Seward Place in Schenectady, New York, on the west side of the Union College campus.
- Seward Park in Auburn, New York.
- Seward Park in the Lower East Side of Manhattan.
- Seward Park in Seattle, Washington.
- Seward Square park in Washington, D.C..
- The Seward Peninsula in Alaska.
- City of Seward, on Alaska's Kenai Peninsula
- Seward, Illinois; Seward, Kansas; Seward, New York; Seward, Nebraska; and Seward, Alaska.
- A hamburger is called 'Seward's Folly' at West Rib Deli ' Pub in Talkeetna, Alaska is named for him.
- Seward County, Nebraska
- Seward's Success, Alaska, an unbuilt community to be enclosed by a dome.
- The Seward neighborhood of Minneapolis, Minnesota
- Seward Mountain (4,361 feet, 1,329 m), one of the Adirondack High Peaks, the highest point in Franklin County.
- At Union College, the campus bus is known as Seward's Trolley, a pun on Seward's Folly
- Seward High School in his hometown of Florida is named for his father, Dr. Samuel

Columbia	The Columbia was a 310 ton, 6 gun barque in the service of the Columbia District of the Hudson's Bay Company on the Columbia River and elsewhere in the Pacific Northwest in the 1830s and 1840s. The vessel's complement of crew was 24 men.
Fugitive slave	The phenomenon of slaves running away and seeking to regain their freedom is as old as the institution of slavery itself. In the history of slavery in the United States, 'fugitive slaves' (or runaway slaves) were slaves who had escaped from their master to travel to a place where slavery was banned or illegal. Many went to northern territories including Pennsylvania and Massachusetts until the Fugitive Slave Act of 1850 was passed.

PRACTICE QUIZ
Chapter 11. Westward Expansion

1. The _________ was the acquisition by the United States of America of 828,800 square miles (2,147,000 km^2) of France's claim to the territory of Louisiana in 1803. The U.S. paid 60 million francs ($11,250,000) plus cancellation of debts worth 18 million francs ($3,750,000), for a total sum of 15 million dollars for the Louisiana territory ($219 million in 2010 dollars). What was purchased was France's claim only, not the actual territory, which belonged to the tribes which inhabited the area. The territory itself was acquired slowly throughout the nineteenth century by purchases to Native American tribes and wars.

   a. Digital Transition Content Security Act
   b. Chiaha
   c. Louisiana Purchase
   d. James Buchanan

2. The _________ was founded June 23, 1810, in New York City. Half of the stock of the company was held by the American Fur Company, owned exclusively by John Jacob Astor, and Astor provided all of the capital for the enterprise. The other half of the stock was ascribed to working partners or kept in reserve.

   a. Pitfall trap
   b. Promyshlenniki
   c. Pacific Fur Company
   d. Rocky Mountain Fur Company

3. _________ is a 1997 blockbuster Bollywood war film based on the Indo-Pakistani War of 1971. J. P. Dutta directed and produced this war epic which stars Sunny Deol, Jackie Shroff, Sunil Shetty, Akshay Khanna, Pooja Bhatt, Sharbani Mukherjee and Tabu.

   Director J.P. Dutta won Best Director at the same award function, while his father O.P. Dutta won for Best Dialogues.

   The movie is an adaptation from real life events that happened at the Battle of Longewala fought in Rajasthan (Western Theatre) during the Indo-Pakistani War of 1971 and Bangladesh Liberation War.

   a. Digital Transition Content Security Act
   b. Border
   c. Jessica's Law
   d. Respect for America's Fallen Heroes Act

---

4. The Territory South of the River Ohio, more commonly known as the _________, was an organized incorporated territory of the United States that existed from May 26, 1790, until June 1, 1796, when it was admitted to the United States as the State of Tennessee.

   The _________ was created by the Southwest Ordinance enacted on May 26, 1790, out of land (the Washington District) that was ceded to the U.S. federal government by the State of North Carolina. The name 'Territory South of the River Ohio' suggests a much larger territory than modern-day Tennessee.

   a. Southwest Territory
   b. Wisconsin Territory
   c. Digital Transition Content Security Act
   d. Federal Funding Accountability and Transparency Act of 2006

5. The phenomenon of slaves running away and seeking to regain their freedom is as old as the institution of slavery itself. In the history of slavery in the United States, '_________s' (or runaway slaves) were slaves who had escaped from their master to travel to a place where slavery was banned or illegal. Many went to northern territories including Pennsylvania and Massachusetts until the _________ Act of 1850 was passed.

   a. Fugitive slave
   b. Fort Gadsden
   c. Cyrus Gates Farmstead
   d. Genius of Universal Emancipation

ANSWER KEY
Chapter 11. Westward Expansion

---

1. c
2. c
3. b
4. a
5. a

CHAPTER OUTLINE: KEY TERMS, PEOPLE, PLACES, CONCEPTS
Chapter 12

The Sections Go Their Own Ways

__________ Republican Party

__________ Black Codes

__________ Dred Scott

__________ Missouri Compromise

__________ Puritan

__________ Sharecropping

__________ England

__________ Sojourner Truth

__________ Charles Deslondes

__________ Turners

__________ Denmark Vesey

__________ Early American currency

__________ Continental Congress

__________ Massachusetts

__________ Factory

__________ American Revolution

__________ Tenement

__________ York

__________ Union

Horace Greeley

Commonwealth v. Hunt

Emancipation Proclamation

Middle Colonies

Commerce

Erie Canal

New York Central Railroad

Land grant

Chicago

Republican Party	The Republican Party is one of the two major contemporary political parties in the United States, along with the Democratic Party. Founded by anti-slavery expansion activists in 1854, it is often called the Grand Old Party (GOP). The party's platform generally reflects American conservatism in the U.S. political spectrum and is considered center-right, in contrast to the more liberal-leaning Democrats.
Black Codes	The Black Codes were unofficial laws put in place in the United States to limit the basic human rights and civil liberties of blacks. Even though the U.S. constitution originally discriminated against blacks (as 'other persons') and both Northern and Southern states had passed discriminatory legislation from the early 19th century, the term Black Codes is used most often to refer to legislation passed by Southern states at the end of the Civil War to control the labor, migration and other activities of newly-freed slaves. In Texas, the Eleventh Legislature produced these codes in 1866, right after the United States Civil War.
Dred Scott	Dred Scott was an African-American slave in the United States who unsuccessfully sued for his freedom and that of his wife and their two daughters in the Dred Scott v. Sandford case of 1857, popularly known as 'the Dred Scott Decision.' His case was based on the fact that although he and his wife Harriet Scott were slaves, he had lived with his master Dr. John Emerson in states and territories where slavery was illegal according to both state laws and the Northwest Ordinance of 1787, including Illinois and Minnesota (which was then part of the Wisconsin Territory). The United States Supreme Court decided 7-2 against Scott, finding that neither he nor any other person of African ancestry could claim citizenship in the United States, and therefore Scott could not bring suit in federal court under diversity of citizenship rules. Moreover, Scott's temporary residence outside Missouri did not bring about his emancipation under the Missouri Compromise, which the court ruled unconstitutional as it would improperly deprive Scott's owner of his legal property.
Missouri Compromise	The Missouri Compromise was an agreement passed in 1820 between the pro-slavery and anti-slavery factions in the United States Congress, involving primarily the regulation of slavery in the western territories. It prohibited slavery in the former Louisiana Territory north of the parallel 36° 30′ north except within the boundaries of the proposed state of Missouri. Prior to the agreement, the House of Representatives had refused to accept this compromise, and a conference committee was appointed.

Puritan	The Puritans were a significant grouping of English Protestants in the 16th and 17th centuries, including, but not limited to, English Calvinists. Puritanism in this sense was founded by some Marian exiles from the clergy shortly after the accession of Elizabeth I of England in 1558, as an activist movement within the Church of England. The designation 'Puritan' is often incorrectly used, notably based on the assumption that hedonism and puritanism are antonyms: Historically, the word was used pejoratively to characterize the Protestant group as extremists similar to the Cathari of France, and according to Thomas Fuller in his Church History dated back to 1564, Archbishop Matthew Parker of that time used it and 'precisian' with the sense of modern 'stickler'.
Sharecropping	Sharecropping is a system of agriculture in which a landowner allows a tenant to use the land in return for a share of the crop produced on the land (e.g., 50% of the crop). This should not be confused with a crop fixed rent contract, in which a landowner allows a tenant to use the land in return for a fixed amount of crop per unit of land (e.g., 1 T/ha). Sharecropping has a long history and there are a wide range of different situations and types of agreements that have encompassed the system.
England	England is a country that is part of the United Kingdom. It shares land borders with Scotland to the north and Wales to the west; the Irish Sea is to the north west, the Celtic Sea to the south west and the North Sea to the east, with the English Channel to the south separating it from continental Europe. Most of England comprises the central and southern part of the island of Great Britain in the North Atlantic.
Sojourner Truth	Sojourner Truth was the self-given name, from 1843 onward, of Isabella Baumfree, an African-American abolitionist and women's rights activist. Truth was born into slavery in Swartekill, New York, but escaped with her infant daughter to freedom in 1826. After going to court to recover her son, she became the first black woman to win such a case against a white man. Her best-known extemporaneous speech on racial inequalities, Ain't I a Woman?, was delivered in 1851 at the Ohio Women's Rights Convention in Akron, Ohio.
Charles Deslondes	Charles Deslondes was one of the slave leaders of the 1811 German Coast Uprising, a slave revolt that began on January 8, 1811 in the Territory of Orleans. He led more than 200 rebels against the plantations along the Mississippi River toward New Orleans. White planters formed militias and ended up hunting down the rebels.
Turners	Turners are members of German-American gymnastic clubs. A German gymnastic movement was started by Turnvater (turners' father) Friedrich Ludwig Jahn in the early 19th century when Germany was occupied by Napoleon. The Turnvereine ('gymnastic unions') were not only athletic, but also political, reflecting their origin in similar 'nationalistic gymnastic' organizations in Europe.

Chapter 12. The Sections Go Their Own Ways

Denmark Vesey	Denmark Vesey, (1767? - July 2, 1822) was an African American slave brought to the United States from the Caribbean of Coromantee background. After purchasing his freedom, he planned what would have been one of the largest slave rebellions in the United States. Word of the plans was leaked, and at Charleston, South Carolina, authorities arrested the plot's leaders before the uprising could begin.
Early American currency	Early American currency went through several stages of development in the colonial and post-Revolutionary history of the United States. Because few coins were minted in the thirteen colonies that became the United States in 1776, foreign coins like the Spanish dollar were widely circulated. Colonial governments sometimes issued paper money to facilitate economic activity.
Continental Congress	The Continental Congress was a convention of delegates called together from the Thirteen Colonies that became the governing body of the United States during the American Revolution. The Congress met from 1774 to 1789 in three incarnations. The first call for a convention was made over issues of mounting taxation without representation in Parliament and because of the British blockade.
Massachusetts	'Massachusetts', words and music by Arlo Guthrie, was made the official folk song of Massachusetts in July, 1981.
Factory	Factory was the English term for the trading posts system originally established by Europeans in foreign territories, first within different states of medieval Europe, and later in their colonial possessions. Factories served simultaneously as market, warehouse, customs, defense and support to the navigation or exploration, headquarters or de facto government of local communities, with the head of the factory being called a factor. This system was adopted by Americans to exchange goods with local non western societies.
American Revolution	The American Revolution was the political upheaval during the last half of the 18th century in which thirteen colonies in North America joined together to break free from the British Empire, combining to become the United States of America. They first rejected the authority of the Parliament of Great Britain to govern them from overseas without representation, and then expelled all royal officials. By 1774, each colony had established a Provincial Congress, or an equivalent governmental institution, to govern itself, but still within the empire. The British responded by sending combat troops to re-impose direct rule.

Tenement

A tenement is, in most English-speaking areas, a substandard multi-family dwelling, usually old, occupied by the poor.

History

Originally the term tenement referred to tenancy and therefore to any rented accommodation. The New York State legislature defined it in the Tenement House Act of 1867 in terms of rental occupancy by multiple households, as

Any house, building, or portion thereof, which is rented, leased, let, or hired out to be occupied or is occupied, as the home or residence of more than three families living independently of one another and doing their own cooking upon the premises, or by more than two families upon a floor, so living and cooking and having a common right in the halls, stairways, yards, water-closets, or privies, or some of them.

York

York was an African American slave best known for his participation with the Lewis and Clark Expedition. As William Clark's slave, he had to do diffficult manual labour without pay. After the expedition's return he pressed for his freedom, which Clark opposed, he possibly agreed ten years later, though some historians dispute this and say he was never freed.

Union

During the American Civil War, the Union was a name used to refer to the federal government of the United States, which was supported by the twenty free states and five border slave states. It was opposed by 11 Southern slave states that had declared a secession to join together to form the Confederacy. Although the Union states included the Western states of California, Oregon, and (after 1864) Nevada, as well as states generally considered to be part of the Midwest, the Union has been also often loosely referred to as 'the North', both then and now.

Horace Greeley

Horace Greeley was an American newspaper editor, a founder of the Liberal Republican Party, a reformer, and a politician. His New York Tribune was America's most influential newspaper from the 1840s to the 1870s and 'established Greeley's reputation as the greatest editor of his day.' Greeley used it to promote the Whig and Republican parties, as well as opposition to slavery and a host of reforms ranging from vegetarianism to socialism.

Crusading against the corruption of Ulysses S. Grant's Republican administration, he was the new Liberal Republican Party's candidate in the 1872 U.S. presidential election.

Chapter 12. The Sections Go Their Own Ways

Commonwealth v. Hunt	Commonwealth v. Hunt was a landmark legal decision issued by the Massachusetts Supreme Judicial Court on the subject of labor unions. Before this decision, based on Commonwealth v. Pullis, labor unions which attempted to 'close' or create a unionized workplace could be charged with conspiracy. However, in March 1842, Chief Justice Lemuel Shaw ruled that unions were legal organizations and had the right to organize a strike.
Emancipation Proclamation	The Emancipation Proclamation is an executive order issued by United States President Abraham Lincoln on January 1, 1863, during the American Civil War using his war powers. It proclaimed the freedom of slaves in the ten states then in rebellion, thus applying to 3.1 million of the 4 million slaves in the U.S. at that time. The Proclamation immediately freed 50,000 slaves, with nearly all the rest (of the 3.1 million) freed as Union armies advanced.
Middle Colonies	The Middle Colonies comprised the middle region of the Thirteen British Colonies in Northern America. Following the American Revolution, the Middle Colonies became the states of New Jersey, Pennsylvania, New York and Delaware. Much of the area was part of the New Netherland until the British exerted control over the region. The British captured much of the area in its war with the Dutch around 1664, and the majority of the conquered land became the Province of New York.
Commerce	While business refers to the value-creating activities of an organization for profit, commerce means the whole system of an economy that constitutes an environment for business. The system includes legal, economic, political, social, cultural, and technological systems that are in operation in any country. Thus, commerce is a system or an environment that affects the business prospects of an economy or a nation-state.
Erie Canal	The Erie Canal is a waterway in New York that runs about 363 miles (584 km) from Albany, New York, on the Hudson River to Buffalo, New York, at Lake Erie, completing a navigable water route from the Atlantic Ocean to the Great Lakes. The canal contains 36 locks and encompasses a total elevation differential of around 565 ft. (169 m).

New York Central Railroad	The New York Central Railroad known simply as the New York Central in its publicity, was a railroad operating in the Northeastern United States. Headquartered in New York, the railroad served most of the Northeast, including extensive trackage in the states of New York, Pennsylvania, Ohio, Michigan, Indiana, Illinois, and Massachusetts, plus additional trackage in the Canadian provinces of Ontario and Quebec. The railroad primarily connected greater New York and Boston in the east with Chicago and St.Louis in the midwest along with the intermediate cities of Albany, Buffalo, Cleveland, Cincinnati, and Detroit.
Land grant	A land grant is a gift of real estate - land or its privileges - made by a government or other authority as a reward for services to an individual, especially in return for military service. Grants of land are also awarded to individuals and companies as incentives to develop unused land in relatively unpopulated countries; the process of awarding land grants are not limited to the countries named below. Ancient Rome Roman soldiers were given rewards at the end of their service including cash or land (praemia).
Chicago	Chicago is the largest city in the state of Illinois. With 2,851,268 residents, it is the most populous city in the Midwestern United States and the third most populous city in the USA. Its metropolitan area, commonly named 'Chicagoland,' is the 27th most populous metropolitan area in the world, home to an estimated 9.7 million people spread across the U.S. states of Illinois, Indiana, and Wisconsin. Chicago is the world's largest inland city that does not serve as either a national or provincial capital city.

PRACTICE QUIZ
Chapter 12. The Sections Go Their Own Ways

1. The _________ were unofficial laws put in place in the United States to limit the basic human rights and civil liberties of blacks. Even though the U.S. constitution originally discriminated against blacks (as 'other persons') and both Northern and Southern states had passed discriminatory legislation from the early 19th century, the term _________ is used most often to refer to legislation passed by Southern states at the end of the Civil War to control the labor, migration and other activities of newly-freed slaves.

   In Texas, the Eleventh Legislature produced these codes in 1866, right after the United States Civil War.

   a. Digital Transition Content Security Act
   b. Write-in candidate
   c. Black Codes
   d. Jessica's Law

2. While business refers to the value-creating activities of an organization for profit, _________ means the whole system of an economy that constitutes an environment for business. The system includes legal, economic, political, social, cultural, and technological systems that are in operation in any country. Thus, _________ is a system or an environment that affects the business prospects of an economy or a nation-state.

   a. Commerce
   b. Federal Funding Accountability and Transparency Act of 2006
   c. Jessica's Law
   d. John L. Stevens

3. _________ is a system of agriculture in which a landowner allows a tenant to use the land in return for a share of the crop produced on the land (e.g., 50% of the crop). This should not be confused with a crop fixed rent contract, in which a landowner allows a tenant to use the land in return for a fixed amount of crop per unit of land (e.g., 1 T/ha). _________ has a long history and there are a wide range of different situations and types of agreements that have encompassed the system.

   a. Digital Transition Content Security Act
   b. Sharecropping
   c. Royal Charter of 1663
   d. Richard Saltonstall

4. The _________ is one of the two major contemporary political parties in the United States, along with the Democratic Party. Founded by anti-slavery expansion activists in 1854, it is often called the Grand Old Party (GOP). The party's platform generally reflects American conservatism in the U.S. political spectrum and is considered center-right, in contrast to the more liberal-leaning Democrats.

   a. Republican Party
   b. Write-in candidate
   c. Digital Transition Content Security Act
   d. Federal Funding Accountability and Transparency Act of 2006

5. _________ was the English term for the trading posts system originally established by Europeans in foreign territories, first within different states of medieval Europe, and later in their colonial possessions. Factories served simultaneously as market, warehouse, customs, defense and support to the navigation or exploration, headquarters or de facto government of local communities, with the head of the _________ being called a factor. This system was adopted by Americans to exchange goods with local non western societies.

   a. Thomas Gage
   b. Factory
   c. Committee of the States
   d. Declaration and Resolves of the First Continental Congress

ANSWER KEY
Chapter 12. The Sections Go Their Own Ways

---

1. c
2. a
3. b
4. a
5. b

CHAPTER OUTLINE: KEY TERMS, PEOPLE, PLACES, CONCEPTS

Chapter 13

The Coming of the Civil War

______________ Fugitive slave

______________ Alabama

______________ CSS Alabama

______________ Central America

______________ Millard Fillmore

______________ Manifest Destiny

______________ Ostend Manifesto

______________ Franklin Pierce

______________ Young America movement

______________ Frederick Douglass

______________ Underground Railroad

______________ Josiah Henson

______________ James Buchanan

______________ Missouri Compromise

______________ John Brown

______________ Emancipation Proclamation

______________ Lecompton Constitution

______________ Radical Republicans

______________ Republican Party

_______________ England

_______________ Northwest Ordinance

_______________ Dred Scott

_______________ Freeport Doctrine

_______________ Robert E. Lee

_______________ Washington

_______________ Black Codes

_______________ Hinton Rowan Helper

_______________ William H. Seward

_______________ John Bell

_______________ Constitutional Union Party

_______________ South Carolina

_______________ Union

_______________ Union Party

_______________ Gettysburg Campaign

Fugitive slave	The phenomenon of slaves running away and seeking to regain their freedom is as old as the institution of slavery itself. In the history of slavery in the United States, 'fugitive slaves' (or runaway slaves) were slaves who had escaped from their master to travel to a place where slavery was banned or illegal. Many went to northern territories including Pennsylvania and Massachusetts until the Fugitive Slave Act of 1850 was passed.
Alabama	Alabama is a state located in the southeastern region of the United States of America. It is bordered by Tennessee to the north, Georgia to the east, Florida and the Gulf of Mexico to the south, and Mississippi to the west. Alabama ranks 30th in total land area and ranks second in the size of its inland waterways. The state ranks 23rd in population with 4.7 million residents in 2009.
CSS Alabama	CSS Alabama was a screw sloop-of-war built for the Confederate States Navy at Birkenhead, United Kingdom, in 1862 by John Laird Sons and Company. Alabama served as a commerce raider, attacking Union merchant and naval ships over the course of her two-year career, during which she never anchored in a Southern port. She was sunk in battle by the USS Kearsarge in 1864 near the Port of Cherbourg, France.
Central America	Central America is the central geographic region of the Americas. It is the southernmost, isthmian portion of the North American continent, which connects with South America on the southeast. When considered part of the unified continental model, it is considered a subcontinent.
Millard Fillmore	Millard Fillmore was the 13th President of the United States, serving from 1850 until 1853, and the last member of the Whig Party to hold the office of president. Being Zachary Taylor`s Vice President, he assumed the presidency after Taylor`s death. He opposed the proposal to keep slavery out of the territories annexed during the Mexican-American War (to appease the South), and so supported the Compromise of 1850, which he signed, including the Fugitive Slave Act ('Bloodhound Law') which was part of the compromise.
Manifest Destiny	Manifest Destiny was the 19th century American belief that the United States (often in the ethnically specific form of the 'Anglo-Saxon race') was destined to expand across the continent. It was used by Democrat-Republicans in the 1840s to justify the war with Mexico; the concept was denounced by Whigs, and fell into disuse after the mid-19th century.

	Advocates of Manifest Destiny believed that expansion was not only wise but that it was readily apparent (manifest) and inexorable (destiny).
Ostend Manifesto	The Ostend Manifesto was a document written in 1854 that described the rationale for the United States to purchase Cuba from Spain while implying that the U.S. should declare war if Spain refused. Cuba's annexation had long been a goal of U.S. expansionists, particularly as the U.S. set its sights southward following the admission of California to the Union. However, diplomatically, the country had been content to see the island remain in Spanish hands so long as it did not pass to a stronger power such as Britain or France.
Franklin Pierce	Franklin Pierce an American politician and lawyer, was the 14th President of the United States, serving from 1853 to 1857. He is the only President from New Hampshire. Pierce was a Democrat and a 'doughface' (a Northerner with Southern sympathies) who served in the U.S. House of Representatives and Senate. Later, Pierce took part in the Mexican-American War and became a brigadier general.
Young America movement	The Young America Movement was an American political and cultural attitude in the mid-nineteenth century. Inspired by European reform movements of the 1830s , the American group was formed as a political organization in 1845 by Edwin de Leon and George H. Evans. It advocated free trade, social reform, expansion southward into the territories, and support for republican, anti-aristocratic movements abroad.
Frederick Douglass	Frederick Douglass was an American social reformer, orator, writer and statesman. After escaping from slavery, he became a leader of the abolitionist movement, known for his dazzling oratory and incisive antislavery writing. He stood as a living counter-example to slaveholders' arguments that slaves did not have the intellectual capacity to function as independent American citizens.
Underground Railroad	The Underground Railroad was an informal network of secret routes and safe houses used by 19th-century black slaves in the United States to escape to free states and Canada with the aid of abolitionists and allies who were sympathetic to their cause. The term is also applied to the abolitionists, both black and white, free and enslaved, who aided the fugitives. Other various routes led to Mexico or overseas.

Chapter 13. The Coming of the Civil War

Josiah Henson

Josiah Henson was an author, abolitionist, and minister. Born into slavery in Charles County, Maryland, he escaped to Ontario, Canada in 1830, and founded a settlement and laborer's school for other fugitive slaves at Dawn, near Dresden in Kent County. At the time of his arrival, Ontario was known as the Province of Upper Canada (U.C)., becoming the Province of Canada in 1841, then Ontario in 1867, all within Henson's lifetime there.

James Buchanan

James Buchanan, Jr. was the 15th President of the United States, from 1857 to 1861, and the last president to be born in the 18th century. He is the only president from Pennsylvania and the only president who was a life-long bachelor.

Missouri Compromise

The Missouri Compromise was an agreement passed in 1820 between the pro-slavery and anti-slavery factions in the United States Congress, involving primarily the regulation of slavery in the western territories. It prohibited slavery in the former Louisiana Territory north of the parallel 36° 30' north except within the boundaries of the proposed state of Missouri. Prior to the agreement, the House of Representatives had refused to accept this compromise, and a conference committee was appointed.

John Brown

John Brown was a revolutionary abolitionist from the United States, who advocated and practiced armed insurrection as a means to abolish slavery for good. He led the Pottawatomie Massacre in 1856 in Bleeding Kansas and made his name in the unsuccessful raid at Harpers Ferry in 1859. He was tried and executed for treason against the state of Virginia, murder, and conspiracy later that year. Brown has been called 'the most controversial of all 19th-century Americans.'

Brown's attempt in 1859 to start a liberation movement among enslaved African Americans in Harpers Ferry, Virginia (now West Virginia) electrified the nation.

Emancipation Proclamation

The Emancipation Proclamation is an executive order issued by United States President Abraham Lincoln on January 1, 1863, during the American Civil War using his war powers. It proclaimed the freedom of slaves in the ten states then in rebellion, thus applying to 3.1 million of the 4 million slaves in the U.S. at that time. The Proclamation immediately freed 50,000 slaves, with nearly all the rest (of the 3.1 million) freed as Union armies advanced.

Lecompton Constitution	The Lecompton Constitution was the second of four proposed constitutions for the state of Kansas (it was preceded by the Topeka Constitution and was followed by the Leavenworth and Wyandotte). The document was written in response to the anti-slavery position of the 1855 Topeka Constitution of James H. Lane and other free-state advocates. The territorial legislature, consisting mostly of slave-owners, met at the designated capital of Lecompton in September 1857 to produce a rival document.
Radical Republicans	The Radical Republicans were a loose faction of American politicians within the Republican Party from about 1854 (before the American Civil War) until the end of Reconstruction in 1877. They called themselves 'radicals' and were opposed during the war by moderates and conservative factions led by Abraham Lincoln and after the war by self-described 'conservatives' (in the South) and 'Liberals' (in the North). Radicals strongly opposed slavery during the war and after the war and distrusted ex-Confederates, demanding harsh policies for Reconstruction. During the war, Radical Republicans often opposed Lincoln in terms of selection of generals (especially his choice of George B. McClellan for top command) and his efforts to bring states back into the Union.
Republican Party	The Republican Party is one of the two major contemporary political parties in the United States, along with the Democratic Party. Founded by anti-slavery expansion activists in 1854, it is often called the Grand Old Party (GOP). The party's platform generally reflects American conservatism in the U.S. political spectrum and is considered center-right, in contrast to the more liberal-leaning Democrats.
England	England is a country that is part of the United Kingdom. It shares land borders with Scotland to the north and Wales to the west; the Irish Sea is to the north west, the Celtic Sea to the south west and the North Sea to the east, with the English Channel to the south separating it from continental Europe. Most of England comprises the central and southern part of the island of Great Britain in the North Atlantic.
Northwest Ordinance	The Northwest Ordinance was an act of the Congress of the Confederation of the United States. The primary effect of the ordinance was the creation of the Northwest Territory as the first organized territory of the United States out of the region south of the Great Lakes, north and west of the Ohio River, and east of the Mississippi River. On August 7, 1789, the U.S. Congress affirmed the Ordinance with slight modifications under the Constitution.

Chapter 13. The Coming of the Civil War

Dred Scott

Dred Scott was an African-American slave in the United States who unsuccessfully sued for his freedom and that of his wife and their two daughters in the Dred Scott v. Sandford case of 1857, popularly known as 'the Dred Scott Decision.' His case was based on the fact that although he and his wife Harriet Scott were slaves, he had lived with his master Dr. John Emerson in states and territories where slavery was illegal according to both state laws and the Northwest Ordinance of 1787, including Illinois and Minnesota (which was then part of the Wisconsin Territory). The United States Supreme Court decided 7-2 against Scott, finding that neither he nor any other person of African ancestry could claim citizenship in the United States, and therefore Scott could not bring suit in federal court under diversity of citizenship rules. Moreover, Scott's temporary residence outside Missouri did not bring about his emancipation under the Missouri Compromise, which the court ruled unconstitutional as it would improperly deprive Scott's owner of his legal property.

Freeport Doctrine

The Freeport Doctrine was articulated by Stephen A. Douglas at the second of the Lincoln-Douglas debates on August 27, 1858, in Freeport, Illinois. Lincoln tried to force Douglas to choose between the principle of popular sovereignty proposed by the Kansas-Nebraska Act and the majority decision of the United States Supreme Court in the case of Dred Scott v. Sandford, which stated that slavery could not legally be excluded from U.S. territories (since Douglas professed great respect for Supreme Court decisions, and accused the Republicans of disrespecting the court, yet this aspect of the Dred Scott decision was contrary to Douglas' views and politically unpopular in Illinois). Instead of making a direct choice, Douglas' response stated that despite the court's ruling, slavery could be prevented from any territory by the refusal of the people living in that territory to pass laws favorable to slavery.

Robert E. Lee

Robert Edward Lee (January 19, 1807 - October 12, 1870) was a career military officer who is best known for having commanded the Confederate Army of Northern Virginia in the American Civil War. The son of U.S. Revolutionary War hero, Henry ('Light Horse Harry') Lee III, and a top graduate of West Point, Robert E. Lee distinguished himself as an exceptional officer and combat engineer in the United States Army for 32 years before resigning to join the Confederate cause. By the end of the American Civil War, he was commanding general of the Confederate army.

Washington

Washington was one of the first steamboats to operate in the states of California and Oregon.

Operations in California

Washington operated in California on the Sacramento River. The vessel was purchased in California in 1851 by pioneer steamboat captain Alexander Sinclair Murray (b.1828).

Black Codes

The Black Codes were unofficial laws put in place in the United States to limit the basic human rights and civil liberties of blacks. Even though the U.S. constitution originally discriminated against blacks (as 'other persons') and both Northern and Southern states had passed discriminatory legislation from the early 19th century, the term Black Codes is used most often to refer to legislation passed by Southern states at the end of the Civil War to control the labor, migration and other activities of newly-freed slaves.

In Texas, the Eleventh Legislature produced these codes in 1866, right after the United States Civil War.

Hinton Rowan Helper

Hinton Rowan Helper was a Southern US critic of slavery during the 1850s. In 1857, he published a book which he dedicated to the 'nonslaveholding whites' of the South. The Impending Crisis of the South, written partly in North Carolina but published when the author was in the North, argued that slavery hurt the economic prospects of non-slaveholders, and was an impediment to the growth of the entire region of the South.

William H. Seward

William Henry Seward (May 16, 1801 - October 10, 1872) was the 12th Governor of New York, United States Senator and the United States Secretary of State under Abraham Lincoln and Andrew Johnson. A determined opponent of the spread of slavery in the years leading up to the American Civil War, he was a dominant figure in the Republican Party in its formative years, and was widely regarded as the leading contender for the party's presidential nomination in 1860 - yet his very outspokenness may have cost him the nomination. Despite his loss, he became a loyal member of Lincoln's wartime cabinet, and played a role in preventing foreign intervention early in the war. On the night of Lincoln's assassination, he survived an attempt on his life in the conspirators' effort to decapitate the Union government. As Johnson's Secretary of State, he engineered the purchase of Alaska from Russia in an act that was ridiculed at the time as 'Seward's Folly', but which somehow exemplified his character. His contemporary Carl Schurz described Seward as 'one of those spirits who sometimes will go ahead of public opinion instead of tamely following its footprints.'

Early life and career

Seward was born in Florida, New York, on May 16, 1801, one of five children of Samuel Sweezy Seward and his wife Mary Jennings Seward. Samuel Seward, described as 'a prosperous, domineering doctor and businessman,' was the founder of the S. S. Seward Institute, today a secondary school in the Florida Union Free School District.

Seward served as president of the S.S. Seward Institute after the death of his father, even while serving as Secretary of State during the Lincoln and Johnson administrations.

Seward studied law at Union College, graduating in 1820 with highest honors, and as a member of Phi Beta Kappa. He was admitted to the New York State Bar in 1821. In that same year, he met Frances Adeline Miller, a classmate of his sister Cornelia at Emma Willard's Troy Female Seminary and the daughter of Judge Elijah Miller of Auburn, New York. In 1823, he moved to Auburn where he entered into law partnership with Judge Miller, and married Frances Miller on October 20, 1824. They raised five children:

- Augustus Henry Seward (1826-1876)
- Frederick William Seward (1830-1915)
- Cornelia Seward (1836-1837)
- William Henry Seward, Jr. (1839-1920)
- Frances Adeline 'Fanny' Seward (1844-1866)
- Olive Risley Seward (1841-1908), adopted

Seward entered politics with the help of his friend Thurlow Weed, whom he had met by chance after a stagecoach accident. Seward was an as an Anti-Masonic member of the New York State Senate (7th D). from 1831 to 1834, sitting in the 54th, 55th, 56th and 57th New York State Legislatures. In 1834, the 33-year-old Seward was named the Whig party candidate for Governor of New York, but lost to incumbent Democrat William Marcy who won 52% of the vote to Seward's 48%.

From 1836 to 1838, Seward served as agent for a group of investors who had purchased the over 3-million-acre (12,000 km^2) western New York holdings of the Holland Land Company. He moved the land office from Mayville, NY to Westfield, New York, where he was successful in easing tensions between the investors and local landowners. On July 16, 1837, he delivered to the students and faculty of the newly formed Westfield Academy a Discourse on Education, in which he advocated for universal education.

In 1838, Seward again challenged Marcy, and was elected Governor of New York by a majority of 51.4% to Marcy's 48.6%. He was narrowly re-elected to a second two-year term in 1840. As a state senator and governor, Seward promoted progressive political policies including prison reform and increased spending on education. He supported state funding for schools for immigrants operated by their own clergy and taught in their native language. This support, which included Catholic parochial schools, came back to haunt him in the 1850s, when anti-Catholic feelings were high, especially among ex-Whigs in the Republican Party.

Seward developed his views about slavery while still a boy. His parents, like other Hudson Valley residents of the early 19th century, owned several slaves. (Slavery was slowly abolished in New York from 1797 to 1827 through a gradual mandated process). Seward recalled his preference as a child for the company and conversation of the slaves in his father's kitchen to the 'severe decorum' in his family's front parlor. He discerned very quickly the inequality between races, writing in later years 'I early came to the conclusion that something was wrong...and [that] determined me...to be an abolitionist.' This belief would stay with Seward through his life and permeate his career.

Seward's wife Frances was deeply committed to the abolitionist movement. In the 1850s, the Seward family opened their Auburn home as a safehouse to fugitive slaves. Seward's frequent travel and political work suggest that it was Frances who played the more active role in Auburn abolitionist activities. In the excitement following the rescue and safe transport of fugitive slave William 'Jerry' Henry in Syracuse on October 1, 1851, Frances wrote to her husband, 'two fugitives have gone to Canada--one of them our acquaintance John.' Another time she wrote, 'A man by the name of William Johnson will apply to you for assistance to purchase the freedom of his daughter. You will see that I have given him something by his book. I told him I thought you would give him more.'

In 1846 Seward became the center of controversy in his hometown when he defended, in separate cases, two convicts accused of murder. Henry Wyatt, a white man, was charged in the stabbing death of a fellow prison inmate; William Freeman, of African American and Native American ancestry, was accused of breaking into a home and stabbing four people to death. In both cases the defendants were mentally ill and had been severely abused while in prison. Seward, having long been an advocate of prison reform and better treatment for the insane, sought to prevent both men from being executed by using a relatively new defense of insanity. In a case involving mental illness with heavy racial overtones Seward argued, 'The color of the prisoner's skin, and the form of his features, are not impressed upon the spiritual immortal mind which works beneath. In spite of human pride, he is still your brother, and mine, in form and color accepted and approved by his Father, and yours, and mine, and bears equally with us the proudest inheritance of our race--the image of our Maker. Hold him then to be a Man.'

Later, Seward quoted Freeman's brother-in-law, praising his eloquence: 'They have made William Freeman what he is, a brute beast; they don't make anything else of any of our people but brute beasts; but when we violate their laws, then they want to punish us as if we were men.' In the end both men were convicted. Although Wyatt was executed, Freeman, whose conviction was reversed on Seward's successful appeal to the New York Supreme Court, died in his cell of tuberculosis.

United States Senator and Presidential Candidate

Seward supported the Whig candidate, General Zachary Taylor, in the presidential election of 1848. He said of Taylor, 'He is the most gentle-looking and amiable of men.' Taylor was a slaveholding plantation owner, but was friendly to Seward anyway.

William Seward was elected as U.S. Senator from New York as a Whig in 1849, and emerged as the leader of the anti-slavery 'Conscience Whigs'. Seward opposed the Compromise of 1850, and was thought to have encouraged Taylor in his supposed opposition. More recent scholarship suggests that Taylor was not under Seward's influence and would have accepted the Compromise if he had not died. Seward believed that slavery was morally wrong, and said so many times, outraging Southerners. He acknowledged that slavery was legal under the Constitution, but denied that the Constitution recognized or protected slavery. He famously remarked in 1850 that 'there is a higher law than the Constitution'. He continued to argue this point of view over the next ten years. He presented himself as the leading enemy of the Slave Power - that is, the perceived conspiracy of southern slaveowners to seize the government and defeat the progress of liberty.

Seward was an opponent of the Fugitive Slave Act, and he defended runaway slaves in court. He supported personal liberty laws.

In February 1855, he was re-elected as a Whig to the U.S. Senate, and joined the Republican Party when the New York Whigs merged with the Anti-Nebraskans later the same year. Seward did not seriously compete for the presidential nomination (won by John C. Frémont) in 1856, but sought and was expected to receive the nomination in 1860. In October 1858, he delivered a famous speech in which he argued that the political and economic systems of North and South were incompatible, and that, due to this 'irrepressible conflict,' the inevitable 'collision' of the two systems would eventually result in the nation becoming 'either entirely a slaveholding nation, or entirely a free-labor nation.' Like Lincoln, he believed slavery could and should be extinguished by long-run historical forces rather than by coercion or war.

In 1859, confident of gaining the presidential nomination and advised by his political ally and friend Thurlow Weed that he would be better off avoiding political gatherings where his words might be misinterpreted by one faction or another, Seward left the country for an eight-month tour of Europe that included a visit to Syria, where Ayub Beg Tarabulsy gave him several Arabian horses. During that hiatus, his lesser-known rival Abraham Lincoln worked diligently to line up support in case Seward failed to win on the first ballot. After returning to the United States, Seward gave a conciliatory, pro-Union Senate speech that reassured moderates but alienated some radical Republicans. (Observing events from Europe, Karl Marx, who was ideologically sympathetic to Frémont, contemptuously regarded Seward as a 'Republican Richelieu' and the 'Demosthenes of the Republican Party' who had sabotaged Frémont's presidential ambitions). Around the same time, his friend Horace Greeley turned against him, opposing Seward on the grounds that his radical reputation made him unelectable. When Lincoln won the nomination, Seward loyally supported him and made a long speaking tour of the West in the autumn of 1860.

Secretary of State

'Our population is destined to roll its resistless waves to the icy barriers of the north, and to encounter oriental civilization on the shores of the Pacific.' --William H. Seward, 1846

Abraham Lincoln appointed Seward his Secretary of State in 1861. Seward played an integral role in resolving the Trent Affair and in negotiating the ensuing Lyons-Seward Treaty of 1862, which set forth strong measures by which the United States and Great Britain agreed to enforce an end to the Atlantic slave trade.

Seward pursued his vision of American expansion. 'Give me only this assurance, that there never be an unlawful resistance by an armed force to the ... United States, and give me fifty, forty, thirty more years of life, and I will engage to give you the possession of the American continent and the control of the world.' Having argued for taking American possession of vulnerable but useful places such as the Danish West Indies, Samaná, Panama, and Hawaii, Seward oversaw the annexation of only one, that of the Brook Islands in 1867. Despite minimal Congressional support, though, he developed American influence in the Hawaiian Islands, as well as in Japan and China to some extent.

Despite his endorsement of expansionist policies, Seward also strongly advocated non-interventionism. After Tsar Alexander II put down the 1863 January Uprising in Poland, French Emperor Napoleon III asked the United States to 'join in a protest to the Tsar.' Seward declined, 'defending 'our policy of non-intervention -- straight, absolute, and peculiar as it may seem to other nations," and insisted that '[t]he American people must be content to recommend the cause of human progress by the wisdom with which they should exercise the powers of self-government, forbearing at all times, and in every way, from foreign alliances, intervention, and interference.'

Assassination Attempt

On the night of April 14, 1865, Lewis Powell, an associate and co-conspirator of John Wilkes Booth, attempted to assassinate Seward at his Washington D.C. home. Powell's attack on Seward was meticulously coordinated with Booth's attack on President Abraham Lincoln and George Atzerodt's attack on Vice President Andrew Johnson in order to maximize the element of surprise and to sever the continuity of the United States government (it should be noted, however, that Atzerodt failed to follow through on his attack). Another member of the conspiracy, David Herold, led Powell to the Seward home on horseback and was responsible for holding Powell's horse while he committed the attack as well as guiding him out of the city during their escape. Powell was able to gain access to the Seward home by telling the butler, William H. Bell, that he was delivering medicine for Seward (who was bed-ridden from a carriage accident which had gravely injured him on April 5, 1865).

Upon entry to the home, Powell began up the stairs, but was stopped at the top of the stairs by Frederick, the Secretary's eldest son. Frederick told Powell that his father was asleep and that he (Frederick) would take the medicine to him. Unsure of what to do, Powell turned around and began descending the stairs, but then suddenly swung back around, drew a pistol, and pointed it at Frederick's head. The pistol misfired. Realizing he needed to act quickly, Powell ruthlessly began beating Frederick over the head with the barrel of his gun. The force of Powell's blows crippled Frederick Seward and left him sprawled on the floor, floating in and out of consciousness, in a pool of blood. Powell's gun was also rendered completely useless, as it had become jammed during the melee.

In Secretary Seward's bedroom was his daughter, Fanny Seward. Hearing the loud noises coming from the second floor hallway, Fanny opened the door to see her brother slumped on the floor and a wide-eyed Powell charging directly towards her, a dagger in his hand. Powell burst through the door, threw Fanny Seward to the side, and jumped on the Secretary's bed, repeatedly stabbing him in the face and neck area. Powell also attacked and injured another son (Augustus), and a soldier and nurse (Sgt. George Robinson) who had been assigned to stay with Seward. Outside the home, David Herold, who could clearly hear the screams coming from the house, fled with both horses, leaving Powell to fend for himself. Powell, convinced that he had mortally wounded the Secretary, fled down the stairs, and stabbed a messenger, Emerick Hansell, who had arrived just as Powell was escaping; Hansell was rendered permanently paralyzed from the stabbing. All five men that were injured that night survived, although Secretary Seward would carry the facial scars from the attack for the rest of his life. The events of that night took their toll on his wife, Frances, who died June 1865. His daughter Fanny died of tuberculosis in October 1866.

Powell was captured the next day (hiding in a tree in Washington D.C). and was executed on July 7, 1865, along with David Herold, George Atzerodt, and Mary Surratt, the three others convicted as conspirators in the Lincoln assassination.

Although it took Seward several months to recover from his wounds, he emerged as a major force in the administration of the new president, Andrew Johnson. He frequently defended his more moderate reconciliation policies towards the South, to the point of enraging Radical Republicans who had once regarded Seward as their ally.

In the fall of 1866, Seward joined Johnson, as well as Ulysses S. Grant and the young General George Armstrong Custer, along with several other administration figures, on the president's ill-fated 'Swing Around the Circle' campaign trip.

At one point Seward became so ill, probably from cholera, that he was sent back to Washington in a special car. Both Johnson and Grant, as well as several members of the Seward family, thought the Secretary was near death. But as with his April 1865 stabbing, Seward surprised many by making a good recovery.

The purchase of Alaska

Seward's most famous achievement as Secretary of State was his successful acquisition of Alaska from Russia. On March 30, 1867, he completed negotiations for the territory, which involved the purchase of 586,412 square miles (1,518,800 km²) of territory (more than twice the area of Texas) for $7,200,000, or approximately 2 cents per acre (equivalent to US$95 million in 2005). The purchase of this frontier land was variously mocked by the public as Seward's Folly, 'Seward's Icebox,' and Andrew Johnson's 'polar bear garden.' Alaska celebrates the purchase on Seward's Day, the last Monday of March. When asked what he considered to be his greatest achievement as Secretary of State, Seward replied 'The purchase of Alaska--but it will take the people a generation to find it out'.

Later life

Seward retired as Secretary of State after Ulysses S. Grant took office as president. During his last years, Seward traveled and wrote prolifically. Most notably, he traveled around the world in fourteen months and two days from August, 1870 to October, 1871. On October 10, 1872, Seward died in his office in his home in Auburn, New York, after having difficulty breathing. His last words were to his children saying, 'Love one another.' He was buried in Fort Hill Cemetery in Auburn, New York, with his wife and two children, Cornelia and Fanny. His headstone reads, 'He was faithful.'

His son, Frederick, edited and published his memoirs in three volumes.

In 1967, a century after the Alaska Purchase, the actor, Joseph Cotten, portrayed Seward in 'The Freeman Story', a part of his NBC anthology series, The Joseph Cotten Show. Virginia Gregg played Fanny Seward. Popular actor, Richard Mulligan, portrayed William Seward in the 1988 Lincoln mini-series, 'Random Letters'.

Seward's homes in Auburn and Florida, New York

Seward and his family owned a home in Auburn, New York which is now a museum; it was built in 1816 by Seward's father-in-law, Judge Elijah Miller. Seward married the Judge's daughter, Frances, in 1824 on the condition that they would live with Miller in his Auburn home. Seward made many changes to the home, adding an addition in the late 1840s and another one in 1866. When he died, Seward left the home to his son, William Seward, Jr.; it passed on to his grandson, William Henry Seward III, in 1920. At his death in 1951, it became a museum that opened to the public in 1955. Four generations of the family's artifacts are contained within the museum, located at 33 South Street in Auburn. The museum is open Tuesday through Saturday from 10am to 5pm.

Meanwhile, Seward's birthplace in Florida, New York was bought by the village in 2010, with the purpose of refurbishing it. (The property actually contains two houses: one in back--Seward's actual birthplace--which was converted into a barn; and one in front, built in the 1890s, used by the family that lived there for many years). The property (after spending an estimated $200,000, to be raised by private donations) is expected to be turned into a museum and opened to the public by 2013.

Legacy

- The purchase of Alaska.
- The Guano Islands Act of 1856
- The $50-dollar Treasury note, also called the Coin note, of the Series 1891, features a portrait of Seward on the obverse. Examples of this note are very rare and would likely se for about $50,000 at auction.
- His house in Auburn, New York is open as a public museum.
- The house in which he lived in Westfield, New York is now home to a bed and breakfast.
- He was a name partner of the law firm of Blatchford, Seward ' Griswold, today known as Cravath, Swaine ' Moore.
- Was famous in his lifetime for his red hair and energetic way of walking. Henry Adams described him as 'wonderfully resembling' a parrot in 'manner and profile'.

Memorials

- Seward Avenue in Auburn. Also in Auburn, Frances Street, Augustus Street, and Frederick Street are named for members of his family. The four streets form a block.
- Seward Elementary School in Auburn.
- Seward Place in Schenectady, New York, on the west side of the Union College campus.
- Seward Park in Auburn, New York.
- Seward Park in the Lower East Side of Manhattan.
- Seward Park in Seattle, Washington.
- Seward Square park in Washington, D.C..
- The Seward Peninsula in Alaska.
- City of Seward, on Alaska's Kenai Peninsula
- Seward, Illinois; Seward, Kansas; Seward, New York; Seward, Nebraska; and Seward, Alaska.
- A hamburger is called 'Seward's Folly' at West Rib Deli ' Pub in Talkeetna, Alaska is named for him.
- Seward County, Nebraska
- Seward's Success, Alaska, an unbuilt community to be enclosed by a dome.
- The Seward neighborhood of Minneapolis, Minnesota
- Seward Mountain (4,361 feet, 1,329 m), one of the Adirondack High Peaks, the highest point in Franklin County.
- At Union College, the campus bus is known as Seward's Trolley, a pun on Seward's Folly
- Seward High School in his hometown of Florida is named for his father, Dr. Samuel

John Bell	John Bell was a Hudson's Bay Company governor and explorer. In 1839, he was sent to explore the land west of the Mackenzie River. With the assistance of Alexander Kennedy Isbister, he established Fort McPherson, Northwest Territories on the Peel River not far from the Mackenzie, and explored the Peel into what is now the Yukon Territory.
Constitutional Union Party	The Constitutional Union Party was a political party in the United States created in 1860. It was made up of conservative former Whigs who wanted to avoid disunion over the slavery issue. These former Whigs (some of whom had been under the banner of the Opposition Party in 1854-58) teamed up with former Know-Nothings and a few Southern Democrats who were against disunion to form the Constitutional Union Party. Its name comes from its extremely simple platform, a simple resolution 'to recognize no political principle other than the Constitution...the Union...and the Enforcement of the Laws.' They hoped that by failing to take a firm stand either for or against slavery or its expansion, the issue could be pushed aside.
South Carolina	South Carolina is a state in the Deep South that borders Georgia to the south and North Carolina to the north. Originally part of the Province of Carolina, the Province of South Carolina was one of the 13 colonies that declared independence from the British Crown during the American Revolution. The colony was originally named by King Charles II of England in honor of his father Charles I, as Carolus is Latin for Charles.
Union	During the American Civil War, the Union was a name used to refer to the federal government of the United States, which was supported by the twenty free states and five border slave states. It was opposed by 11 Southern slave states that had declared a secession to join together to form the Confederacy. Although the Union states included the Western states of California, Oregon, and (after 1864) Nevada, as well as states generally considered to be part of the Midwest, the Union has been also often loosely referred to as 'the North', both then and now.
Union Party	The Union Party was a short-lived political party in the United States, formed in 1936 by a coalition of radio priest Father Charles Coughlin, old-age pension advocate Francis Townsend, and Gerald L. K. Smith, who had taken control of Huey Long's Share Our Wealth movement after Long's assassination in 1935. Each of those people hoped to channel their wide followings into support for the Union Party, which proposed a populist alternative to the New Deal reforms of Franklin D. Roosevelt during the Great Depression.

Many observers at the time felt that there was a place for a party more radical than Roosevelt and the Democrats but still non-Marxist in the political spectrum of the time.

Rumored political aspirations of Huey Long

Although many people expected Huey Long, the colorful Democratic senator from Louisiana, to run as a third-party candidate with his 'Share Our Wealth' program as his platform, his bid was cut short when he was assassinated in September of 1935.

Gettysburg Campaign

The Gettysburg Campaign was a series of battles fought in June and July 1863, during the American Civil War. After his victory in the Battle of Chancellorsville, Confederate General Robert E. Lee's Army of Northern Virginia moved north for offensive operations in Maryland and Pennsylvania. The Union Army of the Potomac, commanded by Maj.

1. The phenomenon of slaves running away and seeking to regain their freedom is as old as the institution of slavery itself. In the history of slavery in the United States, '_________s' (or runaway slaves) were slaves who had escaped from their master to travel to a place where slavery was banned or illegal. Many went to northern territories including Pennsylvania and Massachusetts until the _________ Act of 1850 was passed.

   a. Fugitive Slave Clause
   b. Fort Gadsden
   c. Fugitive slave
   d. Genius of Universal Emancipation

2. The _________ were unofficial laws put in place in the United States to limit the basic human rights and civil liberties of blacks. Even though the U.S. constitution originally discriminated against blacks (as 'other persons') and both Northern and Southern states had passed discriminatory legislation from the early 19th century, the term _________ is used most often to refer to legislation passed by Southern states at the end of the Civil War to control the labor, migration and other activities of newly-freed slaves.

   In Texas, the Eleventh Legislature produced these codes in 1866, right after the United States Civil War.

   a. Digital Transition Content Security Act
   b. Augustine Warner
   c. Nicolas Martiau
   d. Black Codes

3. William Henry Seward (May 16, 1801 - October 10, 1872) was the 12th Governor of New York, United States Senator and the United States Secretary of State under Abraham Lincoln and Andrew Johnson. A determined opponent of the spread of slavery in the years leading up to the American Civil War, he was a dominant figure in the Republican Party in its formative years, and was widely regarded as the leading contender for the party's presidential nomination in 1860 - yet his very outspokenness may have cost him the nomination. Despite his loss, he became a loyal member of Lincoln's wartime cabinet, and played a role in preventing foreign intervention early in the war. On the night of Lincoln's assassination, he survived an attempt on his life in the conspirators' effort to decapitate the Union government. As Johnson's Secretary of State, he engineered the purchase of Alaska from Russia in an act that was ridiculed at the time as 'Seward's Folly', but which somehow exemplified his character. His contemporary Carl Schurz described Seward as 'one of those spirits who sometimes will go ahead of public opinion instead of tamely following its footprints.'

   Early life and career

Seward was born in Florida, New York, on May 16, 1801, one of five children of Samuel Sweezy Seward and his wife Mary Jennings Seward. Samuel Seward, described as 'a prosperous, domineering doctor and businessman,' was the founder of the S. S. Seward Institute, today a secondary school in the Florida Union Free School District.

Seward served as president of the S.S. Seward Institute after the death of his father, even while serving as Secretary of State during the Lincoln and Johnson administrations.

Seward studied law at Union College, graduating in 1820 with highest honors, and as a member of Phi Beta Kappa. He was admitted to the New York State Bar in 1821. In that same year, he met Frances Adeline Miller, a classmate of his sister Cornelia at Emma Willard's Troy Female Seminary and the daughter of Judge Elijah Miller of Auburn, New York. In 1823, he moved to Auburn where he entered into law partnership with Judge Miller, and married Frances Miller on October 20, 1824. They raised five children:

- Augustus Henry Seward (1826-1876)
- Frederick William Seward (1830-1915)
- Cornelia Seward (1836-1837)
- William Henry Seward, Jr. (1839-1920)
- Frances Adeline 'Fanny' Seward (1844-1866)
- Olive Risley Seward (1841-1908), adopted

Seward entered politics with the help of his friend Thurlow Weed, whom he had met by chance after a stagecoach accident. Seward was an as an Anti-Masonic member of the New York State Senate (7th D). from 1831 to 1834, sitting in the 54th, 55th, 56th and 57th New York State Legislatures. In 1834, the 33-year-old Seward was named the Whig party candidate for Governor of New York, but lost to incumbent Democrat William Marcy who won 52% of the vote to Seward's 48%.

From 1836 to 1838, Seward served as agent for a group of investors who had purchased the over 3-million-acre (12,000 km^2) western New York holdings of the Holland Land Company. He moved the land office from Mayville, NY to Westfield, New York, where he was successful in easing tensions between the investors and local landowners. On July 16, 1837, he delivered to the students and faculty of the newly formed Westfield Academy a Discourse on Education, in which he advocated for universal education.

In 1838, Seward again challenged Marcy, and was elected Governor of New York by a majority of 51.4% to Marcy's 48.6%. He was narrowly re-elected to a second two-year term in 1840. As a state senator and governor, Seward promoted progressive political policies including prison reform and increased spending on education. He supported state funding for schools for immigrants operated by their own clergy and taught in their native language. This support, which included Catholic parochial schools, came back to haunt him in the 1850s, when anti-Catholic feelings were high, especially among ex-Whigs in the Republican Party.

Seward developed his views about slavery while still a boy. His parents, like other Hudson Valley residents of the early 19th century, owned several slaves. (Slavery was slowly abolished in New York from 1797 to 1827 through a gradual mandated process). Seward recalled his preference as a child for the company and conversation of the slaves in his father's kitchen to the 'severe decorum' in his family's front parlor. He discerned very quickly the inequality between races, writing in later years 'I early came to the conclusion that something was wrong...and [that] determined me...to be an abolitionist.' This belief would stay with Seward through his life and permeate his career.

Seward's wife Frances was deeply committed to the abolitionist movement. In the 1850s, the Seward family opened their Auburn home as a safehouse to fugitive slaves. Seward's frequent travel and political work suggest that it was Frances who played the more active role in Auburn abolitionist activities. In the excitement following the rescue and safe transport of fugitive slave William 'Jerry' Henry in Syracuse on October 1, 1851, Frances wrote to her husband, 'two fugitives have gone to Canada--one of them our acquaintance John.' Another time she wrote, 'A man by the name of William Johnson will apply to you for assistance to purchase the freedom of his daughter. You will see that I have given him something by his book. I told him I thought you would give him more.'

In 1846 Seward became the center of controversy in his hometown when he defended, in separate cases, two convicts accused of murder. Henry Wyatt, a white man, was charged in the stabbing death of a fellow prison inmate; William Freeman, of African American and Native American ancestry, was accused of breaking into a home and stabbing four people to death. In both cases the defendants were mentally ill and had been severely abused while in prison. Seward, having long been an advocate of prison reform and better treatment for the insane, sought to prevent both men from being executed by using a relatively new defense of insanity. In a case involving mental illness with heavy racial overtones Seward argued, 'The color of the prisoner's skin, and the form of his features, are not impressed upon the spiritual immortal mind which works beneath. In spite of human pride, he is still your brother, and mine, in form and color accepted and approved by his Father, and yours, and mine, and bears equally with us the proudest inheritance of our race--the image of our Maker. Hold him then to be a Man.'

Later, Seward quoted Freeman's brother-in-law, praising his eloquence: 'They have made William Freeman what he is, a brute beast; they don't make anything else of any of our people but brute beasts; but when we violate their laws, then they want to punish us as if we were men.' In the end both men were convicted. Although Wyatt was executed, Freeman, whose conviction was reversed on Seward's successful appeal to the New York Supreme Court, died in his cell of tuberculosis.

United States Senator and Presidential Candidate

Seward supported the Whig candidate, General Zachary Taylor, in the presidential election of 1848. He said of Taylor, 'He is the most gentle-looking and amiable of men.' Taylor was a slaveholding plantation owner, but was friendly to Seward anyway.

William Seward was elected as U.S. Senator from New York as a Whig in 1849, and emerged as the leader of the anti-slavery 'Conscience Whigs'. Seward opposed the Compromise of 1850, and was thought to have encouraged Taylor in his supposed opposition. More recent scholarship suggests that Taylor was not under Seward's influence and would have accepted the Compromise if he had not died. Seward believed that slavery was morally wrong, and said so many times, outraging Southerners. He acknowledged that slavery was legal under the Constitution, but denied that the Constitution recognized or protected slavery. He famously remarked in 1850 that 'there is a higher law than the Constitution'. He continued to argue this point of view over the next ten years. He presented himself as the leading enemy of the Slave Power - that is, the perceived conspiracy of southern slaveowners to seize the government and defeat the progress of liberty.

Seward was an opponent of the Fugitive Slave Act, and he defended runaway slaves in court. He supported personal liberty laws.

In February 1855, he was re-elected as a Whig to the U.S. Senate, and joined the Republican Party when the New York Whigs merged with the Anti-Nebraskans later the same year. Seward did not seriously compete for the presidential nomination (won by John C. Frémont) in 1856, but sought and was expected to receive the nomination in 1860. In October 1858, he delivered a famous speech in which he argued that the political and economic systems of North and South were incompatible, and that, due to this 'irrepressible conflict,' the inevitable 'collision' of the two systems would eventually result in the nation becoming 'either entirely a slaveholding nation, or entirely a free-labor nation.' Like Lincoln, he believed slavery could and should be extinguished by long-run historical forces rather than by coercion or war.

In 1859, confident of gaining the presidential nomination and advised by his political ally and friend Thurlow Weed that he would be better off avoiding political gatherings where his words might be misinterpreted by one faction or another, Seward left the country for an eight-month tour of Europe that included a visit to Syria, where Ayub Beg Tarabulsy gave him several Arabian horses. During that hiatus, his lesser-known rival Abraham Lincoln worked diligently to line up support in case Seward failed to win on the first ballot. After returning to the United States, Seward gave a conciliatory, pro-Union Senate speech that reassured moderates but alienated some radical Republicans. (Observing events from Europe, Karl Marx, who was ideologically sympathetic to Frémont, contemptuously regarded Seward as a 'Republican Richelieu' and the 'Demosthenes of the Republican Party' who had sabotaged Frémont's presidential ambitions). Around the same time, his friend Horace Greeley turned against him, opposing Seward on the grounds that his radical reputation made him unelectable. When Lincoln won the nomination, Seward loyally supported him and made a long speaking tour of the West in the autumn of 1860.

Secretary of State

'Our population is destined to roll its resistless waves to the icy barriers of the north, and to encounter oriental civilization on the shores of the Pacific.' --_________, 1846

Abraham Lincoln appointed Seward his Secretary of State in 1861. Seward played an integral role in resolving the Trent Affair and in negotiating the ensuing Lyons-Seward Treaty of 1862, which set forth strong measures by which the United States and Great Britain agreed to enforce an end to the Atlantic slave trade.

Seward pursued his vision of American expansion. 'Give me only this assurance, that there never be an unlawful resistance by an armed force to the ... United States, and give me fifty, forty, thirty more years of life, and I will engage to give you the possession of the American continent and the control of the world.' Having argued for taking American possession of vulnerable but useful places such as the Danish West Indies, Samaná, Panama, and Hawaii, Seward oversaw the annexation of only one, that of the Brook Islands in 1867. Despite minimal Congressional support, though, he developed American influence in the Hawaiian Islands, as well as in Japan and China to some extent.

Despite his endorsement of expansionist policies, Seward also strongly advocated non-interventionism. After Tsar Alexander II put down the 1863 January Uprising in Poland, French Emperor Napoleon III asked the United States to 'join in a protest to the Tsar.' Seward declined, 'defending 'our policy of non-intervention -- straight, absolute, and peculiar as it may seem to other nations,'' and insisted that '[t]he American people must be content to recommend the cause of human progress by the wisdom with which they should exercise the powers of self-government, forbearing at all times, and in every way, from foreign alliances, intervention, and interference.'

Assassination Attempt

On the night of April 14, 1865, Lewis Powell, an associate and co-conspirator of John Wilkes Booth, attempted to assassinate Seward at his Washington D.C. home. Powell's attack on Seward was meticulously coordinated with Booth's attack on President Abraham Lincoln and George Atzerodt's attack on Vice President Andrew Johnson in order to maximize the element of surprise and to sever the continuity of the United States government (it should be noted, however, that Atzerodt failed to follow through on his attack). Another member of the conspiracy, David Herold, led Powell to the Seward home on horseback and was responsible for holding Powell's horse while he committed the attack as well as guiding him out of the city during their escape. Powell was able to gain access to the Seward home by telling the butler, William H. Bell, that he was delivering medicine for Seward (who was bed-ridden from a carriage accident which had gravely injured him on April 5, 1865).

Upon entry to the home, Powell began up the stairs, but was stopped at the top of the stairs by Frederick, the Secretary's eldest son. Frederick told Powell that his father was asleep and that he (Frederick) would take the medicine to him. Unsure of what to do, Powell turned around and began descending the stairs, but then suddenly swung back around, drew a pistol, and pointed it at Frederick's head. The pistol misfired. Realizing he needed to act quickly, Powell ruthlessly began beating Frederick over the head with the barrel of his gun. The force of Powell's blows crippled Frederick Seward and left him sprawled on the floor, floating in and out of consciousness, in a pool of blood. Powell's gun was also rendered completely useless, as it had become jammed during the melee.

In Secretary Seward's bedroom was his daughter, Fanny Seward. Hearing the loud noises coming from the second floor hallway, Fanny opened the door to see her brother slumped on the floor and a wide-eyed Powell charging directly towards her, a dagger in his hand. Powell burst through the door, threw Fanny Seward to the side, and jumped on the Secretary's bed, repeatedly stabbing him in the face and neck area. Powell also attacked and injured another son (Augustus), and a soldier and nurse (Sgt. George Robinson) who had been assigned to stay with Seward. Outside the home, David Herold, who could clearly hear the screams coming from the house, fled with both horses, leaving Powell to fend for himself. Powell, convinced that he had mortally wounded the Secretary, fled down the stairs, and stabbed a messenger, Emerick Hansell, who had arrived just as Powell was escaping; Hansell was rendered permanently paralyzed from the stabbing. All five men that were injured that night survived, although Secretary Seward would carry the facial scars from the attack for the rest of his life. The events of that night took their toll on his wife, Frances, who died June 1865. His daughter Fanny died of tuberculosis in October 1866.

Powell was captured the next day (hiding in a tree in Washington D.C). and was executed on July 7, 1865, along with David Herold, George Atzerodt, and Mary Surratt, the three others convicted as conspirators in the Lincoln assassination.

Although it took Seward several months to recover from his wounds, he emerged as a major force in the administration of the new president, Andrew Johnson. He frequently defended his more moderate reconciliation policies towards the South, to the point of enraging Radical Republicans who had once regarded Seward as their ally.

In the fall of 1866, Seward joined Johnson, as well as Ulysses S. Grant and the young General George Armstrong Custer, along with several other administration figures, on the president's ill-fated 'Swing Around the Circle' campaign trip.

At one point Seward became so ill, probably from cholera, that he was sent back to Washington in a special car. Both Johnson and Grant, as well as several members of the Seward family, thought the Secretary was near death. But as with his April 1865 stabbing, Seward surprised many by making a good recovery.

The purchase of Alaska

Seward's most famous achievement as Secretary of State was his successful acquisition of Alaska from Russia. On March 30, 1867, he completed negotiations for the territory, which involved the purchase of 586,412 square miles (1,518,800 km^2) of territory (more than twice the area of Texas) for $7,200,000, or approximately 2 cents per acre (equivalent to US$95 million in 2005). The purchase of this frontier land was variously mocked by the public as Seward's Folly, 'Seward's Icebox,' and Andrew Johnson's 'polar bear garden.' Alaska celebrates the purchase on Seward's Day, the last Monday of March. When asked what he considered to be his greatest achievement as Secretary of State, Seward replied 'The purchase of Alaska--but it will take the people a generation to find it out'.

Later life

Seward retired as Secretary of State after Ulysses S. Grant took office as president. During his last years, Seward traveled and wrote prolifically. Most notably, he traveled around the world in fourteen months and two days from August, 1870 to October, 1871. On October 10, 1872, Seward died in his office in his home in Auburn, New York, after having difficulty breathing. His last words were to his children saying, 'Love one another.' He was buried in Fort Hill Cemetery in Auburn, New York, with his wife and two children, Cornelia and Fanny. His headstone reads, 'He was faithful.'

His son, Frederick, edited and published his memoirs in three volumes.

In 1967, a century after the Alaska Purchase, the actor, Joseph Cotten, portrayed Seward in 'The Freeman Story', a part of his NBC anthology series, The Joseph Cotten Show. Virginia Gregg played Fanny Seward. Popular actor, Richard Mulligan, portrayed William Seward in the 1988 Lincoln mini-series, 'Random Letters'.

Seward's homes in Auburn and Florida, New York

Seward and his family owned a home in Auburn, New York which is now a museum; it was built in 1816 by Seward's father-in-law, Judge Elijah Miller. Seward married the Judge's daughter, Frances, in 1824 on the condition that they would live with Miller in his Auburn home. Seward made many changes to the home, adding an addition in the late 1840s and another one in 1866. When he died, Seward left the home to his son, William Seward, Jr.; it passed on to his grandson, William Henry Seward III, in 1920. At his death in 1951, it became a museum that opened to the public in 1955. Four generations of the family's artifacts are contained within the museum, located at 33 South Street in Auburn. The museum is open Tuesday through Saturday from 10am to 5pm.

Meanwhile, Seward's birthplace in Florida, New York was bought by the village in 2010, with the purpose of refurbishing it. (The property actually contains two houses: one in back--Seward's actual birthplace--which was converted into a barn; and one in front, built in the 1890s, used by the family that lived there for many years). The property (after spending an estimated $200,000, to be raised by private donations) is expected to be turned into a museum and opened to the public by 2013.

Legacy

- The purchase of Alaska.
- The Guano Islands Act of 1856
- The $50-dollar Treasury note, also called the Coin note, of the Series 1891, features a portrait of Seward on the obverse. Examples of this note are very rare and would likely sell for about $50,000 at auction.
- His house in Auburn, New York is open as a public museum.
- The house in which he lived in Westfield, New York is now home to a bed and breakfast.
- He was a name partner of the law firm of Blatchford, Seward ' Griswold, today known as Cravath, Swaine ' Moore.
- Was famous in his lifetime for his red hair and energetic way of walking. Henry Adams described him as 'wonderfully resembling' a parrot in 'manner and profile'.

Memorials

- Seward Avenue in Auburn. Also in Auburn, Frances Street, Augustus Street, and Frederick Street are name for members of his family. The four streets form a block.
- Seward Elementary School in Auburn.
- Seward Place in Schenectady, New York, on the west side of the Union College campus.
- Seward Park in Auburn, New York.
- Seward Park in the Lower East Side of Manhattan.
- Seward Park in Seattle, Washington.
- Seward Square park in Washington, D.C..
- The Seward Peninsula in Alaska.
- City of Seward, on Alaska's Kenai Peninsula
- Seward, Illinois; Seward, Kansas; Seward, New York; Seward, Nebraska; and Seward, Alaska.
- A hamburger is called 'Seward's Folly' at West Rib Deli ' Pub in Talkeetna, Alaska is named for him.
- Seward County, Nebraska
- Seward's Success, Alaska, an unbuilt community to be enclosed by a dome.
- The Seward neighborhood of Minneapolis, Minnesota
- Seward Mountain (4,361 feet, 1,329 m), one of the Adirondack High Peaks, the highest point in Franklin County.
- At Union College, the campus bus is known as Seward's Trolley, a pun on Seward's Folly.
- Seward High School in his hometown of Florida is named for his father, Dr. Samuel Seward.
- Statues of him in Seward Park in Auburn, in Madison Square Park in New York City, on the grounds of the Z J. Loussac Public Library in Anchorage, Alaska, and in Volunteer Park in Seattle (not facing towards Alaska)
- The William Henry Seward Memorial in Florida, with a bust sculpted by Daniel Chester French.
- Seward Park Housing Corporation, a housing cooperative in the Lower East Side of Manhattan

---

a. Thomas Gage
b. William H. Seward
c. Charles Brantley Aycock
d. Francisco de Montejo

4. _________, Jr. was the 15th President of the United States, from 1857 to 1861, and the last president to be born in the 18th century. He is the only president from Pennsylvania and the only president who was a life-long bachelor.

a. James Buchanan
b. Thomas Sumter
c. Martin Van Buren
d. John Tyler

5. The _________ was an agreement passed in 1820 between the pro-slavery and anti-slavery factions in the United States Congress, involving primarily the regulation of slavery in the western territories. It prohibited slavery in the former Louisiana Territory north of the parallel 36°30′ north except within the boundaries of the proposed state of Missouri. Prior to the agreement, the House of Representatives had refused to accept this compromise, and a conference committee was appointed.

a. Missouri Fur Company
b. Hank Monk
c. Missouri Compromise
d. Battle of Mount Gray

ANSWER KEY
Chapter 13. The Coming of the Civil War

1. c
2. d
3. b
4. a
5. c

CHAPTER OUTLINE: KEY TERMS, PEOPLE, PLACES, CONCEPTS
Chapter 14

The War to Save the Union

______ Fort Pickens

______ Fort Sumter

______ William H. Seward

______ Republican Party

______ Union

______ Union Army

______ Niagara

______ President

______ Anaconda Plan

______ Democratic Party

______ Emancipation Proclamation

______ PLANS

______ Politics

______ Copperheads

______ Ex parte Merryman

______ Race riot

______ Radical Republicans

______ Alabama

______ Glorieta Pass Battlefield

Chapter 14. The War to Save the Union

__________ Indian American

__________ Albert Sidney Johnston

__________ James Murray Mason

__________ Plains Indians

__________ USS San Jacinto

__________ Robert Allan Brown

__________ Andrew Jackson

__________ African American

__________ Black Codes

__________ Frederick Douglass

__________ Gettysburg Campaign

__________ Massachusetts

__________ Joseph Hooker

__________ Homestead Act

__________ Land grant

__________ Tecumseh

__________ Andrew Johnson

__________ Absalom Jones

__________ Appomattox Court House

Fort Pickens

Fort Pickens is a pentagonal historic United States military fort on Santa Rosa Island in the Pensacola, Florida, area. It is named after American Revolutionary War hero Andrew Pickens. The fort was completed in 1834 and remained in use until 1947. Fort Pickens is currently part of the Gulf Islands National Seashore, and as such, is administered by the National Park Service.

Fort Sumter

Fort Sumter is a Third System masonry coastal fortification located in Charleston harbor, South Carolina. The fort is best known as the site upon which the shots initiating the American Civil War were fired, at the Battle of Fort Sumter.

Construction

Named after General Thomas Sumter, Revolutionary War hero, Fort Sumter was built following the War of 1812, as one of a series of fortifications on the southern U.S. coast.

William H. Seward

William Henry Seward (May 16, 1801 - October 10, 1872) was the 12th Governor of New York, United States Senator and the United States Secretary of State under Abraham Lincoln and Andrew Johnson. A determined opponent of the spread of slavery in the years leading up to the American Civil War, he was a dominant figure in the Republican Party in its formative years, and was widely regarded as the leading contender for the party's presidential nomination in 1860 - yet his very outspokenness may have cost him the nomination. Despite his loss, he became a loyal member of Lincoln's wartime cabinet, and played a role in preventing foreign intervention early in the war. On the night of Lincoln's assassination, he survived an attempt on his life in the conspirators' effort to decapitate the Union government. As Johnson's Secretary of State, he engineered the purchase of Alaska from Russia in an act that was ridiculed at the time as 'Seward's Folly', but which somehow exemplified his character. His contemporary Carl Schurz described Seward as 'one of those spirits who sometimes will go ahead of public opinion instead of tamely following its footprints.'

Early life and career

Seward was born in Florida, New York, on May 16, 1801, one of five children of Samuel Sweezy Seward and his wife Mary Jennings Seward. Samuel Seward, described as 'a prosperous, domineering doctor and businessman,' was the founder of the S. S. Seward Institute, today a secondary school in the Florida Union Free School District.

Seward served as president of the S.S. Seward Institute after the death of his father, even while serving as Secretary of State during the Lincoln and Johnson administrations.

Seward studied law at Union College, graduating in 1820 with highest honors, and as a member of Phi Beta Kappa. He was admitted to the New York State Bar in 1821. In that same year, he met Frances Adeline Miller, a classmate of his sister Cornelia at Emma Willard's Troy Female Seminary and the daughter of Judge Elijah Miller of Auburn, New York. In 1823, he moved to Auburn where he entered into law partnership with Judge Miller, and married Frances Miller on October 20, 1824. They raised five children:

- Augustus Henry Seward (1826-1876)
- Frederick William Seward (1830-1915)
- Cornelia Seward (1836-1837)
- William Henry Seward, Jr. (1839-1920)
- Frances Adeline 'Fanny' Seward (1844-1866)
- Olive Risley Seward (1841-1908), adopted

Seward entered politics with the help of his friend Thurlow Weed, whom he had met by chance after a stagecoach accident. Seward was an as an Anti-Masonic member of the New York State Senate (7th D). from 1831 to 1834, sitting in the 54th, 55th, 56th and 57th New York State Legislatures. In 1834, the 33-year-old Seward was named the Whig party candidate for Governor of New York, but lost to incumbent Democrat William Marcy who won 52% of the vote to Seward's 48%.

From 1836 to 1838, Seward served as agent for a group of investors who had purchased the over 3-million-acre (12,000 km^2) western New York holdings of the Holland Land Company. He moved the land office from Mayville, NY to Westfield, New York, where he was successful in easing tensions between the investors and local landowners. On July 16, 1837, he delivered to the students and faculty of the newly formed Westfield Academy a Discourse on Education, in which he advocated for universal education.

In 1838, Seward again challenged Marcy, and was elected Governor of New York by a majority of 51.4% to Marcy's 48.6%. He was narrowly re-elected to a second two-year term in 1840. As a state senator and governor, Seward promoted progressive political policies including prison reform and increased spending on education. He supported state funding for schools for immigrants operated by their own clergy and taught in their native language. This support, which included Catholic parochial schools, came back to haunt him in the 1850s, when anti-Catholic feelings were high, especially among ex-Whigs in the Republican Party.

Seward developed his views about slavery while still a boy. His parents, like other Hudson Valley residents of the early 19th century, owned several slaves. (Slavery was slowly abolished in New York from 1797 to 1827 through a gradual mandated process). Seward recalled his preference as a child for the company and conversation of the slaves in his father's kitchen to the 'severe decorum' in his family's front parlor. He discerned very quickly the inequality between races, writing in later years 'I early came to the conclusion that something was wrong...and [that] determined me...to be an abolitionist.' This belief would stay with Seward through his life and permeate his career.

Seward's wife Frances was deeply committed to the abolitionist movement. In the 1850s, the Seward family opened their Auburn home as a safehouse to fugitive slaves. Seward's frequent travel and political work suggest that it was Frances who played the more active role in Auburn abolitionist activities. In the excitement following the rescue and safe transport of fugitive slave William 'Jerry' Henry in Syracuse on October 1, 1851, Frances wrote to her husband, 'two fugitives have gone to Canada--one of them our acquaintance John.' Another time she wrote, 'A man by the name of William Johnson will apply to you for assistance to purchase the freedom of his daughter. You will see that I have given him something by his book. I told him I thought you would give him more.'

In 1846 Seward became the center of controversy in his hometown when he defended, in separate cases, two convicts accused of murder. Henry Wyatt, a white man, was charged in the stabbing death of a fellow prison inmate; William Freeman, of African American and Native American ancestry, was accused of breaking into a home and stabbing four people to death. In both cases the defendants were mentally ill and had been severely abused while in prison. Seward, having long been an advocate of prison reform and better treatment for the insane, sought to prevent both men from being executed by using a relatively new defense of insanity. In a case involving mental illness with heavy racial overtones Seward argued, 'The color of the prisoner's skin, and the form of his features, are not impressed upon the spiritual immortal mind which works beneath. In spite of human pride, he is still your brother, and mine, in form and color accepted and approved by his Father, and yours, and mine, and bears equally with us the proudest inheritance of our race--the image of our Maker. Hold him then to be a Man.'

Later, Seward quoted Freeman's brother-in-law, praising his eloquence: 'They have made William Freeman what he is, a brute beast; they don't make anything else of any of our people but brute beasts; but when we violate their laws, then they want to punish us as if we were men.' In the end both men were convicted. Although Wyatt was executed, Freeman, whose conviction was reversed on Seward's successful appeal to the New York Supreme Court, died in his cell of tuberculosis.

United States Senator and Presidential Candidate

Seward supported the Whig candidate, General Zachary Taylor, in the presidential election of 1848. He said of Taylor, 'He is the most gentle-looking and amiable of men.' Taylor was a slaveholding plantation owner, but was friendly to Seward anyway.

William Seward was elected as U.S. Senator from New York as a Whig in 1849, and emerged as the leader of the anti-slavery 'Conscience Whigs'. Seward opposed the Compromise of 1850, and was thought to have encouraged Taylor in his supposed opposition. More recent scholarship suggests that Taylor was not under Seward's influence and would have accepted the Compromise if he had not died. Seward believed that slavery was morally wrong, and said so many times, outraging Southerners. He acknowledged that slavery was legal under the Constitution, but denied that the Constitution recognized or protected slavery. He famously remarked in 1850 that 'there is a higher law than the Constitution'. He continued to argue this point of view over the next ten years. He presented himself as the leading enemy of the Slave Power - that is, the perceived conspiracy of southern slaveowners to seize the government and defeat the progress of liberty.

Seward was an opponent of the Fugitive Slave Act, and he defended runaway slaves in court. He supported personal liberty laws.

In February 1855, he was re-elected as a Whig to the U.S. Senate, and joined the Republican Party when the New York Whigs merged with the Anti-Nebraskans later the same year. Seward did not seriously compete for the presidential nomination (won by John C. Frémont) in 1856, but sought and was expected to receive the nomination in 1860. In October 1858, he delivered a famous speech in which he argued that the political and economic systems of North and South were incompatible, and that, due to this 'irrepressible conflict,' the inevitable 'collision' of the two systems would eventually result in the nation becoming 'either entirely a slaveholding nation, or entirely a free-labor nation.' Like Lincoln, he believed slavery could and should be extinguished by long-run historical forces rather than by coercion or war.

In 1859, confident of gaining the presidential nomination and advised by his political ally and friend Thurlow Weed that he would be better off avoiding political gatherings where his words might be misinterpreted by one faction or another, Seward left the country for an eight-month tour of Europe that included a visit to Syria, where Ayub Beg Tarabulsy gave him several Arabian horses. During that hiatus, his lesser-known rival Abraham Lincoln worked diligently to line up support in case Seward failed to win on the first ballot. After returning to the United States, Seward gave a conciliatory, pro-Union Senate speech that reassured moderates but alienated some radical Republicans. (Observing events from Europe, Karl Marx, who was ideologically sympathetic to Frémont, contemptuously regarded Seward as a 'Republican Richelieu' and the 'Demosthenes of the Republican Party' who had sabotaged Frémont's presidential ambitions). Around the same time, his friend Horace Greeley turned against him, opposing Seward on the grounds that his radical reputation made him unelectable. When Lincoln won the nomination, Seward loyally supported him and made a long speaking tour of the West in the autumn of 1860.

Secretary of State

'Our population is destined to roll its resistless waves to the icy barriers of the north, and to encounter oriental civilization on the shores of the Pacific.' --William H. Seward, 1846

Abraham Lincoln appointed Seward his Secretary of State in 1861. Seward played an integral role in resolving the Trent Affair and in negotiating the ensuing Lyons-Seward Treaty of 1862, which set forth strong measures by which the United States and Great Britain agreed to enforce an end to the Atlantic slave trade.

Seward pursued his vision of American expansion. 'Give me only this assurance, that there never be an unlawful resistance by an armed force to the ... United States, and give me fifty, forty, thirty more years of life, and I will engage to give you the possession of the American continent and the control of the world.' Having argued for taking American possession of vulnerable but useful places such as the Danish West Indies, Samaná, Panama, and Hawaii, Seward oversaw the annexation of only one, that of the Brook Islands in 1867. Despite minimal Congressional support, though, he developed American influence in the Hawaiian Islands, as well as in Japan and China to some extent.

Despite his endorsement of expansionist policies, Seward also strongly advocated non-interventionism. After Tsar Alexander II put down the 1863 January Uprising in Poland, French Emperor Napoleon III asked the United States to 'join in a protest to the Tsar.' Seward declined, 'defending 'our policy of non-intervention -- straight, absolute, and peculiar as it may seem to other nations," and insisted that '[t]he American people must be content to recommend the cause of human progress by the wisdom with which they should exercise the powers of self-government, forbearing at all times, and in every way, from foreign alliances, intervention, and interference.'

Assassination Attempt

On the night of April 14, 1865, Lewis Powell, an associate and co-conspirator of John Wilkes Booth, attempted to assassinate Seward at his Washington D.C. home. Powell's attack on Seward was meticulously coordinated with Booth's attack on President Abraham Lincoln and George Atzerodt's attack on Vice President Andrew Johnson in order to maximize the element of surprise and to sever the continuity of the United States government (it should be noted, however, that Atzerodt failed to follow through on his attack). Another member of the conspiracy, David Herold, led Powell to the Seward home on horseback and was responsible for holding Powell's horse while he committed the attack as well as guiding him out of the city during their escape. Powell was able to gain access to the Seward home by telling the butler, William H. Bell, that he was delivering medicine for Seward (who was bed-ridden from a carriage accident which had gravely injured him on April 5, 1865).

Upon entry to the home, Powell began up the stairs, but was stopped at the top of the stairs by Frederick, the Secretary's eldest son. Frederick told Powell that his father was asleep and that he (Frederick) would take the medicine to him. Unsure of what to do, Powell turned around and began descending the stairs, but then suddenly swung back around, drew a pistol, and pointed it at Frederick's head. The pistol misfired. Realizing he needed to act quickly, Powell ruthlessly began beating Frederick over the head with the barrel of his gun. The force of Powell's blows crippled Frederick Seward and left him sprawled on the floor, floating in and out of consciousness, in a pool of blood. Powell's gun was also rendered completely useless, as it had become jammed during the melee.

In Secretary Seward's bedroom was his daughter, Fanny Seward. Hearing the loud noises coming from the second floor hallway, Fanny opened the door to see her brother slumped on the floor and a wide-eyed Powell charging directly towards her, a dagger in his hand. Powell burst through the door, threw Fanny Seward to the side, and jumped on the Secretary's bed, repeatedly stabbing him in the face and neck area. Powell also attacked and injured another son (Augustus), and a soldier and nurse (Sgt. George Robinson) who had been assigned to stay with Seward. Outside the home, David Herold, who could clearly hear the screams coming from the house, fled with both horses, leaving Powell to fend for himself. Powell, convinced that he had mortally wounded the Secretary, fled down the stairs, and stabbed a messenger, Emerick Hansell, who had arrived just as Powell was escaping; Hansell was rendered permanently paralyzed from the stabbing. All five men that were injured that night survived, although Secretary Seward would carry the facial scars from the attack for the rest of his life. The events of that night took their toll on his wife, Frances, who died June 1865. His daughter Fanny died of tuberculosis in October 1866.

Powell was captured the next day (hiding in a tree in Washington D.C). and was executed on July 7, 1865, along with David Herold, George Atzerodt, and Mary Surratt, the three others convicted as conspirators in the Lincoln assassination.

Although it took Seward several months to recover from his wounds, he emerged as a major force in the administration of the new president, Andrew Johnson. He frequently defended his more moderate reconciliation policies towards the South, to the point of enraging Radical Republicans who had once regarded Seward as their ally.

In the fall of 1866, Seward joined Johnson, as well as Ulysses S. Grant and the young General George Armstrong Custer, along with several other administration figures, on the president's ill-fated 'Swing Around the Circle' campaign trip.

At one point Seward became so ill, probably from cholera, that he was sent back to Washington in a special car. Both Johnson and Grant, as well as several members of the Seward family, thought the Secretary was near death. But as with his April 1865 stabbing, Seward surprised many by making a good recovery.

The purchase of Alaska

Seward's most famous achievement as Secretary of State was his successful acquisition of Alaska from Russia. On March 30, 1867, he completed negotiations for the territory, which involved the purchase of 586,412 square miles (1,518,800 km²) of territory (more than twice the area of Texas) for $7,200,000, or approximately 2 cents per acre (equivalent to US$95 million in 2005). The purchase of this frontier land was variously mocked by the public as Seward's Folly, 'Seward's Icebox,' and Andrew Johnson's 'polar bear garden.' Alaska celebrates the purchase on Seward's Day, the last Monday of March. When asked what he considered to be his greatest achievement as Secretary of State, Seward replied 'The purchase of Alaska--but it will take the people a generation to find it out'.

Later life

Seward retired as Secretary of State after Ulysses S. Grant took office as president. During his last years, Seward traveled and wrote prolifically. Most notably, he traveled around the world in fourteen months and two days from August, 1870 to October, 1871. On October 10, 1872, Seward died in his office in his home in Auburn, New York, after having difficulty breathing. His last words were to his children saying, 'Love one another.' He was buried in Fort Hill Cemetery in Auburn, New York, with his wife and two children, Cornelia and Fanny. His headstone reads, 'He was faithful.'

His son, Frederick, edited and published his memoirs in three volumes.

In 1967, a century after the Alaska Purchase, the actor, Joseph Cotten, portrayed Seward in 'The Freeman Story', a part of his NBC anthology series, The Joseph Cotten Show. Virginia Gregg played Fanny Seward. Popular actor, Richard Mulligan, portrayed William Seward in the 1988 Lincoln mini-series, 'Random Letters'.

Seward's homes in Auburn and Florida, New York

Seward and his family owned a home in Auburn, New York which is now a museum; it was built in 1816 by Seward's father-in-law, Judge Elijah Miller. Seward married the Judge's daughter, Frances, in 1824 on the condition that they would live with Miller in his Auburn home. Seward made many changes to the home, adding an addition in the late 1840s and another one in 1866. When he died, Seward left the home to his son, William Seward, Jr.; it passed on to his grandson, William Henry Seward III, in 1920. At his death in 1951, it became a museum that opened to the public in 1955. Four generations of the family's artifacts are contained within the museum, located at 33 South Street in Auburn. The museum is open Tuesday through Saturday from 10am to 5pm.

Meanwhile, Seward's birthplace in Florida, New York was bought by the village in 2010, with the purpose of refurbishing it. (The property actually contains two houses: one in back--Seward's actual birthplace--which was converted into a barn; and one in front, built in the 1890s, used by the family that lived there for many years). The property (after spending an estimated $200,000, to be raised by private donations) is expected to be turned into a museum and opened to the public by 2013.

Legacy

- The purchase of Alaska.
- The Guano Islands Act of 1856
- The $50-dollar Treasury note, also called the Coin note, of the Series 1891, features a portrait of Seward on the obverse. Examples of this note are very rare and would likely se for about $50,000 at auction.
- His house in Auburn, New York is open as a public museum.
- The house in which he lived in Westfield, New York is now home to a bed and breakfast.
- He was a name partner of the law firm of Blatchford, Seward ' Griswold, today known as Cravath, Swaine ' Moore.
- Was famous in his lifetime for his red hair and energetic way of walking. Henry Adams described him as 'wonderfully resembling' a parrot in 'manner and profile'.

Memorials

- Seward Avenue in Auburn. Also in Auburn, Frances Street, Augustus Street, and Frederick Street are named for members of his family. The four streets form a block.
- Seward Elementary School in Auburn.
- Seward Place in Schenectady, New York, on the west side of the Union College campus.
- Seward Park in Auburn, New York.
- Seward Park in the Lower East Side of Manhattan.
- Seward Park in Seattle, Washington.
- Seward Square park in Washington, D.C..
- The Seward Peninsula in Alaska.
- City of Seward, on Alaska's Kenai Peninsula
- Seward, Illinois; Seward, Kansas; Seward, New York; Seward, Nebraska; and Seward, Alaska.
- A hamburger is called 'Seward's Folly' at West Rib Deli ' Pub in Talkeetna, Alaska is named for him.
- Seward County, Nebraska
- Seward's Success, Alaska, an unbuilt community to be enclosed by a dome.
- The Seward neighborhood of Minneapolis, Minnesota
- Seward Mountain (4,361 feet, 1,329 m), one of the Adirondack High Peaks, the highest point in Franklin County.
- At Union College, the campus bus is known as Seward's Trolley, a pun on Seward's Folly
- Seward High School in his hometown of Florida is named for his father, Dr. Samuel

Republican Party	The Republican Party is one of the two major contemporary political parties in the United States, along with the Democratic Party. Founded by anti-slavery expansion activists in 1854, it is often called the Grand Old Party (GOP). The party's platform generally reflects American conservatism in the U.S. political spectrum and is considered center-right, in contrast to the more liberal-leaning Democrats.
Union	During the American Civil War, the Union was a name used to refer to the federal government of the United States, which was supported by the twenty free states and five border slave states. It was opposed by 11 Southern slave states that had declared a secession to join together to form the Confederacy. Although the Union states included the Western states of California, Oregon, and (after 1864) Nevada, as well as states generally considered to be part of the Midwest, the Union has been also often loosely referred to as 'the North', both then and now.
Union Army	The Union Army was the land force that fought for the Union during the American Civil War. It was also known as the Federal Army, the U.S. Army, the Northern Army and the National Army. It consisted of the small United States Army (the regular army), augmented by massive numbers of units supplied by the Northern states, composed of volunteers as well as conscripts.
Niagara	The Niagara was a 245-foot (75 m) long sidewheel palace steamer launched in 1846. Like the others of its kind, it carried passengers and cargo around the North American Great Lakes. It was owned by the Collingwood Line. On September 23, 1856, the Niagara left Sheboygan, Wisconsin headed for Port Washington, Wisconsin, on Lake Michigan, carrying 170 passengers and a heavy load of cargo.
President	President was a steamboat which currently lies dismantled in St. Elmo, Illinois. Originally named Cincinnati, it was built in 1924, and is the only remaining 'Western Rivers' style sidewheel river excursion steamboat in the United States. She was listed on the National Register of Historic Places and declared a National Historic Landmark in 1989. Her home ports have been Cincinnati, Ohio, New Orleans, Louisiana, Vicksburg, Mississippi, St. Louis, Missouri and Davenport, Iowa.

Chapter 14. The War to Save the Union

Anaconda Plan	The Anaconda Plan is the name widely applied to an outline strategy for subduing the seceding states in the American Civil War. Proposed by General-in-Chief Winfield Scott, the plan emphasized the blockade of the Southern ports, and called for an advance down the Mississippi River to cut the South in two. Because the blockade would be rather passive, it was widely derided by the vociferous faction who wanted a more vigorous prosecution of the war, and who likened it to the coils of an anaconda suffocating its victim.
Democratic Party	The Democratic Party is one of two major contemporary political parties in the United States, along with the Republican Party. The party's social liberal and progressive platform is largely considered center-left in the U.S. political spectrum. The party has the lengthiest record of continuous operation in the United States.
Emancipation Proclamation	The Emancipation Proclamation is an executive order issued by United States President Abraham Lincoln on January 1, 1863, during the American Civil War using his war powers. It proclaimed the freedom of slaves in the ten states then in rebellion, thus applying to 3.1 million of the 4 million slaves in the U.S. at that time. The Proclamation immediately freed 50,000 slaves, with nearly all the rest (of the 3.1 million) freed as Union armies advanced.
PLANS	People for Legal and Non-Sectarian Schools (PLANS) is an organization based in California in the United States which campaigns against the public funding of Waldorf methods charter schools alleging they violate the United States Constitution's separation of church and state. The group claims independent Waldorf schools and public Waldorf methods charter schools teach anthroposophical content, that this content is religious in nature, and that the schools disguise the anthroposophical content from the public. PLANS filed federal suit in 1998 against two California public school districts, Sacramento City Unified School District and Twin Ridges Elementary School District, to halt the Waldorf methods educational programs implemented in two of their schools.
Politics	Politics is an essay written by Ralph Waldo Emerson. It is part of his Essays: Second Series, published in 1844. A premier philosopher, poet and leader of American transcendentalism, he used this essay to belie his feelings on government, specifically American government. His impact on New England thought and his views on pragmatism influenced the likes of Henry David Thoreau, Orestes Brownson, and Frederich Nietzsche, among others.
Copperheads	The Copperheads were a vocal group of Democrats in the Northern United States (see also Union (American Civil War)) who opposed the American Civil War, wanting an immediate peace settlement with the Confederates. Republicans started calling anti-war Democrats 'Copperheads,' likening them to the poisonous snake. The Peace Democrats accepted the label, but for them the copper 'head' was the likeness of Liberty, which they cut from copper pennies and proudly wore as badges.

Ex parte Merryman	Ex parte Merryman, 17 F. Cas. 144 (C.C.D. Md. 1861) (No. 9487), is a well-known U.S. federal court case which arose out of the American Civil War. It was a test of the authority of the President to suspend 'the privilege of the writ of habeas corpus'. Chief Justice Roger Taney, sitting as a federal circuit court judge, ruled that the authority to suspend habeas corpus lay with Congress, not the president.
Race riot	A race riot is an outbreak of violent civil disorder in which race is a key factor. A phenomenon frequently confused with the concept of 'race riot' is sectarian violence, which involves public mass violence or conflict over non-racial factors.
Radical Republicans	The Radical Republicans were a loose faction of American politicians within the Republican Party from about 1854 (before the American Civil War) until the end of Reconstruction in 1877. They called themselves 'radicals' and were opposed during the war by moderates and conservative factions led by Abraham Lincoln and after the war by self-described 'conservatives' (in the South) and 'Liberals' (in the North). Radicals strongly opposed slavery during the war and after the war and distrusted ex-Confederates, demanding harsh policies for Reconstruction. During the war, Radical Republicans often opposed Lincoln in terms of selection of generals (especially his choice of George B. McClellan for top command) and his efforts to bring states back into the Union.
Alabama	Alabama is a state located in the southeastern region of the United States of America. It is bordered by Tennessee to the north, Georgia to the east, Florida and the Gulf of Mexico to the south, and Mississippi to the west. Alabama ranks 30th in total land area and ranks second in the size of its inland waterways. The state ranks 23rd in population with 4.7 million residents in 2009.
Glorieta Pass Battlefield	Glorieta Pass Battlefield, was the site of a decisive American Civil War battle that ended Confederate ambitions to cut off the West from the Union. The Battle of Glorieta Pass took place on March 26-28, 1862. The battlefield area consists of two sites, a 294-acre (1.19 km^2) parcel and a 150-acre (0.61 km^2) parcel.

Chapter 14. The War to Save the Union

Indian American

Indian Americans are Americans who are of Asian descent and have ancestors who are born or are native to India. To make a clear distinction and difference between Indians of Asian origin and Indians 'named as' who are Indigenous peoples of the Americas, the U.S. Census Bureau popularized the term Asian Indian to avoid confusion with 'American Indian'.

History

The term: Indian

In North America the term Indian has an ambiguous meaning.

Albert Sidney Johnston

Albert Sidney Johnston was a career United States Army officer, a Texas Army general, and a Confederate States general. He saw extensive combat during his military career, fighting actions in the Texas War of Independence, the Mexican-American War, the Utah War, as well as the American Civil War.

Considered by Confederate President Jefferson Davis to be the finest general officer in the Confederacy before the emergence of Robert E. Lee, he was killed early in the Civil War at the Battle of Shiloh and was the highest ranking officer, Union or Confederate, killed during the entire war.

James Murray Mason

James Murray Mason was a United States Representative and United States Senator from Virginia. He was a grandson of George Mason and represented the Confederate States of America as appointed commissioner of the Confederacy to the United Kingdom and France between 1861 and 1865 during the American Civil War.

Early life and education

He was born on Analostan Island (now Theodore Roosevelt Island) in the District of Columbia, and was a graduate of the University of Pennsylvania (1818), receiving a law degree from the College of William and Mary in 1820.

Plains Indians	The Plains Indians are the Indigenous peoples who live on the plains and rolling hills of the Great Plains of North America. Their colorful equestrian culture and resistance to White domination have made the Plains Indians an archetype in literature and art for American Indians everywhere. Plains Indians are usually divided into two broad classifications which overlap to some degree. The first group were fully nomadic, following the vast herds of buffalo, although some tribes occasionally engaged in agriculture; growing tobacco and corn primarily.
USS San Jacinto	Three ships of the United States Navy have been named USS San Jacinto, after the Texas battle of San Jacinto in 1836, and the Navy considered acquiring a fourth ship of the name: • The first San Jacinto was an early screw frigate of the Navy, launched in 1850. Bombarded the Taku Forts in support of British and French troops on the ground during the Second Opium War. Active during the American Civil War, but wrecked at the beginning of 1865. Also known for its role in the Trent Affair. • The U.S. Navy considered acquiring a civilian passenger-cargo ship, SS San Jacinto, for use during World War I as USS San Jacinto but never acquired or commissioned her. • The second San Jacinto (CVL-30) was a light aircraft carrier that saw action in the latter half of World War II and was decommissioned in 1947. • The third San Jacinto (CG-56) is a guided missile cruiser commissioned in 1988 and is in naval service as of 2010. .
Robert Allan Brown	Robert Allan Brown was a well-known and flamboyant prospector and speculator in 19th and early 20th Century in the Canadian province of British Columbia. He was known generally as Volcanic Brown, especially in the province's Kootenay and Boundary districts and in adjoining Eastern Washington, and also as Sunset Brown in the Similkameen District and still also to others as Crazy Brown. His enthusiastic nature contributed to his nickname, and as result of that and his flamboyant personality he was a fixture in mining industry news in a wide region which spanned the British Columbia-United States border.

Chapter 14. The War to Save the Union

Andrew Jackson	Andrew Jackson was the seventh President of the United States (1829-1837). Based in frontier Tennessee, Jackson was a politician and army general who defeated the Creek Indians at the Battle of Horseshoe Bend (1814), and the British at the Battle of New Orleans (1815). A polarizing figure who dominated the Second Party System in the 1820s and 1830s, as president he destroyed the national bank and relocated most Indian tribes from the Southeast to west of the Mississippi River.
African American	African Americans (also referred to as Black Americans or Afro-Americans, and formerly as American Negroes) are citizens or residents of the United States who have origins in any of the black populations of Africa. In the United States, the terms are generally used for Americans with at least partial Sub-Saharan African ancestry. Most African Americans are the direct descendants of captive Africans who survived the slavery era within the boundaries of the present United States, although some are--or are descended from--immigrants from African, Caribbean, Central American or South American nations. As an adjective, the term is usually written as African-American.
Black Codes	The Black Codes were unofficial laws put in place in the United States to limit the basic human rights and civil liberties of blacks. Even though the U.S. constitution originally discriminated against blacks (as 'other persons') and both Northern and Southern states had passed discriminatory legislation from the early 19th century, the term Black Codes is used most often to refer to legislation passed by Southern states at the end of the Civil War to control the labor, migration and other activities of newly-freed slaves. In Texas, the Eleventh Legislature produced these codes in 1866, right after the United States Civil War.
Frederick Douglass	Frederick Douglass was an American social reformer, orator, writer and statesman. After escaping from slavery, he became a leader of the abolitionist movement, known for his dazzling oratory and incisive antislavery writing. He stood as a living counter-example to slaveholders' arguments that slaves did not have the intellectual capacity to function as independent American citizens.
Gettysburg Campaign	The Gettysburg Campaign was a series of battles fought in June and July 1863, during the American Civil War. After his victory in the Battle of Chancellorsville, Confederate General Robert E. Lee's Army of Northern Virginia moved north for offensive operations in Maryland and Pennsylvania. The Union Army of the Potomac, commanded by Maj.

Massachusetts	'Massachusetts', words and music by Arlo Guthrie, was made the official folk song of Massachusetts in July, 1981.
Joseph Hooker	Joseph Hooker was a career United States Army officer, fought in the Mexican-American War, and was a major general in the Union Army during the American Civil War. Although he served throughout the war, usually with distinction, Hooker is best remembered for his stunning defeat by Confederate General Robert E. Lee at the Battle of Chancellorsville in 1863.
Homestead Act	A homestead act is one of three United States federal laws that gave an applicant freehold title to an area called a 'homestead' - typically 160 acres (65 hectares or one-fourth section) of undeveloped federal land west of the Mississippi River. The original homestead act, known as the Homestead Act of 1862, was signed into law by President Abraham Lincoln on May 20, 1862. The law required three steps: file an application, improve the land, and file for deed of title. Anyone who had never taken up arms against the U.S. government, including freed slaves, could file an application to claim a federal land grant.
Land grant	A land grant is a gift of real estate - land or its privileges - made by a government or other authority as a reward for services to an individual, especially in return for military service. Grants of land are also awarded to individuals and companies as incentives to develop unused land in relatively unpopulated countries; the process of awarding land grants are not limited to the countries named below. Ancient Rome Roman soldiers were given rewards at the end of their service including cash or land (praemia).
Tecumseh	Tecumseh also known as Tecumtha or Tekamthi, was a Native American leader of the Shawnee and a large tribal confederacy that opposed the United States during Tecumseh's War and the War of 1812. He grew up in the Ohio country during the American Revolutionary War and the Northwest Indian War, where he was constantly exposed to warfare.

	His brother Tenskwatawa was a religious leader who advocated a return to the ancestral lifestyle of the tribes. A large following and a confederacy grew around his prophetic teachings.
Andrew Johnson	Andrew Johnson was the 17th President of the United States (1865-1869). Following the assassination of President Abraham Lincoln, Johnson presided over the Reconstruction era of the United States in the four years after the American Civil War. His tenure was controversial as his positions favoring the white South came under heavy political attack from Republicans.
Absalom Jones	Absalom Jones was an African-American abolitionist and clergyman. After founding a black congregation in 1794, in 1804 he was the first African-American ordained as a priest in the Episcopal Church of the United States. He is listed on the Episcopal calendar of saints and blessed under the date of his decease, February 13, in the 1979 Book of Common Prayer as 'Absalom Jones, Priest, 1818'.
Appomattox Court House	The Appomattox Court House is the current courthouse in Appomattox, Virginia built in 1892. It is located in the middle of the state about three miles (5 km) northwest of the Appomattox Court House National Historical Park, once known as Clover Hill - home of the original Old Appomattox Court House. The 'new' Appomattox Courthouse is near the Appomattox Station and where the regional county government is located. Before the Civil War, the railroad bypassed Clover Hill, now known as the Appomattox Court House National Historical Park.

1. During the American Civil War, the _________ was a name used to refer to the federal government of the United States, which was supported by the twenty free states and five border slave states. It was opposed by 11 Southern slave states that had declared a secession to join together to form the Confederacy. Although the _________ states included the Western states of California, Oregon, and (after 1864) Nevada, as well as states generally considered to be part of the Midwest, the _________ has been also often loosely referred to as 'the North', both then and now.

   a. Avery O. Craven Award
   b. Union
   c. Opposition to the American Civil War
   d. Ordinance of Secession

2. The _________ is one of two major contemporary political parties in the United States, along with the Republican Party. The party's social liberal and progressive platform is largely considered center-left in the U.S. political spectrum. The party has the lengthiest record of continuous operation in the United States.

   a. Digital Transition Content Security Act
   b. Democratic Party
   c. RV Atlantis II
   d. Federal Funding Accountability and Transparency Act of 2006

3. A _________ is an outbreak of violent civil disorder in which race is a key factor. A phenomenon frequently confused with the concept of '_________' is sectarian violence, which involves public mass violence or conflict over non-racial factors.

   a. Digital Transition Content Security Act
   b. United States ex rel. Murphy v. Porter
   c. United States presidential election, 1860
   d. Race riot

4. William Henry Seward (May 16, 1801 - October 10, 1872) was the 12th Governor of New York, United States Senator and the United States Secretary of State under Abraham Lincoln and Andrew Johnson. A determined opponent of the spread of slavery in the years leading up to the American Civil War, he was a dominant figure in the Republican Party in its formative years, and was widely regarded as the leading contender for the party's presidential nomination in 1860 - yet his very outspokenness may have cost him the nomination. Despite his loss, he became a loyal member of Lincoln's wartime cabinet, and played a role in preventing foreign intervention early in the war. On the night of Lincoln's assassination, he survived an attempt on his life in the conspirators' effort to decapitate the Union government. As Johnson's Secretary of State, he engineered the purchase of Alaska from Russia in an act that was ridiculed at the time as 'Seward's Folly', but which somehow exemplified his character. His contemporary Carl Schurz described Seward as 'one of those spirits who sometimes will go ahead of public opinion instead of tamely following its footprints.'

Early life and career

Seward was born in Florida, New York, on May 16, 1801, one of five children of Samuel Sweezy Seward and his wife Mary Jennings Seward. Samuel Seward, described as 'a prosperous, domineering doctor and businessman,' was the founder of the S. S. Seward Institute, today a secondary school in the Florida Union Free School District.

Seward served as president of the S.S. Seward Institute after the death of his father, even while serving as Secretary of State during the Lincoln and Johnson administrations.

Seward studied law at Union College, graduating in 1820 with highest honors, and as a member of Phi Beta Kappa. He was admitted to the New York State Bar in 1821. In that same year, he met Frances Adeline Miller, a classmate of his sister Cornelia at Emma Willard's Troy Female Seminary and the daughter of Judge Elijah Miller of Auburn, New York. In 1823, he moved to Auburn where he entered into law partnership with Judge Miller, and married Frances Miller on October 20, 1824. They raised five children:

- Augustus Henry Seward (1826-1876)
- Frederick William Seward (1830-1915)
- Cornelia Seward (1836-1837)
- William Henry Seward, Jr. (1839-1920)
- Frances Adeline 'Fanny' Seward (1844-1866)
- Olive Risley Seward (1841-1908), adopted

Seward entered politics with the help of his friend Thurlow Weed, whom he had met by chance after a stagecoach accident. Seward was an as an Anti-Masonic member of the New York State Senate (7th D). from 1831 to 1834, sitting in the 54th, 55th, 56th and 57th New York State Legislatures. In 1834, the 33-year-old Seward was named the Whig party candidate for Governor of New York, but lost to incumbent Democrat William Marcy who won 52% of the vote to Seward's 48%.

From 1836 to 1838, Seward served as agent for a group of investors who had purchased the over 3-million-acre (12,000 km^2) western New York holdings of the Holland Land Company. He moved the land office from Mayville, NY to Westfield, New York, where he was successful in easing tensions between the investors and local landowners. On July 16, 1837, he delivered to the students and faculty of the newly formed Westfield Academy a Discourse on Education, in which he advocated for universal education.

In 1838, Seward again challenged Marcy, and was elected Governor of New York by a majority of 51.4% to Marcy's 48.6%. He was narrowly re-elected to a second two-year term in 1840. As a state senator and governor, Seward promoted progressive political policies including prison reform and increased spending on education. He supported state funding for schools for immigrants operated by their own clergy and taught in their native language. This support, which included Catholic parochial schools, came back to haunt him in the 1850s, when anti-Catholic feelings were high, especially among ex-Whigs in the Republican Party.

Seward developed his views about slavery while still a boy. His parents, like other Hudson Valley residents of the early 19th century, owned several slaves. (Slavery was slowly abolished in New York from 1797 to 1827 through a gradual mandated process). Seward recalled his preference as a child for the company and conversation of the slaves in his father's kitchen to the 'severe decorum' in his family's front parlor. He discerned very quickly the inequality between races, writing in later years 'I early came to the conclusion that something was wrong...and [that] determined me...to be an abolitionist.' This belief would stay with Seward through his life and permeate his career.

Seward's wife Frances was deeply committed to the abolitionist movement. In the 1850s, the Seward family opened their Auburn home as a safehouse to fugitive slaves. Seward's frequent travel and political work suggest that it was Frances who played the more active role in Auburn abolitionist activities. In the excitement following the rescue and safe transport of fugitive slave William 'Jerry' Henry in Syracuse on October 1, 1851, Frances wrote to her husband, 'two fugitives have gone to Canada--one of them our acquaintance John.' Another time she wrote, 'A man by the name of William Johnson will apply to you for assistance to purchase the freedom of his daughter. You will see that I have given him something by his book. I told him I thought you would give him more.'

In 1846 Seward became the center of controversy in his hometown when he defended, in separate cases, two convicts accused of murder. Henry Wyatt, a white man, was charged in the stabbing death of a fellow prison inmate; William Freeman, of African American and Native American ancestry, was accused of breaking into a home and stabbing four people to death. In both cases the defendants were mentally ill and had been severely abused while in prison. Seward, having long been an advocate of prison reform and better treatment for the insane, sought to prevent both men from being executed by using a relatively new defense of insanity. In a case involving mental illness with heavy racial overtones Seward argued, 'The color of the prisoner's skin, and the form of his features, are not impressed upon the spiritual immortal mind which works beneath. In spite of human pride, he is still your brother, and mine, in form and color accepted and approved by his Father, and yours, and mine, and bears equally with us the proudest inheritance of our race--the image of our Maker. Hold him then to be a Man.'

Later, Seward quoted Freeman's brother-in-law, praising his eloquence: 'They have made William Freeman what he is, a brute beast; they don't make anything else of any of our people but brute beasts; but when we violate their laws, then they want to punish us as if we were men.' In the end both men were convicted. Although Wyatt was executed, Freeman, whose conviction was reversed on Seward's successful appeal to the New York Supreme Court, died in his cell of tuberculosis.

United States Senator and Presidential Candidate

Seward supported the Whig candidate, General Zachary Taylor, in the presidential election of 1848. He said of Taylor, 'He is the most gentle-looking and amiable of men.' Taylor was a slaveholding plantation owner, but was friendly to Seward anyway.

William Seward was elected as U.S. Senator from New York as a Whig in 1849, and emerged as the leader of the anti-slavery 'Conscience Whigs'. Seward opposed the Compromise of 1850, and was thought to have encouraged Taylor in his supposed opposition. More recent scholarship suggests that Taylor was not under Seward's influence and would have accepted the Compromise if he had not died. Seward believed that slavery was morally wrong, and said so many times, outraging Southerners. He acknowledged that slavery was legal under the Constitution, but denied that the Constitution recognized or protected slavery. He famously remarked in 1850 that 'there is a higher law than the Constitution'. He continued to argue this point of view over the next ten years. He presented himself as the leading enemy of the Slave Power - that is, the perceived conspiracy of southern slaveowners to seize the government and defeat the progress of liberty.

Seward was an opponent of the Fugitive Slave Act, and he defended runaway slaves in court. He supported personal liberty laws.

In February 1855, he was re-elected as a Whig to the U.S. Senate, and joined the Republican Party when the New York Whigs merged with the Anti-Nebraskans later the same year. Seward did not seriously compete for the presidential nomination (won by John C. Frémont) in 1856, but sought and was expected to receive the nomination in 1860. In October 1858, he delivered a famous speech in which he argued that the political and economic systems of North and South were incompatible, and that, due to this 'irrepressible conflict,' the inevitable 'collision' of the two systems would eventually result in the nation becoming 'either entirely a slaveholding nation, or entirely a free-labor nation.' Like Lincoln, he believed slavery could and should be extinguished by long-run historical forces rather than by coercion or war.

In 1859, confident of gaining the presidential nomination and advised by his political ally and friend Thurlow Weed that he would be better off avoiding political gatherings where his words might be misinterpreted by one faction or another, Seward left the country for an eight-month tour of Europe that included a visit to Syria, where Ayub Beg Tarabulsy gave him several Arabian horses. During that hiatus, his lesser-known rival Abraham Lincoln worked diligently to line up support in case Seward failed to win on the first ballot. After returning to the United States, Seward gave a conciliatory, pro-Union Senate speech that reassured moderates but alienated some radical Republicans. (Observing events from Europe, Karl Marx, who was ideologically sympathetic to Frémont, contemptuously regarded Seward as a 'Republican Richelieu' and the 'Demosthenes of the Republican Party' who had sabotaged Frémont's presidential ambitions). Around the same time, his friend Horace Greeley turned against him, opposing Seward on the grounds that his radical reputation made him unelectable. When Lincoln won the nomination, Seward loyally supported him and made a long speaking tour of the West in the autumn of 1860.

Secretary of State

'Our population is destined to roll its resistless waves to the icy barriers of the north, and to encounter oriental civilization on the shores of the Pacific.' --__________, 1846

Abraham Lincoln appointed Seward his Secretary of State in 1861. Seward played an integral role in resolving the Trent Affair and in negotiating the ensuing Lyons-Seward Treaty of 1862, which set forth strong measures by which the United States and Great Britain agreed to enforce an end to the Atlantic slave trade.

Seward pursued his vision of American expansion. 'Give me only this assurance, that there never be an unlawful resistance by an armed force to the ... United States, and give me fifty, forty, thirty more years of life, and I will engage to give you the possession of the American continent and the control of the world.' Having argued for taking American possession of vulnerable but useful places such as the Danish West Indies, Samaná, Panama, and Hawaii, Seward oversaw the annexation of only one, that of the Brook Islands in 1867. Despite minimal Congressional support, though, he developed American influence in the Hawaiian Islands, as well as in Japan and China to some extent.

Despite his endorsement of expansionist policies, Seward also strongly advocated non-interventionism. After Tsar Alexander II put down the 1863 January Uprising in Poland, French Emperor Napoleon III asked the United States to 'join in a protest to the Tsar.' Seward declined, 'defending 'our policy of non-intervention -- straight, absolute, and peculiar as it may seem to other nations,'' and insisted that '[t]he American people must be content to recommend the cause of human progress by the wisdom with which they should exercise the powers of self-government, forbearing at all times, and in every way, from foreign alliances, intervention, and interference.'

Assassination Attempt

On the night of April 14, 1865, Lewis Powell, an associate and co-conspirator of John Wilkes Booth, attempted to assassinate Seward at his Washington D.C. home. Powell's attack on Seward was meticulously coordinated with Booth's attack on President Abraham Lincoln and George Atzerodt's attack on Vice President Andrew Johnson in order to maximize the element of surprise and to sever the continuity of the United States government (it should be noted, however, that Atzerodt failed to follow through on his attack). Another member of the conspiracy, David Herold, led Powell to the Seward home on horseback and was responsible for holding Powell's horse while he committed the attack as well as guiding him out of the city during their escape. Powell was able to gain access to the Seward home by telling the butler, William H. Bell, that he was delivering medicine for Seward (who was bed-ridden from a carriage accident which had gravely injured him on April 5, 1865).

Upon entry to the home, Powell began up the stairs, but was stopped at the top of the stairs by Frederick, the Secretary's eldest son. Frederick told Powell that his father was asleep and that he (Frederick) would take the medicine to him. Unsure of what to do, Powell turned around and began descending the stairs, but then suddenly swung back around, drew a pistol, and pointed it at Frederick's head. The pistol misfired. Realizing he needed to act quickly, Powell ruthlessly began beating Frederick over the head with the barrel of his gun. The force of Powell's blows crippled Frederick Seward and left him sprawled on the floor, floating in and out of consciousness, in a pool of blood. Powell's gun was also rendered completely useless, as it had become jammed during the melee.

In Secretary Seward's bedroom was his daughter, Fanny Seward. Hearing the loud noises coming from the second floor hallway, Fanny opened the door to see her brother slumped on the floor and a wide-eyed Powell charging directly towards her, a dagger in his hand. Powell burst through the door, threw Fanny Seward to the side, and jumped on the Secretary's bed, repeatedly stabbing him in the face and neck area. Powell also attacked and injured another son (Augustus), and a soldier and nurse (Sgt. George Robinson) who had been assigned to stay with Seward. Outside the home, David Herold, who could clearly hear the screams coming from the house, fled with both horses, leaving Powell to fend for himself. Powell, convinced that he had mortally wounded the Secretary, fled down the stairs, and stabbed a messenger, Emerick Hansell, who had arrived just as Powell was escaping; Hansell was rendered permanently paralyzed from the stabbing. All five men that were injured that night survived, although Secretary Seward would carry the facial scars from the attack for the rest of his life. The events of that night took their toll on his wife, Frances, who died June 1865. His daughter Fanny died of tuberculosis in October 1866.

Powell was captured the next day (hiding in a tree in Washington D.C). and was executed on July 7, 1865, along with David Herold, George Atzerodt, and Mary Surratt, the three others convicted as conspirators in the Lincoln assassination.

Although it took Seward several months to recover from his wounds, he emerged as a major force in the administration of the new president, Andrew Johnson. He frequently defended his more moderate reconciliation policies towards the South, to the point of enraging Radical Republicans who had once regarded Seward as their ally.

In the fall of 1866, Seward joined Johnson, as well as Ulysses S. Grant and the young General George Armstrong Custer, along with several other administration figures, on the president's ill-fated 'Swing Around the Circle' campaign trip.

At one point Seward became so ill, probably from cholera, that he was sent back to Washington in a special car. Both Johnson and Grant, as well as several members of the Seward family, thought the Secretary was near death. But as with his April 1865 stabbing, Seward surprised many by making a good recovery.

The purchase of Alaska

Seward's most famous achievement as Secretary of State was his successful acquisition of Alaska from Russia. On March 30, 1867, he completed negotiations for the territory, which involved the purchase of 586,412 square miles (1,518,800 km²) of territory (more than twice the area of Texas) for $7,200,000, or approximately 2 cents per acre (equivalent to US$95 million in 2005). The purchase of this frontier land was variously mocked by the public as Seward's Folly, 'Seward's Icebox,' and Andrew Johnson's 'polar bear garden.' Alaska celebrates the purchase on Seward's Day, the last Monday of March. When asked what he considered to be his greatest achievement as Secretary of State, Seward replied 'The purchase of Alaska--but it will take the people a generation to find it out'.

Later life

Seward retired as Secretary of State after Ulysses S. Grant took office as president. During his last years, Seward traveled and wrote prolifically. Most notably, he traveled around the world in fourteen months and two days from August, 1870 to October, 1871. On October 10, 1872, Seward died in his office in his home in Auburn, New York, after having difficulty breathing. His last words were to his children saying, 'Love one another.' He was buried in Fort Hill Cemetery in Auburn, New York, with his wife and two children, Cornelia and Fanny. His headstone reads, 'He was faithful.'

His son, Frederick, edited and published his memoirs in three volumes.

In 1967, a century after the Alaska Purchase, the actor, Joseph Cotten, portrayed Seward in 'The Freeman Story', a part of his NBC anthology series, The Joseph Cotten Show. Virginia Gregg played Fanny Seward. Popular actor, Richard Mulligan, portrayed William Seward in the 1988 Lincoln mini-series, 'Random Letters'.

Seward's homes in Auburn and Florida, New York

Seward and his family owned a home in Auburn, New York which is now a museum; it was built in 1816 by Seward's father-in-law, Judge Elijah Miller. Seward married the Judge's daughter, Frances, in 1824 on the condition that they would live with Miller in his Auburn home. Seward made many changes to the home, adding an addition in the late 1840s and another one in 1866. When he died, Seward left the home to his son, William Seward, Jr.; it passed on to his grandson, William Henry Seward III, in 1920. At his death in 1951, it became a museum that opened to the public in 1955. Four generations of the family's artifacts are contained within the museum, located at 33 South Street in Auburn. The museum is open Tuesday through Saturday from 10am to 5pm.

Meanwhile, Seward's birthplace in Florida, New York was bought by the village in 2010, with the purpose of refurbishing it. (The property actually contains two houses: one in back--Seward's actual birthplace--which was converted into a barn; and one in front, built in the 1890s, used by the family that lived there for many years). The property (after spending an estimated $200,000, to be raised by private donations) is expected to be turned into a museum and opened to the public by 2013.

Legacy

- The purchase of Alaska.
- The Guano Islands Act of 1856
- The $50-dollar Treasury note, also called the Coin note, of the Series 1891, features a portrait of Seward on the obverse. Examples of this note are very rare and would likely sell for about $50,000 at auction.
- His house in Auburn, New York is open as a public museum.
- The house in which he lived in Westfield, New York is now home to a bed and breakfast.
- He was a name partner of the law firm of Blatchford, Seward ' Griswold, today known as Cravath, Swaine ' Moore.
- Was famous in his lifetime for his red hair and energetic way of walking. Henry Adams described him as 'wonderfully resembling' a parrot in 'manner and profile'.

Memorials

- Seward Avenue in Auburn. Also in Auburn, Frances Street, Augustus Street, and Frederick Street are name for members of his family. The four streets form a block.
- Seward Elementary School in Auburn.
- Seward Place in Schenectady, New York, on the west side of the Union College campus.
- Seward Park in Auburn, New York.
- Seward Park in the Lower East Side of Manhattan.
- Seward Park in Seattle, Washington.
- Seward Square park in Washington, D.C..
- The Seward Peninsula in Alaska.
- City of Seward, on Alaska's Kenai Peninsula
- Seward, Illinois; Seward, Kansas; Seward, New York; Seward, Nebraska; and Seward, Alaska.
- A hamburger is called 'Seward's Folly' at West Rib Deli ' Pub in Talkeetna, Alaska is named for him.
- Seward County, Nebraska
- Seward's Success, Alaska, an unbuilt community to be enclosed by a dome.
- The Seward neighborhood of Minneapolis, Minnesota
- Seward Mountain (4,361 feet, 1,329 m), one of the Adirondack High Peaks, the highest point in Franklin County.
- At Union College, the campus bus is known as Seward's Trolley, a pun on Seward's Folly.
- Seward High School in his hometown of Florida is named for his father, Dr. Samuel Seward.
- Statues of him in Seward Park in Auburn, in Madison Square Park in New York City, on the grounds of the Z J. Loussac Public Library in Anchorage, Alaska, and in Volunteer Park in Seattle (not facing towards Alaska)
- The William Henry Seward Memorial in Florida, with a bust sculpted by Daniel Chester French.
- Seward Park Housing Corporation, a housing cooperative in the Lower East Side of Manhattan

---

a. William H. Seward
b. Francisco de Montejo
c. Juan de Grijalva
d. Marc Lescarbot

5. The _________ was the land force that fought for the Union during the American Civil War. It was also known as the Federal Army, the U.S. Army, the Northern Army and the National Army. It consisted of the small United States Army (the regular army), augmented by massive numbers of units supplied by the Northern states, composed of volunteers as well as conscripts.

a. Union Army
b. Issues of the American Civil War
c. Opposition to the American Civil War
d. Ordinance of Secession

ANSWER KEY

Chapter 14. The War to Save the Union

1. b
2. b
3. d
4. a
5. a

CHAPTER OUTLINE: KEY TERMS, PEOPLE, PLACES, CONCEPTS

Chapter 15

Reconstruction and the South

_______ Homestead Act

_______ Washington

_______ William D. Washington

_______ Oprah Winfrey

_______ PLANS

_______ Emancipation Proclamation

_______ William H. Seward

_______ Union

_______ Race riot

_______ Radical Republicans

_______ President

_______ Black Codes

_______ Copperheads

_______ Three-Fifths Compromise

_______ George Armstrong Custer

_______ Garfield

_______ James A. Garfield

_______ Reconstruction Acts

_______ Andrew Johnson

Chapter 15. Reconstruction and the South

Tenure of Office Act

Thomas Nast

Nation

American Anti-Slavery Society

Carpetbagger

Literacy test

Scalawag

Elizabeth Cady Stanton

South Carolina

Republican Party

Politics

Columbian Exchange

Crop-lien system

England

Sharecropping

Union League

Lydia Maria Child

Force Acts

Ku Klux Klan

Horace Greeley

Whiskey Ring

Cold Mountain

Constitutional Convention

Louisiana

Louisiana Purchase

Alexander Hamilton

Thomas Jefferson

Napoleonic Wars

John Quincy Adams

John Quincy

York

Democratic Party

Homestead Act	A homestead act is one of three United States federal laws that gave an applicant freehold title to an area called a 'homestead' - typically 160 acres (65 hectares or one-fourth section) of undeveloped federal land west of the Mississippi River. The original homestead act, known as the Homestead Act of 1862, was signed into law by President Abraham Lincoln on May 20, 1862. The law required three steps: file an application, improve the land, and file for deed of title. Anyone who had never taken up arms against the U.S. government, including freed slaves, could file an application to claim a federal land grant.
Washington	Washington was one of the first steamboats to operate in the states of California and Oregon. Operations in California Washington operated in California on the Sacramento River. The vessel was purchased in California in 1851 by pioneer steamboat captain Alexander Sinclair Murray (b.1828).
William D. Washington	William D. Washington was an American painter and teacher of art. He is most famous for his painting The Burial of Latane, which became a symbol of the Lost Cause of the Confederacy in the years following the American Civil War, and for the work he did in establishing the fine arts program of the Virginia Military Institute. Biography Washington was born in Clarke County, Virginia, the child of Perrin Washington and Hannah Fairfax Whiting, and was a descendant of Warner Washington, a first cousin of George Washington.

Oprah Winfrey	Oprah Winfrey is an American television host, actress, producer, and philanthropist, best known for her self-titled, multi-award winning talk show, which has become the highest-rated program of its kind in history and was nationally syndicated from 1986 to 2011. She has been ranked the richest African American of the 20th century, the greatest black philanthropist in American history, and was for a time the world's only black billionaire. She is also, according to some assessments, the most influential woman in the world.
PLANS	People for Legal and Non-Sectarian Schools (PLANS) is an organization based in California in the United States which campaigns against the public funding of Waldorf methods charter schools alleging they violate the United States Constitution's separation of church and state. The group claims independent Waldorf schools and public Waldorf methods charter schools teach anthroposophical content, that this content is religious in nature, and that the schools disguise the anthroposophical content from the public. PLANS filed federal suit in 1998 against two California public school districts, Sacramento City Unified School District and Twin Ridges Elementary School District, to halt the Waldorf methods educational programs implemented in two of their schools.
Emancipation Proclamation	The Emancipation Proclamation is an executive order issued by United States President Abraham Lincoln on January 1, 1863, during the American Civil War using his war powers. It proclaimed the freedom of slaves in the ten states then in rebellion, thus applying to 3.1 million of the 4 million slaves in the U.S. at that time. The Proclamation immediately freed 50,000 slaves, with nearly all the rest (of the 3.1 million) freed as Union armies advanced.
William H. Seward	William Henry Seward (May 16, 1801 - October 10, 1872) was the 12th Governor of New York, United States Senator and the United States Secretary of State under Abraham Lincoln and Andrew Johnson. A determined opponent of the spread of slavery in the years leading up to the American Civil War, he was a dominant figure in the Republican Party in its formative years, and was widely regarded as the leading contender for the party's presidential nomination in 1860 - yet his very outspokenness may have cost him the nomination. Despite his loss, he became a loyal member of Lincoln's wartime cabinet, and played a role in preventing foreign intervention early in the war. On the night of Lincoln's assassination, he survived an attempt on his life in the conspirators' effort to decapitate the Union government. As Johnson's Secretary of State, he engineered the purchase of Alaska from Russia in an act that was ridiculed at the time as 'Seward's Folly', but which somehow exemplified his character. His contemporary Carl Schurz described Seward as 'one of those spirits who sometimes will go ahead of public opinion instead of tamely following its footprints.' Early life and career

Seward was born in Florida, New York, on May 16, 1801, one of five children of Samuel Sweezy Seward and his wife Mary Jennings Seward. Samuel Seward, described as 'a prosperous, domineering doctor and businessman,' was the founder of the S. S. Seward Institute, today a secondary school in the Florida Union Free School District.

Seward served as president of the S.S. Seward Institute after the death of his father, even while serving as Secretary of State during the Lincoln and Johnson administrations.

Seward studied law at Union College, graduating in 1820 with highest honors, and as a member of Phi Beta Kappa. He was admitted to the New York State Bar in 1821. In that same year, he met Frances Adeline Miller, a classmate of his sister Cornelia at Emma Willard's Troy Female Seminary and the daughter of Judge Elijah Miller of Auburn, New York. In 1823, he moved to Auburn where he entered into law partnership with Judge Miller, and married Frances Miller on October 20, 1824. They raised five children:

- Augustus Henry Seward (1826-1876)
- Frederick William Seward (1830-1915)
- Cornelia Seward (1836-1837)
- William Henry Seward, Jr. (1839-1920)
- Frances Adeline 'Fanny' Seward (1844-1866)
- Olive Risley Seward (1841-1908), adopted

Seward entered politics with the help of his friend Thurlow Weed, whom he had met by chance after a stagecoach accident. Seward was an as an Anti-Masonic member of the New York State Senate (7th D). from 1831 to 1834, sitting in the 54th, 55th, 56th and 57th New York State Legislatures. In 1834, the 33-year-old Seward was named the Whig party candidate for Governor of New York, but lost to incumbent Democrat William Marcy who won 52% of the vote to Seward's 48%.

From 1836 to 1838, Seward served as agent for a group of investors who had purchased the over 3-million-acre (12,000 km^2) western New York holdings of the Holland Land Company. He moved the land office from Mayville, NY to Westfield, New York, where he was successful in easing tensions between the investors and local landowners. On July 16, 1837, he delivered to the students and faculty of the newly formed Westfield Academy a Discourse on Education, in which he advocated for universal education.

In 1838, Seward again challenged Marcy, and was elected Governor of New York by a majority of 51.4% to Marcy's 48.6%. He was narrowly re-elected to a second two-year term in 1840. As a state senator and governor, Seward promoted progressive political policies including prison reform and increased spending on education. He supported state funding for schools for immigrants operated by their own clergy and taught in their native language. This support, which included Catholic parochial schools, came back to haunt him in the 1850s, when anti-Catholic feelings were high, especially among ex-Whigs in the Republican Party.

Seward developed his views about slavery while still a boy. His parents, like other Hudson Valley residents of the early 19th century, owned several slaves. (Slavery was slowly abolished in New York from 1797 to 1827 through a gradual mandated process). Seward recalled his preference as a child for the company and conversation of the slaves in his father's kitchen to the 'severe decorum' in his family's front parlor. He discerned very quickly the inequality between races, writing in later years 'I early came to the conclusion that something was wrong...and [that] determined me...to be an abolitionist.' This belief would stay with Seward through his life and permeate his career.

Seward's wife Frances was deeply committed to the abolitionist movement. In the 1850s, the Seward family opened their Auburn home as a safehouse to fugitive slaves. Seward's frequent travel and political work suggest that it was Frances who played the more active role in Auburn abolitionist activities. In the excitement following the rescue and safe transport of fugitive slave William 'Jerry' Henry in Syracuse on October 1, 1851, Frances wrote to her husband, 'two fugitives have gone to Canada--one of them our acquaintance John.' Another time she wrote, 'A man by the name of William Johnson will apply to you for assistance to purchase the freedom of his daughter. You will see that I have given him something by his book. I told him I thought you would give him more.'

In 1846 Seward became the center of controversy in his hometown when he defended, in separate cases, two convicts accused of murder. Henry Wyatt, a white man, was charged in the stabbing death of a fellow prison inmate; William Freeman, of African American and Native American ancestry, was accused of breaking into a home and stabbing four people to death. In both cases the defendants were mentally ill and had been severely abused while in prison. Seward, having long been an advocate of prison reform and better treatment for the insane, sought to prevent both men from being executed by using a relatively new defense of insanity. In a case involving mental illness with heavy racial overtones Seward argued, 'The color of the prisoner's skin, and the form of his features, are not impressed upon the spiritual immortal mind which works beneath. In spite of human pride, he is still your brother, and mine, in form and color accepted and approved by his Father, and yours, and mine, and bears equally with us the proudest inheritance of our race--the image of our Maker. Hold him then to be a Man.'

Later, Seward quoted Freeman's brother-in-law, praising his eloquence: 'They have made William Freeman what he is, a brute beast; they don't make anything else of any of our people but brute beasts; but when we violate their laws, then they want to punish us as if we were men.' In the end both men were convicted. Although Wyatt was executed, Freeman, whose conviction was reversed on Seward's successful appeal to the New York Supreme Court, died in his cell of tuberculosis.

United States Senator and Presidential Candidate

Seward supported the Whig candidate, General Zachary Taylor, in the presidential election of 1848. He said of Taylor, 'He is the most gentle-looking and amiable of men.' Taylor was a slaveholding plantation owner, but was friendly to Seward anyway.

William Seward was elected as U.S. Senator from New York as a Whig in 1849, and emerged as the leader of the anti-slavery 'Conscience Whigs'. Seward opposed the Compromise of 1850, and was thought to have encouraged Taylor in his supposed opposition. More recent scholarship suggests that Taylor was not under Seward's influence and would have accepted the Compromise if he had not died. Seward believed that slavery was morally wrong, and said so many times, outraging Southerners. He acknowledged that slavery was legal under the Constitution, but denied that the Constitution recognized or protected slavery. He famously remarked in 1850 that 'there is a higher law than the Constitution'. He continued to argue this point of view over the next ten years. He presented himself as the leading enemy of the Slave Power - that is, the perceived conspiracy of southern slaveowners to seize the government and defeat the progress of liberty.

Seward was an opponent of the Fugitive Slave Act, and he defended runaway slaves in court. He supported personal liberty laws.

In February 1855, he was re-elected as a Whig to the U.S. Senate, and joined the Republican Party when the New York Whigs merged with the Anti-Nebraskans later the same year. Seward did not seriously compete for the presidential nomination (won by John C. Frémont) in 1856, but sought and was expected to receive the nomination in 1860. In October 1858, he delivered a famous speech in which he argued that the political and economic systems of North and South were incompatible, and that, due to this 'irrepressible conflict,' the inevitable 'collision' of the two systems would eventually result in the nation becoming 'either entirely a slaveholding nation, or entirely a free-labor nation.' Like Lincoln, he believed slavery could and should be extinguished by long-run historical forces rather than by coercion or war.

In 1859, confident of gaining the presidential nomination and advised by his political ally and friend Thurlow Weed that he would be better off avoiding political gatherings where his words might be misinterpreted by one faction or another, Seward left the country for an eight-month tour of Europe that included a visit to Syria, where Ayub Beg Tarabulsy gave him several Arabian horses. During that hiatus, his lesser-known rival Abraham Lincoln worked diligently to line up support in case Seward failed to win on the first ballot. After returning to the United States, Seward gave a conciliatory, pro-Union Senate speech that reassured moderates but alienated some radical Republicans. (Observing events from Europe, Karl Marx, who was ideologically sympathetic to Frémont, contemptuously regarded Seward as a 'Republican Richelieu' and the 'Demosthenes of the Republican Party' who had sabotaged Frémont's presidential ambitions). Around the same time, his friend Horace Greeley turned against him, opposing Seward on the grounds that his radical reputation made him unelectable. When Lincoln won the nomination, Seward loyally supported him and made a long speaking tour of the West in the autumn of 1860.

Secretary of State
'Our population is destined to roll its resistless waves to the icy barriers of the north, and to encounter oriental civilization on the shores of the Pacific.' --William H. Seward, 1846

Abraham Lincoln appointed Seward his Secretary of State in 1861. Seward played an integral role in resolving the Trent Affair and in negotiating the ensuing Lyons-Seward Treaty of 1862, which set forth strong measures by which the United States and Great Britain agreed to enforce an end to the Atlantic slave trade.

Seward pursued his vision of American expansion. 'Give me only this assurance, that there never be an unlawful resistance by an armed force to the ... United States, and give me fifty, forty, thirty more years of life, and I will engage to give you the possession of the American continent and the control of the world.' Having argued for taking American possession of vulnerable but useful places such as the Danish West Indies, Samaná, Panama, and Hawaii, Seward oversaw the annexation of only one, that of the Brook Islands in 1867. Despite minimal Congressional support, though, he developed American influence in the Hawaiian Islands, as well as in Japan and China to some extent.

Despite his endorsement of expansionist policies, Seward also strongly advocated non-interventionism. After Tsar Alexander II put down the 1863 January Uprising in Poland, French Emperor Napoleon III asked the United States to 'join in a protest to the Tsar.' Seward declined, 'defending 'our policy of non-intervention -- straight, absolute, and peculiar as it may seem to other nations," and insisted that '[t]he American people must be content to recommend the cause of human progress by the wisdom with which they should exercise the powers of self-government, forbearing at all times, and in every way, from foreign alliances, intervention, and interference.'

Assassination Attempt

On the night of April 14, 1865, Lewis Powell, an associate and co-conspirator of John Wilkes Booth, attempted to assassinate Seward at his Washington D.C. home. Powell's attack on Seward was meticulously coordinated with Booth's attack on President Abraham Lincoln and George Atzerodt's attack on Vice President Andrew Johnson in order to maximize the element of surprise and to sever the continuity of the United States government (it should be noted, however, that Atzerodt failed to follow through on his attack). Another member of the conspiracy, David Herold, led Powell to the Seward home on horseback and was responsible for holding Powell's horse while he committed the attack as well as guiding him out of the city during their escape. Powell was able to gain access to the Seward home by telling the butler, William H. Bell, that he was delivering medicine for Seward (who was bed-ridden from a carriage accident which had gravely injured him on April 5, 1865).

Upon entry to the home, Powell began up the stairs, but was stopped at the top of the stairs by Frederick, the Secretary's eldest son. Frederick told Powell that his father was asleep and that he (Frederick) would take the medicine to him. Unsure of what to do, Powell turned around and began descending the stairs, but then suddenly swung back around, drew a pistol, and pointed it at Frederick's head. The pistol misfired. Realizing he needed to act quickly, Powell ruthlessly began beating Frederick over the head with the barrel of his gun. The force of Powell's blows crippled Frederick Seward and left him sprawled on the floor, floating in and out of consciousness, in a pool of blood. Powell's gun was also rendered completely useless, as it had become jammed during the melee.

In Secretary Seward's bedroom was his daughter, Fanny Seward. Hearing the loud noises coming from the second floor hallway, Fanny opened the door to see her brother slumped on the floor and a wide-eyed Powell charging directly towards her, a dagger in his hand. Powell burst through the door, threw Fanny Seward to the side, and jumped on the Secretary's bed, repeatedly stabbing him in the face and neck area. Powell also attacked and injured another son (Augustus), and a soldier and nurse (Sgt. George Robinson) who had been assigned to stay with Seward. Outside the home, David Herold, who could clearly hear the screams coming from the house, fled with both horses, leaving Powell to fend for himself. Powell, convinced that he had mortally wounded the Secretary, fled down the stairs, and stabbed a messenger, Emerick Hansell, who had arrived just as Powell was escaping; Hansell was rendered permanently paralyzed from the stabbing. All five men that were injured that night survived, although Secretary Seward would carry the facial scars from the attack for the rest of his life. The events of that night took their toll on his wife, Frances, who died June 1865. His daughter Fanny died of tuberculosis in October 1866.

Powell was captured the next day (hiding in a tree in Washington D.C). and was executed on July 7, 1865, along with David Herold, George Atzerodt, and Mary Surratt, the three others convicted as conspirators in the Lincoln assassination.

Although it took Seward several months to recover from his wounds, he emerged as a major force in the administration of the new president, Andrew Johnson. He frequently defended his more moderate reconciliation policies towards the South, to the point of enraging Radical Republicans who had once regarded Seward as their ally.

In the fall of 1866, Seward joined Johnson, as well as Ulysses S. Grant and the young General George Armstrong Custer, along with several other administration figures, on the president's ill-fated 'Swing Around the Circle' campaign trip.

At one point Seward became so ill, probably from cholera, that he was sent back to Washington in a special car. Both Johnson and Grant, as well as several members of the Seward family, thought the Secretary was near death. But as with his April 1865 stabbing, Seward surprised many by making a good recovery.

The purchase of Alaska

Seward's most famous achievement as Secretary of State was his successful acquisition of Alaska from Russia. On March 30, 1867, he completed negotiations for the territory, which involved the purchase of 586,412 square miles (1,518,800 km²) of territory (more than twice the area of Texas) for $7,200,000, or approximately 2 cents per acre (equivalent to US$95 million in 2005). The purchase of this frontier land was variously mocked by the public as Seward's Folly, 'Seward's Icebox,' and Andrew Johnson's 'polar bear garden.' Alaska celebrates the purchase on Seward's Day, the last Monday of March. When asked what he considered to be his greatest achievement as Secretary of State, Seward replied 'The purchase of Alaska--but it will take the people a generation to find it out'.

Later life

Seward retired as Secretary of State after Ulysses S. Grant took office as president. During his last years, Seward traveled and wrote prolifically. Most notably, he traveled around the world in fourteen months and two days from August, 1870 to October, 1871. On October 10, 1872, Seward died in his office in his home in Auburn, New York, after having difficulty breathing. His last words were to his children saying, 'Love one another.' He was buried in Fort Hill Cemetery in Auburn, New York, with his wife and two children, Cornelia and Fanny. His headstone reads, 'He was faithful.'

His son, Frederick, edited and published his memoirs in three volumes.

In 1967, a century after the Alaska Purchase, the actor, Joseph Cotten, portrayed Seward in 'The Freeman Story', a part of his NBC anthology series, The Joseph Cotten Show. Virginia Gregg played Fanny Seward. Popular actor, Richard Mulligan, portrayed William Seward in the 1988 Lincoln mini-series, 'Random Letters'.

Seward's homes in Auburn and Florida, New York

Seward and his family owned a home in Auburn, New York which is now a museum; it was built in 1816 by Seward's father-in-law, Judge Elijah Miller. Seward married the Judge's daughter, Frances, in 1824 on the condition that they would live with Miller in his Auburn home. Seward made many changes to the home, adding an addition in the late 1840s and another one in 1866. When he died, Seward left the home to his son, William Seward, Jr.; it passed on to his grandson, William Henry Seward III, in 1920. At his death in 1951, it became a museum that opened to the public in 1955. Four generations of the family's artifacts are contained within the museum, located at 33 South Street in Auburn. The museum is open Tuesday through Saturday from 10am to 5pm.

Meanwhile, Seward's birthplace in Florida, New York was bought by the village in 2010, with the purpose of refurbishing it. (The property actually contains two houses: one in back--Seward's actual birthplace--which was converted into a barn; and one in front, built in the 1890s, used by the family that lived there for many years). The property (after spending an estimated $200,000, to be raised by private donations) is expected to be turned into a museum and opened to the public by 2013.

Legacy

- The purchase of Alaska.
- The Guano Islands Act of 1856
- The $50-dollar Treasury note, also called the Coin note, of the Series 1891, features a portrait of Seward on the obverse. Examples of this note are very rare and would likely se for about $50,000 at auction.
- His house in Auburn, New York is open as a public museum.
- The house in which he lived in Westfield, New York is now home to a bed and breakfast.
- He was a name partner of the law firm of Blatchford, Seward ' Griswold, today known as Cravath, Swaine ' Moore.
- Was famous in his lifetime for his red hair and energetic way of walking. Henry Adams described him as 'wonderfully resembling' a parrot in 'manner and profile'.

Memorials

- Seward Avenue in Auburn. Also in Auburn, Frances Street, Augustus Street, and Frederick Street are named for members of his family. The four streets form a block.
- Seward Elementary School in Auburn.
- Seward Place in Schenectady, New York, on the west side of the Union College campus.
- Seward Park in Auburn, New York.
- Seward Park in the Lower East Side of Manhattan.
- Seward Park in Seattle, Washington.
- Seward Square park in Washington, D.C..
- The Seward Peninsula in Alaska.
- City of Seward, on Alaska's Kenai Peninsula
- Seward, Illinois; Seward, Kansas; Seward, New York; Seward, Nebraska; and Seward, Alaska.
- A hamburger is called 'Seward's Folly' at West Rib Deli ' Pub in Talkeetna, Alaska is named for him.
- Seward County, Nebraska
- Seward's Success, Alaska, an unbuilt community to be enclosed by a dome.
- The Seward neighborhood of Minneapolis, Minnesota
- Seward Mountain (4,361 feet, 1,329 m), one of the Adirondack High Peaks, the highest point in Franklin County.
- At Union College, the campus bus is known as Seward's Trolley, a pun on Seward's Folly
- Seward High School in his hometown of Florida is named for his father, Dr. Samuel

Union	During the American Civil War, the Union was a name used to refer to the federal government of the United States, which was supported by the twenty free states and five border slave states. It was opposed by 11 Southern slave states that had declared a secession to join together to form the Confederacy. Although the Union states included the Western states of California, Oregon, and (after 1864) Nevada, as well as states generally considered to be part of the Midwest, the Union has been also often loosely referred to as 'the North', both then and now.
Race riot	A race riot is an outbreak of violent civil disorder in which race is a key factor. A phenomenon frequently confused with the concept of 'race riot' is sectarian violence, which involves public mass violence or conflict over non-racial factors.
Radical Republicans	The Radical Republicans were a loose faction of American politicians within the Republican Party from about 1854 (before the American Civil War) until the end of Reconstruction in 1877. They called themselves 'radicals' and were opposed during the war by moderates and conservative factions led by Abraham Lincoln and after the war by self-described 'conservatives' (in the South) and 'Liberals' (in the North). Radicals strongly opposed slavery during the war and after the war and distrusted ex-Confederates, demanding harsh policies for Reconstruction. During the war, Radical Republicans often opposed Lincoln in terms of selection of generals (especially his choice of George B. McClellan for top command) and his efforts to bring states back into the Union.
President	President was a steamboat which currently lies dismantled in St. Elmo, Illinois. Originally named Cincinnati, it was built in 1924, and is the only remaining 'Western Rivers' style sidewheel river excursion steamboat in the United States. She was listed on the National Register of Historic Places and declared a National Historic Landmark in 1989. Her home ports have been Cincinnati, Ohio, New Orleans, Louisiana, Vicksburg, Mississippi, St. Louis, Missouri and Davenport, Iowa.
Black Codes	The Black Codes were unofficial laws put in place in the United States to limit the basic human rights and civil liberties of blacks. Even though the U.S. constitution originally discriminated against blacks (as 'other persons') and both Northern and Southern states had passed discriminatory legislation from the early 19th century, the term Black Codes is used most often to refer to legislation passed by Southern states at the end of the Civil War to control the labor, migration and other activities of newly-freed slaves.

	In Texas, the Eleventh Legislature produced these codes in 1866, right after the United States Civil War.
Copperheads	The Copperheads were a vocal group of Democrats in the Northern United States (see also Union (American Civil War)) who opposed the American Civil War, wanting an immediate peace settlement with the Confederates. Republicans started calling anti-war Democrats 'Copperheads,' likening them to the poisonous snake. The Peace Democrats accepted the label, but for them the copper 'head' was the likeness of Liberty, which they cut from copper pennies and proudly wore as badges.
Three-Fifths Compromise	The Three-Fifths Compromise was a compromise between Southern and Northern states reached during the Philadelphia Convention of 1787 in which three-fifths of the enumerated population of slaves would be counted for representation purposes regarding both the distribution of taxes and the apportionment of the members of the United States House of Representatives. It was proposed by delegates James Wilson and Roger Sherman. Delegates opposed to slavery generally wished to count only the free inhabitants of each state.
George Armstrong Custer	George Armstrong Custer was a United States Army officer and cavalry commander in the American Civil War and the Indian Wars. Today he is most remembered for a disastrous military engagement known as the Battle of the Little Bighorn. Raised in Michigan and Ohio, Custer was admitted to West Point in 1858, where he graduated last in his class. However, with the outbreak of the Civil War, all potential officers were needed, and Custer was called to serve with the Union Army.
Garfield	Garfield is a comic strip created by Jim Davis. Published since June 19, 1978, it chronicles the life of the title character, Jon Arbuckle; and Arbuckle's dog, Odie. As of 2007, it was syndicated in roughly 2,580 newspapers and journals, and held the Guinness World Record for being the world's most widely syndicated comic strip.
James A. Garfield	The James A. Garfield was an American 3-masted bark which sunk off of the Florida gulf coast.

The Garfield transported lumber and operated in and out of Apalachee Bay. During this time, the bay served as an anchorage for timber concerns in northern Florida and provided access to the port towns of Apalachicola, Carrabelle, and St. Marks.

Reconstruction Acts

After the end of the Civil War, as part of the on-going process of Reconstruction, the United States Congress passed four statutes known as Reconstruction Acts. Fulfillment of the requirements of the Acts were necessary for the former Confederate States to be readmitted to the Union. The Acts excluded Tennessee, which had already ratified the Thirteenth Amendment to the United States Constitution and had been readmitted to the Union.

Andrew Johnson

Andrew Johnson was the 17th President of the United States (1865-1869). Following the assassination of President Abraham Lincoln, Johnson presided over the Reconstruction era of the United States in the four years after the American Civil War. His tenure was controversial as his positions favoring the white South came under heavy political attack from Republicans.

Tenure of Office Act

Tenure of Office Act may refer to:

- Tenure of Office Act
- Tenure of Office Act

.

Thomas Nast

Thomas Nast was a German-born American caricaturist and editorial cartoonist who is considered to be the 'Father of the American Cartoon'. Among his notable works were the creation of the modern version of Santa Claus, the male personification of the United States government, Uncle Sam, as well as the political symbols of both major United States political parties: the Republican elephant and the Democratic donkey.

Youth and education

He was born in the barracks of Landau, Germany, the son of a trombonist in the 9th regiment Bavarian band.

Chapter 15. Reconstruction and the South

Nation	Nation has different meanings in different contexts. In worldwide diplomacy, nation can mean country or sovereign state. The United Nations, for instance, speaks of how it was founded after the Second World War with '51 countries' and currently has '192 member states'.
American Anti-Slavery Society	The American Anti-Slavery Society was an abolitionist society founded by William Lloyd Garrison and Arthur Tappan. Frederick Douglass was a key leader of this society and often spoke at its meetings. William Wells Brown was another freed slave who often spoke at meetings.
Carpetbagger	In United States history, carpetbagger was a pejorative term Southerners gave to Northerners (also referred to as Yankees) who moved to the South during the Reconstruction era, between 1865 and 1877. The term referred to the observation that these newcomers tended to carry 'carpet bags,' a common form of luggage at the time (sturdy and made from used carpet). It was used as a derogatory term, suggesting opportunism and exploitation by the outsiders.
Literacy test	A literacy test, in the context of United States political history, refers to the government practice of testing the literacy of potential citizens at the federal level, and potential voters at the state level. The federal government first employed literacy tests as part of the immigration process in 1917. Southern state legislatures employed literacy tests as part of the voter registration process as early as the late 19th century. Literacy tests, along with poll taxes and extra-legal intimidation, were used to deny suffrage to African-Americans.
Scalawag	In United States history, scalawag was a derogatory nickname for southern whites who supported Reconstruction following the Civil War. History Scalawags formed a winning coalition with black freedmen and Northern newcomers (pejoratively labeled carpetbaggers) to take control of their state and local governments.

	Despite being a minority, they gained power by taking advantage of the Reconstruction laws of 1867 that disenfranchised the majority of Southern whites who could not or did not wish to take the Ironclad oath certifying that they did not serve in Confederate military or hold any office under the previous regime.
Elizabeth Cady Stanton	Elizabeth Cady Stanton was an American social activist, abolitionist, and leading figure of the early woman's movement. Her Declaration of Sentiments, presented at the first women's rights convention held in 1848 in Seneca Falls, New York, is often credited with initiating the first organized woman's rights and woman's suffrage movements in the United States. Before Stanton narrowed her political focus almost exclusively to women's rights, she had been an active abolitionist together with her husband, Henry Brewster Stanton and cousin, Gerrit Smith.
South Carolina	South Carolina is a state in the Deep South that borders Georgia to the south and North Carolina to the north. Originally part of the Province of Carolina, the Province of South Carolina was one of the 13 colonies that declared independence from the British Crown during the American Revolution. The colony was originally named by King Charles II of England in honor of his father Charles I, as Carolus is Latin for Charles.
Republican Party	The Republican Party is one of the two major contemporary political parties in the United States, along with the Democratic Party. Founded by anti-slavery expansion activists in 1854, it is often called the Grand Old Party (GOP). The party's platform generally reflects American conservatism in the U.S. political spectrum and is considered center-right, in contrast to the more liberal-leaning Democrats.
Politics	Politics is an essay written by Ralph Waldo Emerson. It is part of his Essays: Second Series, published in 1844. A premier philosopher, poet and leader of American transcendentalism, he used this essay to belie his feelings on government, specifically American government. His impact on New England thought and his views on pragmatism influenced the likes of Henry David Thoreau, Orestes Brownson, and Frederich Nietzsche, among others.

Chapter 15. Reconstruction and the South

Columbian Exchange	The Columbian Exchange was a dramatically widespread exchange of animals, plants, culture, human populations (including slaves), communicable diseases, and ideas between the Eastern and Western hemispheres (Old World and New World). It was one of the most significant events concerning ecology, agriculture, and culture in all of human history. Christopher Columbus' first voyage to the Americas in 1492 launched the era of large-scale contact between the Old and the New Worlds that resulted in this ecological revolution, hence the name 'Columbian' Exchange.
Crop-lien system	The crop-lien system is a credit system that became widely used by farmers in the United States in the South from the 1860s to the 1920s After the American Civil War, farmers in the South had little cash. The crop-lien system was a way for farmers to get credit before the planting season by borrowing against the value for anticipated harvests. Local merchants provided food and supplies all year long on credit; when the cotton crop was harvested farmers turned it over to the merchant to pay back their loan.
England	England is a country that is part of the United Kingdom. It shares land borders with Scotland to the north and Wales to the west; the Irish Sea is to the north west, the Celtic Sea to the south west and the North Sea to the east, with the English Channel to the south separating it from continental Europe. Most of England comprises the central and southern part of the island of Great Britain in the North Atlantic.
Sharecropping	Sharecropping is a system of agriculture in which a landowner allows a tenant to use the land in return for a share of the crop produced on the land (e.g., 50% of the crop). This should not be confused with a crop fixed rent contract, in which a landowner allows a tenant to use the land in return for a fixed amount of crop per unit of land (e.g., 1 T/ha). Sharecropping has a long history and there are a wide range of different situations and types of agreements that have encompassed the system.
Union League	A Union League is one of a number of organizations established starting in 1862, during the American Civil War to promote loyalty to the Union and the policies of Abraham Lincoln. They were also known as Loyal Leagues. They comprised upper middle class men who supported efforts such as the United States Sanitary Commission, which helped treat wounded soldiers after battle.

Lydia Maria Child	Lydia Maria Child was an American abolitionist, women's rights activist, opponent of American expansionism, Indian rights activist, novelist, and journalist and Unitarian. Her journals, fiction and domestic manuals reached wide audiences from the 1820s through the 1850s. She at times shocked her audience, as she tried to take on issues of both male dominance and white supremacy in some of her stories.
Force Acts	Force Acts can refer to several groups of acts passed by the United States Congress. The term usually refers to the events after the American Civil War. Andrew Jackson's Tariff Enforcement (1833) The Force Bill, 4 Stat. 632 (1833), was passed by Congress at Andrew Jackson's request, as part of the Nullification Crisis.
Ku Klux Klan	Ku Klux Klan, often abbreviated ku\ klux\ klan and informally known as the Klan, is the name of three distinct past and present far-right organizations in the United States, which have advocated extremist reactionary currents such as white supremacy, white nationalism, and anti-immigration, historically expressed through terrorism. Since the mid-20th century, the ku\ klux\ klan has also been anti-communist. The current manifestation is splintered into several chapters and is classified as a hate group.
Horace Greeley	Horace Greeley was an American newspaper editor, a founder of the Liberal Republican Party, a reformer, and a politician. His New York Tribune was America's most influential newspaper from the 1840s to the 1870s and 'established Greeley's reputation as the greatest editor of his day.' Greeley used it to promote the Whig and Republican parties, as well as opposition to slavery and a host of reforms ranging from vegetarianism to socialism. Crusading against the corruption of Ulysses S. Grant's Republican administration, he was the new Liberal Republican Party's candidate in the 1872 U.S. presidential election.

Chapter 15. Reconstruction and the South

Whiskey Ring

In the United States, the Whiskey Ring was a scandal, exposed in 1875, involving diversion of tax revenues in a conspiracy among government agents, politicians, whiskey distillers, and distributors. The Whiskey Ring began in St. Louis but was also organized in Chicago, Milwaukee, Cincinnati, New Orleans, and Peoria.Before they were caught, a group of mostly Republican politicians were able to siphon off millions of dollars in federal taxes on liquor; the scheme involved an extensive network of bribes involving distillers, rectifiers, gaugers, storekeepers, and internal revenue agents.

U.S. Secretary of the Treasury Benjamin H. Bristow, working without the knowledge of the President or the Attorney General, broke the tightly connected and politically powerful ring in 1875 using secret agents from outside the Treasury department to conduct a series of raids across the country on May 10, 1875. The trials began at Jefferson City, Mo.

Cold Mountain

Cold Mountain is the original soundtrack of the 2003 film Cold Mountain starring Jude Law, Nicole Kidman and Renée Zellweger.

The album won the BAFTA Award for Best Film Music and the World Soundtrack Award for Best Original Soundtrack of the Year in 2003. It was also nominated for the Academy Award for Best Original Score and the Grammy Award for Best Compilation Soundtrack Album for a Motion Picture, Television or Other Visual Media. The songs 'The Scarlet Tide' and 'You Will Be My Ain True Love' were nominated for the Grammy Award for Best Song Written for a Motion Picture, Television or Other Visual Media.

Constitutional Convention

The United States Constitutional Convention took place from May 25 to September 17, 1787, in Philadelphia, Pennsylvania, to address problems in governing the United States of America, which had been operating under the Articles of Confederation following independence from Great Britain. Although the Convention was purportedly intended only to revise the Articles of Confederation, the intention from the outset of many of its proponents, chief among them James Madison and Alexander Hamilton, was to create a new government rather than fix the existing one. The delegates elected George Washington to preside over the convention.

Louisiana

Louisiana was the name of an administrative district of the Viceroyalty of New Spain from 1764 to 1803 that represented territory west of the Mississippi River basin, plus New Orleans. Spain acquired the territory from France: see Louisiana.

History

The area, comprising what is now known as the Louisiana Purchase, was turned over to the French for a few days in 1803 before it, in turn, was turned over to the United States.

Louisiana Purchase

The Louisiana Purchase was the acquisition by the United States of America of 828,800 square miles (2,147,000 km^2) of France's claim to the territory of Louisiana in 1803. The U.S. paid 60 million francs ($11,250,000) plus cancellation of debts worth 18 million francs ($3,750,000), for a total sum of 15 million dollars for the Louisiana territory ($219 million in 2010 dollars). What was purchased was France's claim only, not the actual territory, which belonged to the tribes which inhabited the area. The territory itself was acquired slowly throughout the nineteenth century by purchases to Native American tribes and wars.

Alexander Hamilton

Alexander Hamilton was the first United States Secretary of the Treasury, a Founding Father, economist, and political philosopher.

Aide-de-camp to General George Washington during the American Revolutionary War, he was a leader of American nationalists calling for a new Constitution; he was one of America's first constitutional lawyers, and wrote most of the Federalist Papers, a primary source for Constitutional interpretation. Hamilton was the primary author of the economic policies of the George Washington Administration, especially the funding of the state debts by the Federal government, the establishment of a national bank, a system of tariffs, and friendly trade relations with Britain.

Thomas Jefferson

Thomas Jefferson was the third President of the United States (1801-1809) and the principal author of the Declaration of Independence (1776). Jefferson was one of the most influential Founding Fathers, known for his promotion of the ideals of republicanism in the United States. Jefferson envisioned America as the force behind a great 'Empire of Liberty' that would promote republicanism and counter the imperialism of the British Empire.

Chapter 15. Reconstruction and the South

Napoleonic Wars	The Napoleonic Wars were a series of conflicts declared against Napoleon's French Empire and changing sets of European allies by opposing coalitions that ran from 1803 to 1815. As a continuation of the wars sparked by the French Revolution of 1789, they revolutionized European armies and played out on an unprecedented scale, mainly due to the application of modern mass conscription. French power rose quickly, conquering most of Europe, but collapsed rapidly after France's disastrous invasion of Russia in 1812. Napoleon's empire ultimately suffered complete military defeat resulting in the restoration of the Bourbon monarchy in France. The wars resulted in the dissolution of the Holy Roman Empire and sowed the seeds of nascent nationalism in Germany and Italy that would lead to the two nations' consolidation later in the century.
John Quincy Adams	John Quincy Adams was the sixth President of the United States from 1825 to 1829. He was also an American diplomat and served in both the Senate and House of Representatives. He was a member of the Federalist, Democratic-Republican, National Republican, and later Anti-Masonic and Whig parties. Adams was the son of President John Adams and Abigail Adams.
John Quincy	Colonel John Quincy was an American soldier, politician and member of the Quincy political family. His granddaughter Abigail Adams named her son, John Quincy Adams, in his honor. The city of Quincy, Massachusetts is named in his honor, as well.
York	York was an African American slave best known for his participation with the Lewis and Clark Expedition. As William Clark's slave, he had to do diffficult manual labour without pay. After the expedition's return he pressed for his freedom, which Clark opposed, he possibly agreed ten years later, though some historians dispute this and say he was never freed.
Democratic Party	The Democratic Party is one of two major contemporary political parties in the United States, along with the Republican Party. The party's social liberal and progressive platform is largely considered center-left in the U.S. political spectrum. The party has the lengthiest record of continuous operation in the United States.

1. _________ was an American social activist, abolitionist, and leading figure of the early woman's movement. Her Declaration of Sentiments, presented at the first women's rights convention held in 1848 in Seneca Falls, New York, is often credited with initiating the first organized woman's rights and woman's suffrage movements in the United States.

   Before Stanton narrowed her political focus almost exclusively to women's rights, she had been an active abolitionist together with her husband, Henry Brewster Stanton and cousin, Gerrit Smith.

   a. Mary Greenleaf Clement Leavitt
   b. Thomas Gage
   c. Francisco de Montejo
   d. Elizabeth Cady Stanton

2. _________ was one of the first steamboats to operate in the states of California and Oregon.

   Operations in California

   _________ operated in California on the Sacramento River. The vessel was purchased in California in 1851 by pioneer steamboat captain Alexander Sinclair Murray (b.1828).

   a. Washington
   b. Mother Orange Tree
   c. South 40
   d. Henry Synck

3. _________ was a German-born American caricaturist and editorial cartoonist who is considered to be the 'Father of the American Cartoon'. Among his notable works were the creation of the modern version of Santa Claus, the male personification of the United States government, Uncle Sam, as well as the political symbols of both major United States political parties: the Republican elephant and the Democratic donkey.

   Youth and education

He was born in the barracks of Landau, Germany, the son of a trombonist in the 9th regiment Bavarian band.

a. Thomas Nast
b. The American Political Tradition
c. Bennett Law
d. Broad Seal War

4. _________ is an American television host, actress, producer, and philanthropist, best known for her self-titled, multi-award winning talk show, which has become the highest-rated program of its kind in history and was nationally syndicated from 1986 to 2011. She has been ranked the richest African American of the 20th century, the greatest black philanthropist in American history, and was for a time the world's only black billionaire. She is also, according to some assessments, the most influential woman in the world.

a. Executive Branch Reform Act
b. Elizabeth Blair Lee
c. Philip Richard Fendall II
d. Oprah Winfrey

ANSWER KEY
Chapter 15. Reconstruction and the South

1. d
2. a
3. a
4. d

Other Cram101 e-Books and Tests

Other Cram101 e-Books and Tests

CPSIA information can be obtained at www.ICGtesting.com
Printed in the USA
LVOW10s2350250814

400898LV00001B/28/P

9 781478 408659